T0295879

Saving Ourselves

Interviews
with
World Leaders
on the
Sustainable
Transition

Interviews
with
World Leaders
on the
Sustainable
Transition

Editor

Yacine Belhaj-Bouabdallah

King's College London, UK

World Scientific

NEW JERSEY · LONDON · SINGAPORE · BEIJING · SHANGHAI · HONG KONG · TAIPEI · CHENNAI · TOKYO

Published by

WS Professional, an imprint of
World Scientific Publishing Co. Pte. Ltd.
5 Toh Tuck Link, Singapore 596224
USA office: 27 Warren Street, Suite 401-402, Hackensack, NJ 07601
UK office: 57 Shelton Street, Covent Garden, London WC2H 9HE

Library of Congress Cataloging-in-Publication Data
Names: Belhaj-Bouabdallah, Yacine.
Title: Saving ourselves : interviews with world leaders on the sustainable transition /
    Yacine Belhaj-Bouabdallah (King's College London, UK).
Description: New Jersey : World Scientific, 2017. | Includes bibliographical references.
Identifiers: LCCN 2016059814| ISBN 9789813220744 (hc : alk. paper) |
    ISBN 9789813220751 (pbk : alk. paper)
Subjects: LCSH: Sustainability--Social aspects. | Environmental policy--Social aspects.
Classification: LCC HC79.E5 B434 2017 | DDC 304.2--dc23
LC record available at https://lccn.loc.gov/2016059814

Copyright © Yacine Belhaj-Bouabdallah 2017

All rights reserved.

Desk Editors: Suraj Kumar/Philly Lim

Typeset by Stallion Press
Email: enquiries@stallionpress.com

Printed in Singapore by B & Jo Enterprise Pte Ltd

Contents

Reviews of the Book   vii

About the Author   ix

Contents by Contributors   xi

Introduction   1

Chapter 1 Climate Change   7

Chapter 2 Fossil Fuels   31

Chapter 3 Biodiversity   57

Chapter 4 Nourishing Our Planet   83

Chapter 5 Population, Health and Consumption   113

Chapter 6 Protecting the Global Commons   143

Chapter 7 Sustainable Cities   167

Chapter 8 Sustainable Governance   189

Chapter 9 Towards a Sustainable Economy   211

Chapter 10 Religion   225

Chapter 11 Philosophy   233

Chapter 12 Education 241
Chapter 13 Advice and Skills for the Next Generation 257

References 269
Abbreviations 277
Acknowledgements 279

Reviews of the Book

"Reading these interviews with the world's top decision makers and experts on sustainable development and global warming will make you have your tail in the air urging action to save the planet."

Professor Rick van der Ploeg
Professor of Economics, Oxford University

"An impressive list of contributors provide thought-provoking answers to a set of well-chosen questions covering many different aspects of sustainability."

Professor Richard Green
Alan and Sabine Howard Professor of
Sustainable Energy Business
Imperial College Business School

About the Author

 **Yacine Belhaj-Bouabdallah** is President of the King's College London (KCL) Future Society. Having visited 63 countries, he graduates with a Bachelor's degree in International Politics from King's College London at the age of 19 in 2017. He was also a member of the Moroccan government delegations to the COP21 and COP22 UN climate conferences in Paris and Marrakech. Yacine is currently working on a second book examining how the successful initiatives and programs linked to the Sustainable Development Goals can be replicated in other parts of the world.

Contents by Contributors

Inger Andersen, Director-General of the
International Union for Conservation of
Nature (IUCN).   60, 72, 75, 82

Prof. Kenneth Arrow, Joan Kenney Professor of   214, 215
Economics and Emeritus Professor of Operations
Research at Stanford University and winner of the
1972 Nobel Memorial Prize in Economics.

Prof. Victoria Arroyo, Executive Director of the   33, 34, 37
Georgetown Climate Center, Assistant Dean for
Centers and Institutes, and Director of the
Environmental Law Program at Georgetown
University (USA).

Ida Auken, Danish Social Liberal MP and   18, 23, 133
Former Danish Minister for the Environment
(2011–2014).

H.E. Michelle Bachelet, President of Chile.   201, 236, 246

Peter Bakker, President of the World Business   38, 219, 221
Council for Sustainable Development.

Dr. Joop de Beer, Head of the Department of   114, 123, 129
Population Dynamics at the Netherlands
Interdisciplinary Demographic Institute,
Nidi (Netherlands).

Prof. Sally Benson, Director of the Precourt   27, 40, 50
Institute for Energy and Professor of Energy
Engineering at Stanford University (USA).

Prof. Frans Berkhout, Executive Dean of the   19, 152, 158, 166
Faculty of Social Science & Public Policy at
King's College London (UK).

Prof. Eugenie Birch, Lawrence C. Nussdorf   170, 176, 185
Professor of Urban Research, and Co-Director
of the Penn Institute for Urban Research at the
University of Pennsylvania (USA).

Stephanie Brancaforte, Global Campaign   35, 207, 213, 223
Leader on Climate & Energy at Greenpeace.

Prof. Michael Braungart, CEO of EPEA   132, 138, 140, 142
Internationale Umweltforschung GmbH,
Co-founder and Scientific Director of
McDonough Braungart Design Chemistry
(MBDC), and inventor of "Cradle to Cradle" Design.

Simon Bridges, Minister of Transport, Minister   45, 52
of Energy and Resources, and Associate Minister
for Climate Change Issues of New Zealand.

Carol Browner, Former Administrator of the   234
Environmental Protection Agency (1993–2001)
and Director of the White House Office of Energy
and Climate Change Policy (2009–2011).

Dr. Gro Harlem Brundtland, Former Prime Minister   21, 146, 153
of Norway (1986–1989; 1990–1996) and Director
of the World Health Organization (1998–2003).

Dr. Hans Bruyninckx, Executive Director of the   146, 147, 203
European Environment Agency.

Dr. Jet Bussemaker, Minister of Education,   248–250
Culture, and Science of the Netherlands.

Winnie Byanyima, Executive Director of Oxfam   163, 190
International.

Dr. Ray Chambers, UN Secretary-General's Special   124–126
Envoy for Health in Agenda 2030 and for Malaria.

H.E. Marie Louise Coleiro Preca, President   191, 194, 202
of Malta.

Prof. Sir Gordon Conway, Professor and Chair   85, 89, 98, 106
in International Development at Imperial College
London (UK).

Prof. Robert Costanza, Professor and Chair   137, 196, 214, 261
in Public Policy at the Australian National
University (Australia).

Prof. Paul Crutzen, Professor of Atmospheric   11, 12, 28
Chemistry at the Max Planck Institute for
Chemistry and recipient of the 1995 Nobel Prize
in Chemistry (Netherlands).

Dr. John J. DeGioia, President of Georgetown   239, 244, 255
University (USA).

Dr. Jos Delbeke, Director-General of the   22, 41, 47, 48, 50
Directorate-General for the Climate Action
at the European Commission.

Dr. Braulio Ferreira de Souza Dias, Executive   67, 69, 73, 76
Secretary of the Convention on Biological
Diversity.

Carole Dieschbourg, Minister for the Environment   153, 155
of Luxembourg.

Dr. Mark Diesendorf, Associate Professor   36, 38, 42, 53
and Deputy Director of Interdisciplinary
Environmental Studies at the University of
New South Wales (Australia).

Caroline Drummond, Chief Executive   104, 109, 112, 253
of LEAF UK.

Jostein Eikeland, Founder, Chairman   54, 55
and CEO of Alevo.

Hakima El Haite, Minister for the   8, 157, 199, 264
Environment of Morocco.

José María Figueres, President and Chairman   39, 196, 266
of the Carbon War Room and Former President
of Costa Rica (1994–1998).

Theressa Frantz, Head of Environmental   66, 77, 79, 164
Programmes at WWF-South Africa.

Vitor Gaspar, Director of the Fiscal Affairs   209, 217, 262
Department at the International Monetary
Fund (IMF)and Former Finance Minister
of Portugal (2011–2013).

Dr. Jane Goodall, Founder of the Jane Goodall   61, 64, 66, 73
Institute and UN Messenger of Peace.

Prof. Quentin Grafton, Professor of   107, 111, 136, 260
Economics at the Australian National
University (Australia) and the UNESCO Chair
in Water Economics and Transboundary
Water Governance.

H.E. Ameenah Gurib-Fakim, President of Mauritius.   68, 74, 201

Tenzin Gyatso, His Holiness the 14th   226, 227, 237, 239, 265
Dalai Lama.

Tarja Halonen, Former President of   193, 197, 205, 253
Finland (2000–2012) and Minister of Foreign
Affairs (1995–2000).

H.E. Sheikh Hasina, Prime Minister   71, 206, 247, 266
of Bangladesh.

Connie Hedegaard, Former European   41, 134, 153, 161, 265
Commissioner for Climate Action
(2010–2014), Former Danish Minister of
Climate and Energy (2007–2009) and of the
Environment (2004–2007).

Prof. Cameron Hepburn, Professor of   35, 46, 166, 209
EnvironmentalEconomics at the University
of Oxford (UK).

Anne Hidalgo, Mayor of Paris (France).   174, 177, 183

Jay Inslee, Governor of Washington (USA).   43, 70, 205

Frank Jensen, Lord Mayor of Copenhagen   173, 179, 181, 183
(Denmark).

Prof. Sir David King, Foreign Secretary's   15, 21, 154, 156
Special Representative for Climate Change,
Emeritus Professor in Physical Chemistry at the
University of Cambridge, Chairman of the Future
Cities Catapult and former Chief Scientific Advisor
to the British Government (2000–2007).

John Kufuor, Former President of Ghana   94, 96, 102, 258
(2001–2009).

Prof. Klaus Lackner, Director of the Center   25, 29, 32, 39, 48
for Negative Carbon Emissions at Arizona
State University (USA).

Ricardo Lagos, Former President of Chile   150, 156, 172
(2000–2006) and UN Special Envoy for
Climate Change.

Brice Lalonde, Executive Coordinator of   21, 155, 238, 266
United Nations Conference on Sustainable
Development (Rio+20; 2012), Former French
Ambassador on Climate Change Negotiations
(2007–2010) and former French Minister for
the Environment (1988–1992).

Dr. Marco Lambertini, Director-General   59, 63, 65, 71, 81, 259
of WWF International.

Dr. Alessia Lefebure, Director of the Alliance   244, 245, 254
Program and Adjunct Professor at the School
of International and Public Affairs (SIPAs) at
Columbia University (USA).

Prof. Thomas Lovejoy, University Professor at George   68
Mason University (USA).

Prof. Jess Lowenberg-DeBoer, Professor of   92, 95, 99, 109
Agricultural Economics and Associate Dean
and Director of International Programs in
Agriculture at Purdue University (USA).

Prof. Wolfgang Lutz, Director of the   115, 116, 122, 126, 130
Vienna Institute of Demography at the
Austrian Academy of Sciences and Founding
Director of the Wittgenstein Centre for
Demography and Global Human Capital (Austria).

H.E. Mogens Lykketoft, President of the   149, 162, 198, 205
UN General Assembly (2015–2016)
and Former Minister of Finance of
Denmark (1993–2000).

Prof. Georgina Mace, Professor of Biodiversity   61, 74, 80
and Ecosystems and Director of the Centre
for Biodiversity and Environment at University
College London (UK).

Prof. Edward Maibach, University Professor and   18, 20
Director of the Center for Climate Change
Communication at George Mason University (USA).

Prof. Pamela Matson, Dean of the School of Earth,   24, 89, 262
Energy & Environmental Studies at Stanford
University (USA).

Prof. Lord Robert May of Oxford, Professor at the   10, 16
University of Oxford, Former President of the Royal
Society (2000–2005) and Former Chief Scientific
Advisor to the British Government (1995–2000).

Prof. Federico Mayor Zaragoza,   235, 246, 249, 251, 264
Former Director of UNESCO (1987–1999)
and Current President of the Foundation for
a Culture of Peace.

Catherine McKenna, Minister of Environment   192
and Climate Change of Canada.

Clover Moore, Lord Mayor of Sydney   171, 174, 180, 187
(Australia).

Dr. David Nabarro, UN   87, 100, 101, 103, 268
Secretary-General's Special Representative
for Food Security and Nutrition, Special Envoy
on Ebola and Special Adviser to the UN
Secretary-General on the 2030 Agenda
for Sustainable Development and Climate Change.

Janos Pasztor, Director of the Carnegie   51, 149, 158, 165, 263
Climate Geoengineering Governance Project

and former United Nations Assistant Secretary-General
on Climate Change (2015–2016).

Prof. Andy Pitman, Director of the ARC Centre   9, 13, 17, 259
of Excellence for Climate System Science at the
University of New South Wales (Australia).

David Pitt-Watson, Chair of the United Nations   212, 213, 222
Environment Program Finance Initiative (UNEP-FI)
and Executive Fellow of Finance at the London
Business School.

Mary Polak, Minister of the Environment of British   39, 49, 220
Columbia (Canada).

Paul Polman, CEO of Unilever.   216, 218, 222

Prof. Ian Pool, Professor Emeritus of   122, 124, 128
Demography and Founding Director of the
Population Studies Centre at the University
of Waikato (New Zealand).

Prof. Tariq Ramadan, HH Sheikh Hamad Bin Khalifa   227–230
Al Thani Professor of Contemporary Islamic Studies
at the University of Oxford and Director of the
Research Centre of Islamic Legislation and Ethics (UK).

Prof. Steve Rayner, James Martin Professor   26, 27, 168, 237
of Science and Civilization and Director of the
Institute for Science, Innovation and Society
(InSIS) at the University of Oxford (UK).

Prof. William Rees, Professor Emeritus and   133, 135, 139, 262
former Director of the School of Community
and Regional Planning at the University of
British Columbia (Canada).

H.E. Tumusiime Rhoda Peace, African Union   88, 90, 93, 97
Commissioner for Agriculture and the Rural
Economy.

Mary Robinson, President of the   160, 195, 199, 264
Mary Robinson Foundation for Climate Justice,
UN Special Envoy for Climate Change, Former
President of Ireland (1990–1997), and UN High
Commissioner for Human Rights (1997–2002).

Prof. Johan Rockström, Executive Director of the   62, 78, 80
Stockholm Resilience Centre and Professor in
Environmental Science at Stockholm University (Sweden).

Andrä Rupprechter, Federal Minister of Agriculture,   154, 201
Forests, Environment and Water Management of Austria.

H.E. Enele Sopoaga, Prime Minister of Tuvalu.   64, 151, 252, 268

Prof. Will Steffen, Adjunct Professor at the   9, 16, 17, 24, 261
Australian National University (Australia) and
Former Director of the ANU Climate Change Institute.

Achim Steiner, Director of the Oxford Martin   144, 200, 243
School at the University of Oxford and Former
Executive Director of the UN Environment Program
(UNEP; 2006–2016).

Sir Crispin Tickell, Director of the Policy Foresight   131
Programme at the James Martin School for the
twenty-first Century at Oxford University (UK).

H.E. Justin Trudeau, Prime Minister of Canada.   203, 208, 248

Cardinal Peter Turkson, President of the   228, 229, 231
Pontifical Council for Justice and Peace
and Archbishop Emeritus of Cape Coast.

Gino Van Begin, Secretary General of the   170, 171, 182, 186
International Council for Local Government
Initiatives (ICLEI) — Local Governments
for Sustainability.

Laura Vaught, Associate Administrator Responsible   22, 75
for the Office of Policy at the Environmental
Protection Agency (United States).

Margrethe Vestager, European Commissioner   43, 219, 223
for Competition.

Celia Wade-Brown, Mayor of Wellington   175, 177, 178, 184
(New Zealand).

Dr. Rebecca Winthrop, Director of the Center   242, 245, 255
for Universal Education at the Brookings
Institution (USA).

Prof. John Wiseman, Deputy Director of the   42, 53, 134, 263
Melbourne Sustainable Society Institute at the
University of Melbourne (Australia).

Park Won-soon, Mayor of Seoul (South Korea).   171, 173

Introduction

Thirty years ago, the Internet was relatively new and was used almost exclusively by academics. Since then, it has revolutionised the way we live and has changed the types of activities we devote our time to. In the same way, sdustainability today is discussed almost exclusively by academics and politicians, with little participation from most people around the world, despite the important repercussions it will have on the way we live in 30 years' time. But this time, the transition to sustainability will be very different: instead of being primarily technological, it will be much more social and institutional in character. Sustainability not only implies that we will not pollute more than the Earth can sustain but also implies good governance that promotes social inclusivity, cooperation between stakeholders in ensuring that we remain sustainable and increased awareness about the effects of our actions on our environment. The latter quality will be important in enabling and facilitating our transition.

Nevertheless, we have faced several obstacles to this transition, all linked to the way we think of the world. The first one has been psychological: how we react to change. Why is change so hard to achieve? Firstly, change is expensive, both in terms of monetary costs and in personal mental costs. As much as most of us wish the environment well, it is often hard to change our behaviour accordingly. Why change when staying the same or doing the same things is so much easier? My goal in this book is to show that, contrary to popular belief, sustainability does not require radical changes and sacrifices to be made in the way we live our lives. It will more likely be about redesigning our institutions, businesses and production patterns so that they benefit both us and the environment rather than benefiting the former at the expense of the latter. But despite the importance of institutional change in transitioning towards more sustainable societies, individual change should not be neglected. And this is why innovative sustainable practices are useful in encouraging us to change our behaviour, or at least in making it simpler for us to do so. Taxes and bans on plastic bags compel us to consume less plastic, more efficient homes and showers ensure that we consume less water or energy, cheaper renewable energies encourage us to make the switch. In all likelihood, the transition to sustainability will become progressively easier to implement as 'business as usual' becomes harder to pursue than making the switch.

Though individuals do not find it easy to act, a prerequisite to action is awareness, a trait which many people around the world are dangerously lacking. Though the Internet and the big data revolution that emerged over the past two decades have allowed us to become more aware of our actions and their detrimental effects on our environment, we often choose to ignore such information because we lack the necessary solutions. This is understandable because many of us learn about climate change through news stories. News channels and newspapers usually carry stories about climate change only when it is linked to its detrimental consequences, such as an increase in the number and strength of hurricanes. Though plenty of innovative solutions have been developed and are implemented every day around the world, they are rarely featured prominently in news stories because they are not deemed as important as daily news. Sustainability, which is likely to take decades to implement, is usually featured only when major events linked to it, such as international conferences or world expositions, are held. These events are short enough, and attract enough stakeholders, to be featured in the daily news. Such news stories help raise our awareness about the problems at hand, but awareness of our planet's problems is not of much help, as many argue in this book, if we lack potential solutions to them.

Climate activist movements and, more generally, younger generations argue that not enough is being done while our planet's future is in peril. Such movements, though they often have positive intentions, are extremely negative in their arguments. Declaring that the environment is dying, that rising sea levels and increasingly frequent hurricanes threaten our cities, that population and consumption levels must be reduced, that economic growth is detrimental to the environment and that massive changes are required to our societies simply turns people away from such movements. The anger and dissatisfaction that is often felt at climate protests cannot be expected to encourage participation and understanding among the general population. The discourse needs to be positive and it needs to encourage people to participate in the process by appealing to what we can achieve if we transition to a sustainable planet rather than what could happen if we don't. Instead of focusing on the issues at hand, we should focus on the solutions.

Appealing to people's fears is easy, but it rarely results in positive change and often instills false assumptions in people's minds. Arguments common among activists in the run-up to the Conference of the Parties (COP21) international climate conference were that no deal would be reached because developed nations were unwilling to compensate developing ones, or that any deal reached would be ineffective because of the influence of oil nations and corporate interests. They argued that even if a deal were reached, it would simply be a cover to justify business as usual with minimal changes made to prevent environmental harm. These cynical depictions of international institutions, governments and the private sector as uncaring in the face of a degrading environment fortunately do not hold up.

In conducting interviews for this book, I was allowed to be part of the Moroccan delegation to COP21, where I was able to witness diplomats, negotiators, politicians and members of civil society organisations working passionately day and night in order to reach an agreement. While getting 196 nations to agree to every word of a 12-page treaty[i] is truly a feat, and getting the international community to agree to limit temperature rise to 1.5°C was a challenge, this did not stop many activists from nevertheless portraying the resulting deal as a failure.[ii] But, as in many other political situations, pursuing incremental, yet sustained, changes in the right direction is likely to be better than enacting radical, far-reaching changes that may destabilise our societies. As many of the experts interviewed in this book argue, many of the incremental changes we are making and will be making in transitioning towards more sustainable societies have the beneficial side-effect of improving well-being.

Reducing pollution from fossil fuels improves health in cities, increasing the number of green places in urban areas improves well-being, making government policies socially inclusive increases societal cohesiveness, preserving biodiversity allows our societies to feed themselves and function, incorporating the cost of environmental harm into the prices of goods increases social responsibility and economic efficiency, and educating all children so that they can contribute to these changes benefits all mankind. In all these ways, and others, pursuing sustainable development and transitioning towards sustainable societies will improve prospects in health, education, inclusivity, environmental protection, job creation and economic growth.

While sustainability is often seen through an environmental and scientific lens, it will affect and be affected by people from all walks of life. Ensuring that we preserve the environment, improve the well-being of present generations and plan for the long-term implications of our actions is not something that can be resolved in any single field of study. Climate change alone is caused by many activities: from industrial production and transportation to agriculture and energy production. Adapting to and mitigating it will require cooperation between citizens, civil society organisations, local and regional governments, academic institutions, businesses and corporations, national governments and international institutions.

As we live in an increasingly connected and interdependent world, global issues such as climate change and the pursuit of sustainable development will be increasingly numerous. Issues such as management of ecosystems and common resources (resources that are used by many countries), the accommodation of environmentally displaced people, and technology-sharing between developed and developing countries will need to be planned for on a global level if they are to be resolved. By learning to cooperate and develop frameworks to resolve such global issues, we may ensure that our societies thrive in this century.

And most importantly, we need to remember that transitioning to a more sustainable model is not costly, unfeasible and radical. In most cases, the technology and infrastructure necessary is both available and affordable. For example, solar energy is already competitive with or cheaper than most forms of fossil fuels. Making sure that incentives facilitate the development of sustainable energy, resilient cities, environmentally friendly modes of production, inclusive government and healthier, wealthier and better educated societies hardly sounds radical. And ensuring the right incentives are in place to facilitate the pursuit of these goals will help ensure our societies flourish in the twenty first century.

Chapter 1

Climate Change

Mitigating the effects of climate change is at the centre of our quest to become sustainable. It has come about through our overuse of fossil fuels, which released more CO_2 into the atmosphere than the planet could naturally absorb. This, in turn, led to the accumulation of CO_2 in our atmosphere, which has been leading and is leading to serious climate and environmental effects.

Climate change is leading to warmer weather and increased droughts, which are likely to affect food production and water availability. It is leading to more frequent and intense weather-related events, such as hurricanes and floods. It is easing desertification, which is threatening biodiversity, and among other things, it is resulting in the melting of the ice caps, which usually reflect heat from the Sun back into space.

On the one hand, we seek sustainability by ensuring that we do not release more CO_2 into the atmosphere than the planet can absorb through natural processes. This means reducing CO_2 emissions to limit the effects of climate change as much as possible. But on the other hand, we also try to ensure that countries are equipped to handle the effects of climate change that we cannot prevent.

Climate change is, in this sense, both an environmental and developmental challenge.

While the goal of limiting the effects of climate change mainly focuses on reducing CO_2 emissions, the goal of adapting to climate change focuses on building resilient infrastructures and cities that can cope with these changes. As the poorest countries are often the ones that are the most affected by and the most vulnerable to the effects of climate change, building up their resilience provides them with an opportunity to develop in an environmentally friendly way. Though these countries produce a small proportion of all CO_2 emissions worldwide, they are increasingly finding themselves needing to adapt to the effects of climate change. This necessity, combined with the declining cost of renewable energy, helps ensure that their development is sustainable and that their cities are cleaner and greener. This is why the Moroccan Environment Minister Hakima El Haite called this opportunity a 'climate chance' at COP21.

The way we handle the many risks of climate change will be crucial in determining how we will emerge from the sustainable transition. As with all topics discussed in this book, education and awareness will be necessary to ensure that the general population is involved in the development and implementation of solutions. With participation and understanding, we can ensure the transition is successful.

Why has climate change alarmed the scientific community and why should it alarm the general public?

The concern about climate change has been growing for over 50 years as observations, new science and analyses have gradually reinforced our confidence that the increasing CO_2 emissions are having a profound effect on our planet and this effect will continue to intensify in the future. Overall, however, there are few areas where science has changed so little as climate science. The early predictions of the impact of doubled CO_2 emissions suggested that warming would occur. These are very similar to more recent projections, and the lack of any evidence to suggest there are problems with the basic science provides a very firm foundation for alarm.

The general public should be alarmed about climate change and our role in causing it. It is going to have a major impact on our societies; indeed, it has been having a major impact for some decades now in many parts of the planet. The critical factor is that the sooner decisions are made to transition from a carbon-based economy to a non-carbon-based one, the easier it will be. The lack of serious progress on this means that the general public is committing their children and grandchildren to solving problems that will be even harder to solve than they are now, and that is an ethical disgrace.

Prof. Andy Pitman
Director of the ARC Centre of Excellence for Climate System Science
University of New South Wales, Australia

At its most fundamental level, climate change represents a rapid and significant change in the energy balance at the Earth's surface. This is an absolutely fundamental indicator of the state of the Earth system and it shows that we are destabilising our planet at a rapid rate. This should alarm the general public because human civilisations, starting with agriculture, then becoming villages and cities and more complex societies, all developed in the Holocene, the most recent state of the Earth system and one with a very stable energy balance. Because of climate change, we are now leaving the relatively stable climate of the Holocene into a rapidly changing one with an unknown end point (or different state of the Earth system). Such rapid changes to our global environment may prove to be too much for our society to cope with.

Prof. Will Steffen
Climate Change Institute
Australian National University, Australia

Why are we in great part responsible for instigating climate change? Which of our collective actions in particular is at fault for causing it?

Climate change is being driven by the increase in the number of humans wanting to use energy (to heat or cool homes, to travel around in cars or the like and to produce a great variety of things). The energy required to achieve all this is basically produced by burning various fuels (coal, trees, you name it) which release carbon into the atmosphere. This input of fossil fuels and other forms of carbon into the atmosphere results in a hotter planet Earth.

Prof. Lord Robert May of Oxford
Professor at the University of Oxford, UK
Former President of the Royal Society (2000–2005)
Former Chief Scientific Adviser to the British
Government (1995–2000)

In the context of what we call 'the great acceleration', humans exponentially increased their consumption of natural resources, especially after the Second World War, and thus, CO_2, methane and nitrous oxide levels in the atmosphere increased dramatically compared to pre-industrial times. CO_2 emissions increased by 40%, CH_4 by more than 100%. There is a clear correlation between Greenhouse Gas (GHG) emissions and changes in temperature, between sea levels and the northern hemisphere snow cover.

There is no single reason for climate change. It is, rather, the sum of our industrial and agricultural activities. Let me give you a few examples. During the past 3 centuries, the human population has increased tenfold to 7 billion, the cattle population has increased to 1.4 billion. There are currently some 20 billion farm animals worldwide. Urbanisation grew more than tenfold in the past century, and now almost half of the human population live in cities and megacities. Industrial output increased fortyfold during the past century, energy use 16 times. Almost 80% of the Earth's land surface has been transformed by human action and the annual carbon emission values from fossil fuel burning are at 6×10^{15} g and 10^{15} g from deforestation.

We definitely must reduce consumption. As Mahatma Gandhi pointed out, the Earth provides enough to satisfy every man's needs, but not for every man's greed. In order to accommodate the current Western lifestyle around the world, we would need several more Earths, which we will never have.

Mankind will remain a major environmental force for many millennia. A daunting task lies ahead for scientists and engineers to guide society towards environmentally sustainable management during the era of the Anthropocene, especially as this will require appropriate human behaviour at all scales.

Prof. Paul Crutzen
Professor of Atmospheric Chemistry at the Max Planck
Institute for Chemistry, Germany
Recipient of the 1995 Nobel Prize in Chemistry

Why have some scientists stated that we live in the Anthropocene? What is the Anthropocene and what differentiates it from other geological epochs?

With the term 'Anthropocene' as a new geological era following the Holocene, I wanted to express the fact that humans are and will remain a major environmental force for many millennia. Humans are shaping planet Earth to a greater degree than any natural processes — we have modified 80% of the land surface, while our actions have influenced the biological, geological and meteorological characteristics of Earth.

One can argue about the precise beginning of the Anthropocene. It could be placed at the invention of steam engines or in the late eighteenth century, when, according to analyses of air trapped in polar ice, the growing global concentrations of CO_2 and methane occurred due to industrialisation. Or we could say it started with the Trinity test, the test of the first atomic weapons on 16 July 1945 in the USA. Even though the scientific community has not finalised the discussion when the Anthropocene started, there is, however, no doubt about the fact that we live in it.

Personally, I view the term and the discussion about it as an opportunity for smart development because everything depends on how wisely and fairly we use the Earth's resources and how good we are at developing smart technology and medicine. If humanity does not change its mode of operation, the future of the Anthropocene might be very short. I thus hope that the term emphasises the responsibility we have for the Earth and for our future.

Prof. Paul Crutzen
Professor of Atmospheric Chemistry at the Max Planck
Institute for Chemistry, Germany
Recipient of the 1995 Nobel Prize in Chemistry

What repercussions is climate change likely to have on our societies and the processes they are dependent on?

I could name all the environmental issues linked to climate change, such as the risks associated with the melting of permafrost soils in the Northern Hemisphere, which will cause the release of even more CO_2, or the increase in ocean water acidity resulting in the inability of carbonate-secreting microorganisms to build their skeletons and thus to lower CO_2 fixation rates. Both, for example, would lead to an additional rise in temperature.

However, what worries me is the fact that we will most likely face more and more mass migration due to climate issues, which will have huge impacts on societies here and abroad, such as in countries like Bangladesh, for which the UN estimates predict 20 million refugees alone. Global warming, sea-level rises and the increase in the number of extreme weather events will also affect agriculture and our access to water resources in the future. This will cause millions of people to leave their homes in order to find better living conditions for themselves and their families.

Prof. Paul Crutzen
Professor of Atmospheric Chemistry at the Max Planck
Institute for Chemistry, Germany
Recipient of the 1995 Nobel Prize in Chemistry

How can we adapt to climate change and/or mitigate its effects? What types of strategies would be effective in this regard?

That is simple. Policies that reduce the emission of GHG, policies that deeply cut emissions very urgently, policies that invest in alternative energy sources, energy efficiencies, that stop the subsidising of fossil fuels, improve energy efficiency use, and that honestly tax the cost of energy production to include the costs associated with the damage caused by CO_2 emissions among others.

Prof. Andy Pitman
ARC Centre of Excellence for Climate System Science
University of New South Wales, Australia

The essential response to the scientific understanding of climate change is to mitigate its effects by both decarbonising the global economy and avoiding all deforestation of natural forests as well as by undergoing an extensive programme of reforestation. The aim is to reach CO_2 neutrality — to emit only as much as captured by the forest sinks — this century.

The EU countries have already initiated the process of decarbonisation by introducing extensive subsidies in the form of feed-in tariffs[iii] for the installation of renewable energy sources. These have created an increasing market for renewables, which has resulted in a learning curve leading to a substantial decrease in their installation costs over the past 25 years. Renewable energy is now cheaper to install than fossil fuel energy sources for most parts of the world, and in 2014, more renewable energy sources were installed around the world than fossil fuel sources.

However, renewable sources such as solar photovoltaic and wind turbines are intermittent: when the sun doesn't shine and the wind doesn't blow, no electricity is produced. We now need a mission-oriented surge in publicly funded research, development and demonstration to address the need for storage technologies, in addition to the lithium ion batteries currently being rolled out into the market, and to develop sophisticated smart grid systems.[iv] I led a group of British authors who proposed such a programme, the Global Apollo Programme, aimed at corralling about $15 billion a year from willing counties to fund this effort over 10 years. The object is to achieve cheaper electricity from renewables than from fossil fuels 24 hours a day, 365 days a year, for all countries within this 10-year period. This notion has received support from the G7 heads of government at their meeting in Germany in June 2015.

This programme was launched by Obama, Modi, Cameron and Hollande on the first day of the Paris COP21. Twenty two countries have joined the programme, now called Mission Innovation, and have agreed to double their public spending in clean energy research, development demonstration. This will amount to $30 billion per year by 2020. In addition, a Breakthrough Energy Coalition was also announced by Bill Gates and 28 other wealthy individuals, offering private funding to accelerate the best technologies into the market place.

Managing the forests was the subject of the New York Forests Declaration made at the UN Secretary-General's heads of government climate change meeting in 2014. In essence, this states that the deforestation of natural forests will be brought to an end by 2030 and an area the size of India will have been reforested by then. Funded by Britain, Norway and Germany, this commitment has now gained the support of 37 forested nations as its signatories.

Every country will also have to begin the process of developing resilience against the impacts of climate change. Currently, the global surface temperature is about 0.8°C higher than in the pre-industrial period, and it will probably rise to 1.5–2°C this century even if the mitigation efforts described above are rapidly achieved worldwide. This will bring quite severe challenges to all parts of the world, but these will differ considerably from one region to another. Adaptation measures can be determined only through a detailed climate analysis for each region at a small scale of around 12×12 km. The models developed at the UK Met Office, the Hadley Centre and at the National Oceanic and Atmospheric Administration in the USA are capable of producing these analyses for every region of the world. The biggest challenge for the UK, for example, as I explained to the Cabinet and Parliament when I served as Chief Scientific Adviser to the British government in 2003, is from flooding, arising from storms both at sea and inland. The government therefore increased funding for flood defences and flood water management and this will need to continue into the future.

If the action to mitigate is not taken in the immediate future, temperatures will rise to levels that will lead to consequences that cannot be tackled by adaptation measures for most parts of the world.

The risks associated with climate change have recently been analysed using the approach used by the insurance industry and conducted with experts, political advisers, generals and admirals drawn from China, India, the UK and the USA. Specific risks, such as the failure of rice crops in a given year in China or the flooding of major cities, such as Calcutta, New York and Shanghai, as well as systemic or global risks were analysed. The conclusion of this study was clear: without major mitigation measures, the global economy, and with it our modern civilisation, will be at severe risk.

Prof. Sir David King
Foreign Secretary's Special Representative for Climate Change
Emeritus Professor in Physical Chemistry at the University of
Cambridge, UK
Chairman of the Future Cities Catapult
Former Chief Scientific Adviser to the British Government
(2000–2007)

Why has action to stop climate change, or at least mitigate its effects, been so slow? What types of changes (e.g., policy and social) are needed to speed up the process?

There are a number of reasons why action to stabilise the climate system has been slow (although it is picking up momentum now). The first is inertia in the global socioeconomic system (the problem of turning around a battleship quickly). The second is the lack of a clear way forward (until recently) for decarbonising societies. The third is that in some countries, the climate change denial movement has gained political traction (an example is the Abbott government in Australia) and that has slowed action, combined with the power of the incumbents — the fossil fuel and related industries — to push for policies that will delay action on the transition to a clean energy future.

Prof. Will Steffen
Climate Change Institute
Australian National University, Australia

Action has indeed been disgracefully slow. As things get worse and worse, it will ultimately be impossible to dodge the problem, and to say it is not 'my fault'. The really unfortunate aspect of all this is that once the problem becomes really bad, people will wish to take action, even though such action would have been vastly more effective had it been implemented earlier.

Looking wider at other parts of our galaxy where other planets circle around their suns, it is possible that they, too, may have encountered such problems (which ultimately must arise). And when they did, did they get together and take effective action, or did they behave as we seem to be doing, wishfully hoping the problem would go away and strenuously resisting serious attempts to deal with it until things have gone so far that they are beyond recovery. To put it another way, given that there may well be other sentient entities on other planets in our galaxy, similar problems would probably arise. But is our reaction of putting our head in the sand rather than taking effective action something that would be likely to happen on any such planet, or is our failure to take effective action on an appropriately large scale essentially pathological?

Prof. Lord Robert May of Oxford
Professor at the University of Oxford, UK
Former President of the Royal Society (2000–2005)
Former Chief Scientific Adviser to the British Government
(1995–2000)

Why has climate change denial managed to become popular in some areas? How can we convince those who adhere to it that climate change is indeed happening and that it requires urgent action?

Climate change denial isn't as popular as many people think. Even in countries like Australia and the USA, climate deniers are still a small minority. They tend to exist primarily in the English-speaking world, and even there, primarily in the resource-rich 'new lands' like the USA, Canada and Australia. They also tend to be concentrated on the far right of the political spectrum, such as the Tea Party in the USA and their equivalents here in Australia. By contrast, there are very few climate deniers in the Scandinavian countries and even those who did exist there a decade or two ago were convinced once the scientific evidence that they were wrong became overwhelming. In Scandinavian countries, the few deniers tended to be persuaded by the evidence because they took a scientific approach to the question, whereas in the USA, Canada and Australia, climate deniers are mostly motivated by political and ideological belief systems and so no amount of incontrovertible science can change their minds.

Prof. Will Steffen
Climate Change Institute
Australian National University, Australia

Is the lack of citizen awareness about the potential solutions (mitigation and adaptation strategies) to climate change responsible for the lack of action on their part?

I think there is a high level of awareness. There may not be a high level of understanding, but the awareness is high. There is considerable enthusiasm in some sectors, but it is true that the scale of general public engagement in this problem lacks the urgency necessary. It is partially a willingness to put off hard choices for someone else to make; it is partly a hope that the problem will disappear, it is partly a lack of knowledge of what one can do, and it is partly a lack of leadership amongst national and international leaders in communicating the scale of the challenge.

Prof. Andy Pitman
ARC Centre of Excellence for Climate System Science
University of New South Wales, Australia

How can people be motivated and galvanised to take action to mitigate climate change and to transition to a sustainable society? What methods are effective in getting people to change their unsustainable behaviour?

When people understand the problem, and understand the options for solving the problem, they can participate effectively in the process of making informed decisions about how best to address it. Limiting climate change, and taking all possible steps to ensure that people are not needlessly hurt, requires we get the policies right — public policies in cities, counties, states, nations and internationally. We have a collective problem that requires collective solutions, and the only way to accomplish them will be through effective policies, not through individual behaviour change.

Prof. Edward Maibach
Director of the Centre for Climate Change Communication
George Mason University, USA

We need to create positive scenarios. The Intergovernmental Panel of Climate Change is focused on scenarios of how bad things can become if we do not take action. We need someone to show us positive scenarios. People are not moved and inspired by long-term threats. They are moved by hope, by stories of a better quality of life, by job creation and by greener and more liveable cities. These are the scenarios we need to show people.

Ida Auken
Danish Social Liberal MP
Former Danish Minister for the Environment (2011–2014)

Though information and awareness are part of the solution, they are never enough. Sometimes, we may be very aware of some things, but behave in a different way. There is often a dissonance between what people feel is right and how they behave in relation to those sorts of things that they know about: food, alcohol, etc. So, for example, even if people are very aware about more environmentally sustainable ways of travelling, most have a car and prefer to use it. Many social scientists argue that you also really need to look at social practices: how people travel to work or university, for instance, and the conditions that determine the choices they make. Do they ride a bike, catch a bus, or maybe drive a car?

And the interesting challenge is how you can get people to reconsider some of the choices they're making and how you can build new practices into their lives, making them available but also reinforcing them and making them normal, such as not to drive to work but to cycle to work. A lot of people have made that switch, and once that happens, then other people will switch, and so on. And that is more than just awareness, it's about building new behaviour, a new social practice into your day, into your sense of yourself. The reason you cycle to work may have nothing to do with emissions at all, it may have to do with health and wanting to breathe fresh air on your way to work, or the fact that you're a cyclist and you love cycling and there's a fitness thing there. There are all sorts of reasons why people might do that; we must try to understand social practices as much as to make people aware.

Prof. Frans Berkhout
Executive Dean of the Faculty of Social Science and Public Policy
King's College London, UK

Could using marketing strategies be effective in convincing people to abandon (or change) their unsustainable and environmentally harmful behaviour? How would such strategies manifest themselves in practice?

Marketing strategies can help, especially if we use them to market effective policies to public policy and corporate decision-makers. The essence of marketing is to make the behaviour we are attempting to promote easy, fun and popular. When we succeed in doing that, members of the target audience become much more willing to embrace the kind of behaviour being promoted.

An important lesson we have learned in public health is that the best way to change people's behaviour — by encouraging them to give up an existing practice in preference for a new form of behaviour — is to make the new practice at least as easy, if not easier, than the practice we are trying to replace. For example, in the case of climate change, we need to make use of clean renewable fuels easier than using dirty fossil fuels. And we need to make energy conservation as easy, if not easier, as wasting energy.

Prof. Edward Maibach
Director of the Centre for Climate Change Communication
George Mason University, USA

What are the consequences of not changing our mentalities and behaviour to mitigate or stop climate change?

Failure to limit climate change to 2°C would be tantamount to allowing a global public health catastrophe to happen. Over the past 50–100 years, the world's nations have done so much to help people emerge from poverty and to live healthfully, but these gains — and more — are at risk if we don't now deal effectively with climate change.

Prof. Edward Maibach
Director of the Centre for Climate Change Communication
George Mason University, USA

In the face of a slow-moving crisis with complex causes and repercussions, would governments and NGOs not be better off by initiating a massive awareness campaign to inform people of the effects of their actions and the various potential solutions and alternatives?

Certainly, but this effort is undertaken very differently in different countries, and interest groups often hinder such campaigns. Indeed, we need the support of 7 billion human beings to combat climate change, but humanity is divided into 195 states that defend their national interests before that of humanity's. Perhaps, the development of global goals (such as the Sustainable Development Goals and the Millennium Development Goals) will allow the establishment of coalitions made up of governments, local governments, businesses, NGOs and others, which can undertake change more efficiently.

Brice Lalonde
Executive Coordinator of the UN Conference on Sustainable
Development (Rio+20; 2012)
Former French Ambassador on Climate Change Negotiations
(2007–2010)
Former French Minister for the Environment (1988–1992)

Indeed, government action is crucial to the whole situation. However, given the still wide range of different opinions, and the complexity of the situation, I am not sure that asking governments to launch campaigns while they are still in dialogue about the necessary international agreements would help.

Dr. Gro Harlem Brundtland
Former Prime Minister of Norway (1986–1989; 1990–1996)
Director-General of the World Health Organization (1998–2003)

The British government has, for example, been running an awareness campaign through its Carbon Trust over the past 15 years. In 2005, when the UK was in the Presidency of the G8, we put climate change and African development on the agenda and invited a +5 group of heads of state — Brazil, China, India, Mexico and South Africa — to attend. Globally, this campaign has many facets: the UN Framework Convention on Climate Change (UNFCCC) meets once a year in open forum and the meetings are widely attended. Many other actions are taken to give the issue the widest publicity, including the Encyclical on Climate Change by Pope Francis. What is now required is for governments to introduce legislation for private sector companies to reduce their carbon footprint and for individuals to change their behaviour and use less energy.

Prof. Sir David King
Foreign Secretary's Special Representative for Climate Change

Emeritus Professor in Physical Chemistry at the
University of Cambridge
Chairman of the Future Cities Catapult
Former Chief Scientific Adviser to the British Government
(2000–2007)

One of the US Environmental Protection Agency's main purposes is to ensure that all parts of society — communities, individuals, businesses, and state, local and tribal governments — have access to accurate information so they can manage health and environmental risks. We do this through environmental education grants that promote awareness and help provide people with the skills to take responsible actions to protect the environment. We also do so through voluntary partnership programmes like Energy Star that helps people save money and protect our climate through energy efficiency.

Laura Vaught
Associate Administrator for the Office of Policy
Environmental Protection Agency, USA

Citizens can play a role in pushing the climate agenda forward by adopting climate-friendly habits in their everyday lives and by encouraging businesses and governments to act. Many innovative low-carbon solutions already exist — they now need to be scaled up. Active citizens, innovative businesses and effective policies will all play a role, but this may well require forms of action that are very different from just information campaigns. For instance, the EU is developing new legislation to improve our internal electricity market and at the same time deal with the impact of large amounts of renewable energy on the reliability of our energy system. Part of the answer will lie in more flexible ways of using energy, which can also reduce costs for consumers. This will require not only informing consumers on potential solutions and alternatives but also developing the rules that will enable consumers and producers to put them into practice in real life.

Dr. Jos Delbeke
Director-General at the Directorate General for Climate Action
European Commission

I think education and information are important. As a government you need the legitimacy of having a population that supports important decisions or at least understands them. It is important to let people know the cost of inaction in the environmental field. The World Bank says that up to 8% of GDP is lost in developing countries due to climate change, environmental degradation and pollution. But you should also tell people the positive story of how you can create a more resilient country and economy if we transition to an inclusive green economy.

Ida Auken
Danish Social Liberal MP
Former Danish Minister for the Environment (2011–2014)

Prior to industrialisation, the Earth's natural processes were relatively balanced, with little significant variation in climate over the past several millennia. This meant that these natural processes were self-sustaining with little to no waste or byproducts resulting from them. Our use of fossil fuels since the late eighteenth century has resulted in a disruption of this state of balance as CO_2 accumulated in the atmosphere. Some have viewed this issue in terms of planetary limits: what types of excesses the planet can sustain.

In what ways have we exceeded Earth's planetary limits?

I don't have evidence that we have exceeded planetary limits. There is no doubt that we are driving down the natural capital of the planet, with some regions losing the capacity for natural assets to support the needs of people today, let alone in the longer term. Agriculture is certainly one of the most important drivers of loss of natural capital assets through land changes and biodiversity loss, soil erosion, nutrient losses, over-enrichment, emissions of air pollutants and so on. Our past and current efforts to meet the needs of people for food have many unintentional negative consequences. Likewise, the production and use of energy resources of all kinds has negative consequences, as do industrial and urban activities. The sustainability challenge we face for the future is to find ways of meeting social needs while dramatically reducing the negative consequences. I don't think the planetary boundaries perspective is very useful in this, but we definitely need metrics and measures of the rate of change, up or down, in our global assets and we need to manage to sustain then.

Prof. Pamela Matson
Dean of the School of Earth, Energy & Environmental Studies
Stanford University, USA

As climate change has been caused by the accumulation of CO_2 in the atmosphere, some have proposed expanding the Earth's capacity to absorb it. The sinks which absorb CO_2, such as forests and oceans, have been the natural means the planet has used to prevent the accumulation of excess carbon. Others, though, have argued that the creation of artificial sinks are necessary to reduce excess CO_2.

How do sinks absorb CO_2? Can we increase the number of sinks?

Carbon 'sinks' won't solve the problem. The numbers just don't add up. For example, land systems can indeed take up CO_2, but any credible analysis comes up with something around 5% of annual human emissions that can be stored in terrestrial sinks. And even there, the permanency issue is a big problem — wildfires can reemit carbon stored for decades in forests in a couple of days. More fundamentally, the Second Law of Thermodynamics is against the absorption of CO_2 as a solution. The gas is highly dispersed in the atmosphere, especially as it is in its fully oxidised form. It takes a lot of energy to capture it and then put it back into reduced form. By far, the best solution is not to emit CO_2 in the first place, that is, to leave fossil fuels in the ground.

Prof. Will Steffen
Climate Change Institute
Australian National University, Australia

Geo-engineering has been proposed as a scientific method to delay or mitigate some of the effects of climate change, especially in case more time is necessary to transition to a more sustainable and less CO_2 polluting world.

What is geo-engineering? What would be the physical manifestations and repercussions of geo-engineering techniques?

Geo-engineering means many different things to different people. It usually refers to technologies that can control the climate in a way that is desirable. Albedo manipulations, which reflect sunlight and heat back into space, might fall into this category. The removal of CO_2 from the air is often considered to be a geo-engineering technology. In my view, it can become that, but initially it is more akin to a technology for collecting the CO_2 from emissions. At this scale, it is not an attempt to change the climate, but an attempt to mop up the CO_2 that has escaped from our various points of emissions. It becomes a geo-engineering effort once we designate a target and use the technology only if we are above the designated value. Generally, technologies that use very large amplification to make big changes to the Earth with very little input are risky. If they work differently from the way intended, then there are usually no options to counter the change. Emissions of CO_2 to the atmosphere fall into this category because the resulting warming is much larger than the heat released in the combustion. This amplification is due to the greenhouse effect. On the other hand, not keeping the atmosphere at an elevated level removes the problem rather than creating a new state. Leaving the CO_2 in the air and hoping that countermeasures cancel it out is far more difficult. It can help; it may work in an emergency, but clearly one cannot let the CO_2 accumulate indefinitely. You cannot throw garbage in the street indefinitely. Putting houses on stilts may keep you out of the garbage, but it does not solve the root cause of the problem.

Prof. Klaus Lackner
Director of Center for Negative Carbon Emissions
Arizona State University, USA

What are the ethical dilemmas posed by geo-engineering? Can they be resolved?

Geo-engineering covers a wide range of technologies with very different implications. While scientists emphasise the distinction between reflecting sunlight away from the planet (for example, by putting sulphate aerosols in the stratosphere) and methods that could remove CO_2 from the ambient air (so-called artificial trees, for example), the ethical and social concerns seem to fall out along the distinction between putting things into the environment to reduce sunlight or draw down carbon (iron-enrichment of the oceans to absorb CO_2, for instance) and self-contained engineering devices (such as space mirrors or artificial trees). There are no truly unprecedented ethical issues raised by either kind of technology, but there are real reasons to be concerned about the unintended consequences and inequitable distribution of benefits and burdens of deploying any such technology on a large scale.

Prof. Steve Rayner
James Martin Professor of Science and Civilisation
Director of the Institute for Science, Innovation and Society
University of Oxford, UK

In practice, would geo-engineering be legal without the agreement of all nations? Who would fund and implement it?

Air capture technology based on any sovereign territory could be implemented under existing national environmental and planning laws. While there is currently no international law that specifically prevents experiments with or even the deployment of sulphate aerosols, there are customary duties of care under international law that would apply. While there is no legal barrier to using this technology without an international treaty, I would argue that it would be politically unwise, as a unilateral actor is likely to be be blamed for any subsequent weather-related disaster, regardless of whether it was actually related to their actions or not. Given the world's poor record on climate treaties, I think that such a treaty is unlikely to come into being.

Prof. Steve Rayner
James Martin Professor of Science and Civilisation
Director of the Institute for Science, Innovation and Society
University of Oxford, UK

Is geo-engineering simply a temporary solution to give the international community more time to adequately respond to the challenges posed by climate change? Do the benefits of such a solution (truly) outweigh the costs?

Geo engineering should be viewed as an option of last resort. We should focus our efforts on transforming our energy system to avoid CO_2 emissions. Anything that takes our attention away from this is a distraction and can lead to complacency. There are many benefits from a transition to a low-emission or no-emission energy system in addition to addressing the climate change problem. Air pollution can be reduced, people can rely on more distributed energy resources and energy supplies will be more secure.

Prof. Sally Benson
Director of the Precourt Institute for Energy and Professor of Energy
Resources Engineering
Stanford University, USA

I have always stated this might only be an ultimate possibility to rapidly combat potentially drastic climate heating if we fail to reduce CO_2 and other GHG emissions, which is still our top priority. These should be reduced to such an extent that geo-engineering such as albedo modification by stratospheric sulphur injections would not need to take place.

I would not apply geo-engineering at present, but research should continue on its possible positive as well as its potential negative side-effects. I share the fear, however, that researching geo-engineering will lead to an attitude that CO_2 reductions can be postponed because of the belief that sulphur injection technology will save us from dangerous climate change. That would be totally wrong. I am doubtful that geo-engineering will be used because of its costs and its side-effects. We should definitely not count on it.

Prof. Paul Crutzen
Professor of Atmospheric Chemistry at the Max Planck Institute for
Chemistry, Germany
Recipient of the 1995 Nobel Prize in Chemistry

Would it not be safer and more effective to use natural processes (e.g., planting more trees) to remove CO_2 from the atmosphere than to use scientific ones like geo-engineering?

I do not see it as an either-or scenario. Planting trees on a large scale would definitely be a geo-engineering measure. However, even if we were able to afforest or reforest large areas of land today, it would take decades until forests could act as valuable carbon sinks. This is not a short-term measure, and additionally, we would need to be clear on the issue of land use, e.g., there would be more trees but less agricultural land.

What I regard as an urgent and globally needed agreement is stopping deforestation as this contributes to global warming. Trees contain large amounts of carbon and much of it is released as CO_2 into the atmosphere when we cut them down. According to the FAO, natural forests have decreased by a net 6.6 million ha per year from 2010 to 2015, an area that corresponds to the size of Lithuania.

Prof. Paul Crutzen
Professor of Atmospheric Chemistry at the Max Planck Institute for
Chemistry, Germany
Recipient of the 1995 Nobel Prize in Chemistry

Not really. At present we have added more than 400 Gt (400 billion tons) of carbon into the atmosphere since the beginning of the industrial revolution. About half of it is still there, most of the rest has gone into the ocean. The entire standing forest holds around 600 Gt of carbon. Doubling the forests would have strong environmental consequences, especially in the case of forest fires. Also, the carbon tied up in trees won't stay there as the trees will die and fall apart. As far as efficiency is concerned, the CO_2 collection rate of a tree is about 1,000 times slower than one could collect from the air with a comparably sized collector.

Prof. Klaus Lackner
Director of Center for Negative Carbon Emissions
Arizona State University, USA

Adapting to and mitigating climate change will take time — putting the right infrastructure, incentives, policies and agreements in place will not happen overnight. It will require the coordination and participation of all stakeholders, governments, international institutions, corporations, NGOs and the general public. Geo-engineering allows us to extend the time we have to perform these transitions, but comes with (too) many risks.

This is why, as the previous respondents have argued, transitioning to a sustainable energy system should be our priority. If we wish to avoid the worst effects of climate change, we should replace fossil fuels with renewable energy sources such as solar, wind and geothermal energy.

Chapter 2

Fossil Fuels

Over the past two centuries, our societies have been powered by fossil fuels. These sources, such as oil, coal and natural gas, were easy to extract and convert into usable energy.

Despite catalysing great human progress and innovation, this has had adverse environmental effects. Extracting fossil fuels from the ground often risks contaminating nearby ecosystems and water sources, while consuming them releases CO_2, which accumulates in the atmosphere. The latter consequence is a source of great concern as it is one of the main causes of climate change, and because we consume fossil fuels at a rate greater than the Earth can sustain, the presence of CO_2 in our atmosphere has been raised to a level not seen in 3 million years.[v]

This is especially worrying because human civilisation has developed benefiting from a relatively stable climate over the past 10,000 years, and because the consequences of future climate change on our societies imply important risks. This is why governments are focusing their efforts on reducing CO_2 emissions both by promoting carbon-efficient technologies and transitioning to cleaner forms of energy.

In what ways is the increased concentration of CO_2 in the atmosphere detrimental to us and to the environment?

Adding CO_2 to the atmosphere interferes with the natural carbon cycle. The atmosphere, biosphere and oceans are in close contact with each other. So, some of the carbon will redistribute itself between these reservoirs. While the surface ocean and the biosphere tend to react fast, the deep ocean will take up to a 1,000 years to equilibrate with the surface of the planet. These reservoirs comprise the mobile carbon pool. Beyond these reservoirs, a large amount of carbon is tied up in the soil and in mineral carbonates. Smaller amounts are present as reduced carbon. This carbon is quite immobile and its interaction with the mobile carbon is very slow. Roughly half the CO_2 added to the atmosphere will stay for a few hundred years. Over a 1,000 years, the ocean will equilibrate with the air and take on 75–80% of the total. For the excess carbon to leave the mobile carbon pool will take tens of thousands of years. The ability of the CO_2 to stick around makes changes in the CO_2 from a human perspective virtually permanent.

The most immediate impact is global warming. This in turn affects the hydrological cycle and causes dramatic changes in weather patterns. This is hard on human societies because infrastructures are designed for a particular climate. Warming also leads to the melting of glaciers, which in turn will result in ocean rises, putting at risk a large fraction of the world population. Beyond warming, CO_2 dissolved in water becomes carbonic acid and the acidification of the surface ocean will lead to significant ecological changes.

Prof. Klaus Lackner
Director of Center for Negative Carbon Emissions
Arizona State University, USA

What contribution do fossil fuels make to climate change?

Carbon pollution from fossil fuels is far and away the dominant driver of climate change. The overwhelming amount of scientific evidence makes this abundantly clear. People are the cause of this pollution through our daily activities, from the oil we use in our cars to the coal and natural gas that generate our electricity. But, it's also people, through our intellect, creativity and resiliency, who can develop and implement technology and policy solutions to attack this problem.

The challenges of transitioning to a low-carbon future naturally present problems of collective action, reducing our dependence on fossil-based energy being one of the toughest tests. But we're seeing important progress. In the USA, the Clean Power Plan announced in 2015 represents the first ever US national standards that address carbon pollution from power plants. The policy aims to reduce carbon pollution from the power sector by 32% below 2005 levels by 2030. The measures taken by US states to meet their targets will increase efficiency, reduce coal use and increase our use of renewables such as wind and solar power.

Globally, the 2015 Paris agreement brings together all countries in advancing a more sustainable, low-carbon future. Many believed that forces against collective action might prevent such a deal from being reached. But the bottom-up approach of the Paris agreement that allows countries to define their contributions to control carbon pollution provides a framework that can strengthen over time. China, for instance, led the world in developing clean energy projects in 2015 while taking steps to reduce its coal use. Actions of states, cities and other subnational governments also played an important role in setting the stage for the Paris agreement and will continue to play important roles in helping countries across the world take actions to reduce carbon pollution and build resilience to climate change.[vi]

Prof. Victoria Arroyo
Executive Director of the Georgetown Climate Center
Georgetown University, USA

What encourages fossil fuel consumption and prevents us from switching to a more sustainable source of energy?

Inertia is a big factor. Much of the world relies on a fossil-based energy system. Breaking the mould and finding ways to make big changes in the face of deeply rooted interests is always a tough challenge. But we've met great challenges before and we can do it again.

Market forces are also important in our transition to cleaner energy. For instance, the availability of inexpensive natural gas in recent years has been a big driver in a shift away from coal-based electricity generation. Wind and solar power are increasingly cost-competitive with fossil-based energy and the market share of these renewable sources continues to grow.[vii] Polices at all levels of government that support carbon pollution reductions and promote clean energy are critical to maintaining this progress. Sensible and robust policy provides the clear market signal that business and industry need to invest in cleaner energy sources. Progress made in 2015 both internationally with the Paris agreement and within the USA with the Clean Power Plan are two significant examples of policy changes that will drive us toward a more sustainable energy future — along with innovation at the subnational level (states, cities and businesses).

Prof. Victoria Arroyo
Executive Director of the Georgetown Climate Center
Georgetown University, USA

What types of costs are associated with a transition to a sustainable energy system? How can governments finance such a transition and how can they be galvanised to do so?

The potential human costs are enormous if we fail to transition early and gradually to a low-carbon energy system. A delayed and precipitous adjustment could lead to large-scale job losses, early 'stranding' of assets before the end of their useful life and other forms of potential economic and financial disruption, not to mention the loss of human life from climate change. These costs can be managed. When polluting energy capital stock is retired, it should be replaced with clean energy. Our research at Oxford shows that we do not have the carbon budget to build new polluting capital stock. Similarly, the gradual winding down of polluting sectors would allow for the retraining of people to take up jobs created elsewhere in the economy, including in new clean sectors.

Governments are vital in financing the transition. While private capital will be extremely important, the cost of that capital will depend very strongly upon the perceived risks of policy reversals. So, a clear commitment by government to the transition, using mechanisms (including legal mechanisms) to limit the possibility of future policy backtracks, will make financing the transition much less risky and hence cheaper.

Prof. Cameron Hepburn
Professor of Environmental Economics
University of Oxford, UK

Constructing sustainable energy systems means that the present generation is able to access the resources it needs to live a particular quality of life without impinging on the abilities of future generations to live a similar quality of life. The costs of business as usual, of not transitioning to a 100% renewable energy system for all, have already contributed to catastrophe-inducing climate change and the devastating pollution of air, water and land. Numerous studies have shown the costs of inaction on climate change far outstrip the price tag for a clean energy transition. The true costs of dirty energy, including environmental clean up and social harm, are rarely included in the price tag.

For the sake of argument, let us nevertheless isolate the costs of a renewable energy roll-out versus (still highly subsidised) dirty energy use. The upfront costs of some renewable energy may be steeper than some sources of dirty energy, though this is not a given. What is certain is that over time the costs of sustainable energy are almost invariably far lower. The costs of renewable technologies have plummeted and the unit costs of renewable electricity may well approach zero in the coming decades. The lifespan of solar panels is longer than what the economic projections take into account, making them an even better deal for many consumers. Additionally, studies show that adding renewables to the grid in fact lowers all consumers' energy costs.

Stephanie Brancaforte
Global Campaign Leader on Climate & Energy at Greenpeace

Sustainable energy has zero fuel costs (except for bioenergy) and low operation and maintenance costs compared with fossil fuel and nuclear technologies. The principal costs of sustainable energy systems are the capital costs, and these can be paid for by consumers, not governments. Large-scale renewable electricity systems can be funded by electricity consumers paying for feed-in tariffs or renewable energy certificates. Government finance can be restricted to grants for research, development and demonstration, new transmission lines and other infrastructure, and the initial funding of low-interest loans distributed by a sustainable energy finance corporation, which would become self-sustaining as loans are repaid. Governments can further assist the transition by setting targets for renewable electricity and heat and energy efficiency, regulating to require electricity utilities to accept feed-ins and to pay a fair price for them, setting energy performance standards for buildings, appliances and other equipment, energy labelling of buildings, appliances and other equipment and removing subsidies for the production and use of fossil fuels.

To galvanise governments, community, faith, academic, professional and union organisations must exert strong pressure through public meetings, media and non-violent actions.

Dr. Mark Diesendorf
Associate Professor and Deputy Director of Interdisciplinary
Environmental Studies
University of New South Wales, Australia

What are the social benefits (e.g., jobs) that a transition to a sustainable energy system is likely to provide?

We at the Georgetown Climate Center support US states in their efforts to reduce carbon pollution and to transition to a clean energy economy as well as to prepare for the impacts of climate change. Many states are achieving cost-effective carbon pollution reductions and with benefits to their economies, while reducing energy costs for consumers, driving clean energy innovation and improving public health. These benefits are occurring in part because of changes in the markets, including the availability of inexpensive natural gas and more cost-competitive solar and wind power. However, these positive changes are also driven by innovative and ambitious state policies. For example, at the end of 2015, 37 states had renewable standards or goals, 27 states had energy efficiency standards or goals, and ten states had some kind of cap-and-trade programme to reduce CO_2 emissions. The Clean Power Plan builds on state successes to bring greater clean energy benefits to all states. States are also working together to promote a shift to zero emission vehicles (such as electric vehicles). Weaning our cars from gasoline and shifting our energy grid to cleaner fuels together can result in significant carbon reductions, while also reducing air pollution and improving public health.

In addition to the social benefits of a transition to clean energy, building more resilient communities in the face of climate change is vital. While much work remains, important progress is underway in several US states and communities. For example, New York City, which suffered $19 billion in damage from Hurricane Sandy in 2012, requires in its Waterfront Revitalisation Program that new development and redevelopment projects consider and mitigate risks posed by climate change and sea-level rise. Maryland counties are developing plans to prepare for sea-level rise and the state's coastal smart guidelines require that all state projects and investments be designed to account for a future rise in sea levels. More information about climate adaptation efforts of states and cities is readily accessible in our Adaptation Clearinghouse.[viii]

Prof. Victoria Arroyo
Executive Director of the Georgetown Climate Center
Georgetown University, USA

Our world is in a systemic crisis characterised by poverty, accelerating environmental degradation and inequality. What's at stake is the capacity of our planet to sustain life. The Sustainable Development Goals (SDGs) provide a solid framework for all stakeholders to collaborate in tackling these issues. A resilient and inclusive low-carbon economy represents new business opportunities, further innovation, sustainable growth and job creation on a massive scale: in other words, integrated benefits for our economies, societies and the environment.

Growth strategies aligned with the SDGs will boost development in emerging markets unlocking trillions in US$ trapped by economic stagnation and social instability. They will guide us to encourage sustainable production and consumption patterns while improving the well-being of people and communities worldwide. An increasing number of companies are already realising enormous savings through investments in energy efficiency, renewables and emission reduction initiatives. Scaled up, these measures have the potential to boost global economic output significantly, which would in turn translate into numerous social benefits through employment and economic and political stability.

Peter Bakker
President of the World Business Council for Sustainable Development

Benefits include a better environment and better health through reducing Greenhouse Gas (GHG) emissions, the pollution of air and water and land degradation, improved energy security and a cap on energy prices, once the initial investments have been made. Many new jobs are created by the manufacture, installation and sales of sustainable energy technologies.

Dr. Mark Diesendorf
Associate Professor and Deputy Director of Interdisciplinary
Environmental Studies
University of New South Wales, Australia

In British Columbia, the Clean Energy Act came into force in 2010, setting out 16 energy objectives including conservation and GHG reduction. The Act commits British Columbia to generating at least 93% of electricity from clean or renewable resources. In fact, British Columbia's electricity supply was 97.9% clean for the year ending 31 March 2015, and 25% came from private renewables.

We are seeing innovative companies generating green jobs, creating sustainable businesses and stimulating low-carbon investments.

Using the best new technologies in British Columbia means our industries are gaining a competitive edge that only clean technology can provide. All the while, we continue to export innovations around the globe, helping businesses save money and the environment.

Our green economy provides this foundation for a secure future through investments and job creation around the province. For instance, we have seen a 48% growth in the clean technology sector sales since 2008.

Mary Polak
Minister of the Environment of British Columbia, Canada

How can we decarbonise? What steps need to be taken and policies enacted in order for us to transition to a post-carbon society?

Decarbonisation entails balancing the carbon budget. For every ton of carbon that enters the mobile carbon pool, another ton will have to leave. Since the atmosphere retains half the CO_2 that is injected into it for a very long time, it is also necessary that for every ton of CO_2 injected into the atmosphere, another ton will have to be removed from it. This can be done by growing biomass, by technical means or other ways of accelerating the removal of CO_2 from the air.

Prof. Klaus Lackner
Director of Center for Negative Carbon Emissions
Arizona State University, USA

Global CO_2 emissions can be divided into two groups. One group, representing approximately 50% of the total, needs intergovernmental agreements to contain or reduce them. The other half provides an extraordinary business opportunity to create jobs, advance new business models and spur economic activity as we transition out of 200 years of industrial revolution into a new age of the low-carbon economy.

José María Figueres
President and Chairman of the Carbon War Room
Former President of Costa Rica (1994–1998)

Decarbonisation is just one component of transforming our energy system. We need to become much more efficient too. More than two-thirds of the energy we use is wasted by inefficiencies. A concerted effort to reduce the carbon intensity (CO_2 emissions per unit of energy used) and energy intensity (energy used per unit of GDP) by 5% a year is needed throughout this century. Policy measures should focus on measuring and achieving this goal. There are already many technological options available, such as solar photovoltaics, wind turbines and natural gas. Many more are coming soon: electric cars, batteries and a more modern electric grid, to name a few. There are also many technologies on the horizon such as making fuels from renewable energy, CO_2, and water. Policies to provide strong government and industry support are crucial to the sustained success of the energy transition.

Prof. Sally Benson
Director of the Precourt Institute for Energy and Professor of Energy
Resources Engineering
Stanford University, USA

Accelerating the low-carbon transition will be a significant innovation and investment challenge, but also a huge opportunity to put our economies and societies on a safer, more sustainable path for the future. This requires action in all sectors of the economy, supported by effective policies.

The low-carbon roadmap published by the European Commission in 2011 examines how the EU can cut its emissions domestically by 80% by 2050. This is in line with science and the EU leaders' commitment to reducing emissions by 80–95% by 2050 in the context of similar reductions to be taken by developed countries as a group.

The roadmap elaborates the way that the main sectors — power generation, industry, transport, buildings and construction, as well as agriculture — can make a cost-effective low-carbon transition. Relatively fast progress can be made for example in power generation. We have already seen rapid developments in the run-up to achieving the EU's target of getting 20% of our energy from renewable sources by 2020, which will require significantly higher increases in the share of renewables in the power sector. Substantial progress is also possible in the buildings sector through sustained efforts to build new, low-energy houses, renovate existing buildings and increase the efficiency of heating and cooling systems.

Furthermore, continued emission reductions can be achieved in transport and industry, mostly through improvements in efficiency. After 2030, however, innovative technologies will be needed, such as the deployment of electric mobility (i.e., electric cars) and carbon capture and storage. According to the roadmap, agricultural emissions will be the ones that are reduced the least, due in part to the growing global food demand and the fact that further reductions will require changes towards consuming less meat.

Dr. Jos Delbeke
Director-General at the Directorate General for Climate Action
European Commission

Are there any easy and economical fixes that can quickly be implemented to reduce our CO_2 emissions?

A price on carbon would help greatly to incentivise action, but governments and politicians also need to emphasise the opportunities, including the jobs potential of going green, instead of talking only about the costs. Yes, the green transition does not come for free — but neither does business as usual (i.e., continuing on our previous path). The sooner we understand this, the sooner we will manage to make choices that are better for the long term.

Connie Hedegaard
Former European Commissioner for Climate Action
(2010–2014)
Former Danish Minister of Climate and Energy (2007–2009)
and of the Environment (2004–2007)

What types of policies can governments enact to reduce their dependence on non-renewable resources and to transition to a sustainable energy system based on renewable resources?

The steps to a rapid shift from non-renewable to renewable resource usage will include removal of the (currently vast) subsidies supporting fossil fuel mining and industries, the establishment of a robust price on carbon, regulatory and legislative measures strengthening investment and innovation in renewable energy industries and encouraging more local and decentralised economic systems and ways of living.

Prof. John Wiseman
Deputy Director of the Melbourne Sustainable Society Institute
University of Melbourne, Australia

To support the transition to sustainable energy, we need targets for renewable electricity, renewable heat and energy efficiency, feed-in tariffs or contracts-for-difference for renewable energy, regulations to require electricity utilities to accept feed-ins, grants for research, development and demonstration, possibly a few new transmission lines, low-interest loans distributed by a sustainable energy finance corporation, energy performance standards and energy labelling for buildings, appliances and other equipment, and removal of subsidies for the production and use of fossil fuels. In addition, a carbon price is needed to discourage potential investors in fossil fuels and to internalise some of the external costs (environmental, health, social) of using these fuels. The revenue raised by the carbon price should be fed back to compensate low-income earners and other individuals (not corporations) who are disadvantaged by the carbon price. My preference is for a carbon tax, not an emissions trading scheme, because it's easy for governments to design an emissions trading scheme that will be ineffective.

Dr. Mark Diesendorf
Associate Professor and Deputy Director of Interdisciplinary
Environmental Studies
University of New South Wales, Australia

Renewable energies like wind and solar are already becoming competitive. However, until they can compete with conventional energies, renewables may still need public support. Several factors can contribute to increasing their competitiveness, starting with gradually integrating them into the market. Our approach is that from 2016, producers receiving state aid will have to sell their electricity in the market and have normal obligations to ensure that the electricity supply is always sufficient to meet demand. From 2017, new installations will compete for support through tenders — an optimal way to stimulate competition and bring costs down.

Moreover, the market has to function well — be open and well connected, reflect the true costs of energy and send the right price signals to investors. A stable and predictable regulatory environment at EU and national level is essential to attract investors and reduce their financial costs. Other important aspects include promoting cross-border investment so that plants are built where conditions are best. Also, to further stimulate technological innovation and cost reductions, burdensome administration should be removed, ensuring adequate R&D policies and support. Our rules for state aid reflect the fact that new technologies need the space and flexibility to develop until they become competitive.

Margrethe Vestager
Commissioner for Competition, European Union

While two-thirds of the electricity generated in Washington state comes from hydropower, the citizens of the state secured a vote of the people to require the state's electric utilities to increase the use of renewable energy over time from sources beyond hydropower. As a result of this renewable portfolio standard policy, Washington is now one of the leading US states in generating wind energy, securing investment and jobs along with additional carbon-free power, and significantly decreasing the costs of wind energy. The state currently produces one-fifth of the renewable energy for the whole of the USA.

Jay Inslee
Governor of Washington, USA

Governments have a variety of options available to them when transitioning to a sustainable energy system based on renewable resources, and their uptake depends on the countries' individual circumstances. In New Zealand, electricity generation is around 80% renewable, and the total primary energy supply is 40% renewable. The government is pursuing a number of diverse policies:

Deregulated electricity markets

The introduction and refinement of a deregulated electricity market has been the key to ensuring that New Zealand's energy is increasingly renewable. The introduction of competition in the electricity market has led to renewable energy projects being economic in the long run compared with thermal generation projects, which are vulnerable to price fluctuations and supply issues. The New Zealand government plays a 'hands off' role in the electricity sector, acting as a regulator and overseer of markets. Government sets targets and strategies but is not involved in price setting of any kind. This approach has led to the electricity market being free of all subsidies, which provides long-term certainty for investors. In 2015, New Zealand's share of renewable electricity generation was 81% and we are making strong progress towards our goal of 90% by 2025 with future generation likely to be wind and geothermal.

Transport

Transport is an area where we can improve fuel efficiency, make savings, reduce CO_2 emissions and improve New Zealand's drive to increase the use of renewables.

Electric vehicles present an opportunity for a serious leap forward, especially given our high percentage of renewable electricity generation. This year, the Government announced an ambitious and wide-ranging package of measures to increase the uptake of electric vehicles in New Zealand, including a target of doubling the number of electric vehicles every year to reach approximately 64,000 by 2021. Other government initiatives include an exemption from the road user charges for electric vehicles. This exemption recognises the importance of encouraging the use of alternative fuel technologies to help reduce CO_2 emissions. The Energy Efficiency and Conservation Agency in New Zealand has put in place initiatives such as a vehicle fuel economy labelling scheme and an online tool that helps provide information to consumers on the total cost of ownership, including energy running costs of both conventional and electric vehicles.

Inefficient fossil fuel subsidy reform

Consistent with our focus on best practice policy settings to promote renewable energy, the New Zealand government believes that it is important to address inefficiencies. We also believe more needs to be done globally to remove inefficient fossil fuel subsidies. Fossil fuel subsidies can lead to wasteful consumption, disadvantage renewable energy and drain scarce public resources that could be better spent on other sustainable forms of energy.

Simon Bridges
Minister of Energy and Resources and Minister of Transport
of New Zealand

One of the main proposals to reduce CO_2 emissions is economic. This states that governments should set the amount of pollution that can be emitted each year, and that emitters can buy permits to pollute. These permits can be kept or traded to other emitters, thus limiting pollution to an overall number. These cap-and-trade systems even allow governments to buy back some permits if they seek to reduce the overall amount of pollution. By limiting CO_2 emissions to certain level, these encourage the transition towards a low-carbon and renewable energy system.

Could establishing a cap-and-trade system and emitting permits be effective in reducing CO_2 emissions? What would be necessary for such a policy to be effective?

Carbon pricing is an important element of a sensible response to climate change for several reasons. Carbon prices increase the price paid by consumers for polluting goods and services and reduce the profit received by those who produce the pollution. Carbon pricing therefore works to reduce both the demand and the supply of pollution. There are few other policies that attack both sides simultaneously. Carbon prices provide a stimulus to substitute dirty with clean products, allowing the private sector to innovate and to work out how to best achieve this. We now have clear evidence that carbon prices reduce short-term CO_2 emissions at low cost.

Cap-and-trade systems are one realistic way of establishing a carbon price. Carbon taxes are another. Taxes have the advantage of fixing the carbon price for a specific period, while trading has the advantage of fixing the level of emissions. While taxes may in some respects be preferred for a problem such as climate change, they have tended to face greater political resistance than cap-and-trade systems. But proposals to "dividend" a proportion of the revenues out to the general public might increase their political appeal.

Prof. Cameron Hepburn
Professor of Environmental Economics
University of Oxford, UK

Putting a price on GHG emissions and using market forces to make the necessary emission reductions has been a core element of the EU climate and energy policy since the launch of the EU Emissions Trading System (EU ETS) in 2005. The EU ETS is the first — and still by far the biggest — international system for trading GHG allowances. It covers more than 11,000 power stations and industrial plants in 31 countries as well as emissions from flights between European airports.

The EU ETS works on the cap-and-trade principle with the overall cap on emissions reducing over time. In 2020, the emissions cap for the sectors covered by the ETS will be 21% lower than in 2005. By 2030, it should be 43% lower. This translates into what economic analysis has shown would be a cost-effective contribution by these sectors to meeting the EU's overall emissions reduction targets, i.e., 20% by 2020 and at least 40% by 2030, compared to 1990 levels.

Several studies show that the carbon price signal has resulted in real emission reductions since the very beginning of the EU ETS. However, over the last few years, a significant surplus of allowances has built up in the system due to lower than expected emissions and a big inflow of international credits. A significant reform in the form of a market stability reserve was recently agreed to make the ETS more robust to unexpected future demand shocks.

Furthermore, a revision for the period 2021–2030 has been proposed by the European Commission to ensure that the system will also continue to deliver cost-effective emission reductions in the coming decade. The intention is to continue to use part of the revenue from the auctioning of emission allowances to stimulate innovation and support the energy transformation in the EU's lower income member states.

Dr. Jos Delbeke
Director-General at the Directorate General for Climate Action
European Commission

One of the drawbacks of cap-and-trade systems is that the government or regional organisation issuing these permits may issue too many, thus failing to discourage CO_2 emissions. Carbon taxes have been proposed as an alternatives. These charge all polluters a fee for their CO_2 emissions, making it more expensive and therefore discouraging pollution. The tax percentage can even be increased after polluters have emitted more than a certain amount of CO_2, thus also limiting excessive quantities of pollution for those who can pay.

How would an effective carbon tax manifest itself? What would be the advantages of implementing such a tax?

An effective carbon tax would tax the carbon the moment it comes out of the ground. The tax should be paid back to those who take CO_2 and sequester it. This would raise the price of fossil carbon by the amount of the tax. If the tax is sufficiently high, it would encourage the removal of all excess carbon from the environment. An easier way to accomplish the same might be requiring those who extract, say, a ton of carbon from the ground to buy a certificate of sequestration beforehand.

Prof. Klaus Lackner
Director of Center for Negative Carbon Emissions
Arizona State University, USA

Market-based measures, such as cap-and-trade systems and carbon taxes, help bring about reductions in emissions by putting a price on carbon, as companies and economic actors are encouraged to include its value in their operational decision-making and long-term investment planning. Such measures also have the potential to generate money that can be used for climate change mitigation and adaptation.

In theory, carbon taxes and cap-and-trade systems are comparable instruments. In practice, in the EU, it has proven impossible to introduce effective harmonised taxation schemes that are sufficiently ambitious. Cap-and-trade systems are better suited to be introduced in a regulatory environment that requires flexibility, for instance, to address the need for a free allocation of emission allowances in certain sectors, while still setting the right incentives to reduce emissions and deliver on the overall environmental goal. In Europe, these considerations led to the development of the EU ETS.

Dr. Jos Delbeke
Director-General at the Directorate General for Climate Action
European Commission

Since the introduction of our Climate Action Plan in 2008, British Columbia has been recognised as a world leader in the fight against climate change. We were the first jurisdiction in North America to introduce a broad-based, revenue-neutral carbon tax and to have a carbon-neutral public sector. Our carbon tax puts a price on GHG, so they have been reduced. We are encouraging individuals and businesses to use less fossil fuel and reduce their GHG, so that those who produce emissions pay for them, and making clean energy alternatives economically appealing.

We have shown we can reduce GHG emissions while continuing to grow the economy. In June 2014, we announced that British Columbia had reached its first interim GHG emissions reduction target of 6% below 2007 levels by 2012. Because the carbon tax is revenue neutral, we've cut taxes. Every dollar generated by the carbon tax is returned to British Columbians through reductions in other taxes. In fact, for 2015/2016, the reduction in provincial revenue is forecasted to exceed carbon tax revenues by $360 million.

There is increasing global recognition that carbon pricing is not only necessary to reduce GHG emissions, but that British Columbia's broad-based, revenue-neutral carbon tax is a successful model to follow.

Mary Polak
Minister for the Environment of British Columbia, Canada

Would policies aiming to change consumer behaviour at the individual level (e.g., encouraging public transport use over car ownership) not be more effective in reducing CO_2 emissions than broad national policies like energy efficiency standards?

Individual behaviour is an important part of the solution. We need to make good buying decisions, opt for a lifestyle that reduces our own energy and carbon intensity and support political leaders who will lead, not hinder, progress. Lifestyle choices are often developed at a young age, so education is also a key component of sustaining the energy transition. At the same time, government and private sector support is needed to provide the infrastructure for more sustainable energy choices. We need excellent public transportation, access to safe lanes for bicycles, charging stations for electric vehicles and policies that drive continuous improvements in appliance and buildings.

Individuals cannot do this alone. Citizens can make good choices but only if good options are available.

Prof. Sally Benson
Director of the Precourt Institute for Energy and Professor of Energy
Resources Engineering
Stanford University, USA

Tackling the climate challenge effectively requires changes by producers and consumers throughout the economy and society. The EU experience has shown that there is no silver bullet that on its own can bring down emissions across so many sectors. Climate policies have to be built up step by step and by putting together a jigsaw of policy approaches.

Surveys show that public attitudes are evolving. According to the latest EU-wide Eurobarometer survey on climate change (March 2015), nine out of ten Europeans consider climate change a serious problem and four out of five recognise that fighting climate change and using energy more efficiently can boost the economy and employment. In the same survey, some 93% of respondents said they had already taken some personal action against climate change, such as reducing and recycling waste (74%) and trying to cut their use of disposable items (57%).

It is clear that certain behavioural changes could play a relatively important role in reducing emissions over time. For this, consumers need to be informed on the impact and options they have. EU policies, such as energy labelling on household appliances, aim to help consumers make such climate-friendly choices.

Dr. Jos Delbeke
Director-General at the Directorate General for Climate Action
European Commission

Could replacing fossil fuel subsidies with renewable energy subsidies ('feed-in tariffs') be effective in making renewables competitive? Is this a plausible policy?

Renewable energy is already competitive with most of the other conventional energy systems in many situations. When subsidies are made available to renewable energy, they may either become more competitive or, in cases when they were not yet competitive, they can become so. So, the use of subsidies has been clearly shown to be helpful for the development of renewable energy. And at some point, when the prices of renewables begin to come down, then you can start removing those subsidies. Now, while there are subsidies for renewables, at the same time, many governments still provide subsidies for producing and consuming fossil fuels. On the one hand, they give money to enhance the use and production of fossil fuels, and on the other hand, they give money to renewables so there will be less fossil fuel pollution. This kind of policy incoherence needs to be resolved. It's important to reduce the fossil fuel subsidies so that then we will perhaps not need any subsidies for renewables.

Janos Pasztor
Director of the Carnegie Climate Geoengineering Governance Project
Former UN Assistant Secretary-General for Climate Change Issues
(2015–2016)

What are the advantages of using renewable sources of energy such as solar and wind power to replace fossil fuels?

Geothermal energy provides a good example of the advantages of using renewable energy. In 2015, electricity generation from geothermal accounted for over 17% of New Zealand's total electricity supply and it is currently one of New Zealand's cheapest sources of electricity generation. It is a reliable, sustainable and clean resource that provides an alternative to using fossil fuels.

In addition to electricity generation, there is a wide range of direct uses of geothermal energy. The benefits of direct geothermal heat have been experienced across a range of sectors, such as aquaculture, forestry, horticulture and agriculture. The wood-processing company, Tenon, for example, uses direct geothermal energy to heat its timber-drying kilns, replacing natural gas in 2006. The result was a 27,900 tonnes reduction in CO_2, and cost savings of over NZ$1 million in energy costs in the first year of operating. Productivity also increased as to the wood dried more efficiently from the use of geothermal energy — all kilns could be ramped up at the same time — something that was not possible with natural gas.

Simon Bridges
Minister of Energy and Minister of Transport of New Zealand

In the 1970s and 1980s, nuclear energy was seen as the best alternative to fossil fuels, considering it emitted fewer CO_2 emissions. Renewable energy was not considered to be an effective alternative at the time as it was deemed too expensive and dilute to be effective or feasible on a large scale.

Why is nuclear energy not an adequate alternative to fossil fuels?

In brief, nuclear energy is too dangerous, too expensive, too slow to build and too intensive of CO_2:

- It is too dangerous because of its contribution to the proliferation of nuclear weapons, the rare but potentially devastating accidents and the need to manage nuclear waste for 100,000 years or more.
- It is too expensive because it is about double the price of onshore wind and new large-scale solar farms in Chile, Brazil and Uruguay are already cheaper. Soon offshore wind will be cheaper too.
- It is too slow because construction times in the USA average nine years plus planning and setting up infrastructure. The European pressurised water reactors under construction in Finland and France are each several years over their planned construction times and 2.7 times the cost of the original estimate.
- It is too intensive of CO_2 over a life cycle, as uranium ore grade is declining and so energy inputs and associated CO_2 emissions from mining and milling uranium are increasing. This applies to generation II and III reactors. Generation IV fast-breeder reactors will

have much lower life cycle CO_2 emissions, but they will not be commercially available for the foreseeable future.

Dr. Mark Diesendorf
Associate Professor and Deputy Director of Interdisciplinary
Environmental Studies
University of New South Wales, Australia

What types of policies can governments enact to facilitate the integration of renewable energies into the national electric grid?

Policies required to facilitate the integration of the renewable energy supply into national electricity grids include regulatory and pricing arrangements that strike an equitable balance between maintaining adequate levels of investment in grid infrastructure and encouraging the exploration of more decentralised and distributed household and industry energy systems.

Prof. John Wiseman
Deputy Director of the Melbourne Sustainable Society Institute
University of Melbourne, Australia

Will there still be a national electric grid when renewable energy technologies (e.g., solar-powered batteries) replace conventional fossil fuel-powered plants? Why?

In the short to medium term, it is likely that the most equitable, reliable and efficient transition to a renewable energy-based economy will involve an ongoing mix of grid-integrated and off-grid energy systems.

Prof. John Wiseman
Deputy Director of the Melbourne Sustainable Society Institute
University of Melbourne, Australia

Yes, there will still be an electric grid, but it will have a very different character and structure from the one that we currently have. The main purpose of the grid is to collect and disseminate energy produced among the widest possible number of people, whether from oil and gas or renewables. Without the grid, investment cost would be significantly greater and establishing more localised infrastructure (solar power on every person's roof) will cause greater instability than the cost of investing in the optimisation of the grid system. Also, different areas would be more heavily reliant on different energy sources, which would make all areas more volatile. The grid is essentially the most democratic and efficient way of utilising our resources.

Jostein Eikeland
CEO of Alevo

Despite the obvious advantages of renewable forms of energy, such as their very low maintenance costs and the fact that they do not harm the environment (as fossil fuels do), they have previously been said to have some deficiencies. Some have argued that solar and wind energy produce energy only when the sun is shining or the wind if blowing and that any energy produced would be too dilute at any one time to sustainably power cities and countries.

Is there any way to make up for the reality that renewable energies like solar and wind power produce electricity only at certain times?

This is far less of a key issue than most people assume. In fact, the problem currently holding back a more accelerated transference towards renewable sources is the same problem that needs to be overcome to optimise the use of traditional energy sources as well. At present, a large proportion of the energy that passes through the grid system is wasted as the technology to retain the surpluses that are injected into the grid during peak consumer usage points has not yet been integrated on a mass scale. Once we have established an effective means of storing energy, the fact that renewables are not constantly providing energy will not matter as we will have been able to process and store maximum energy to be deployed when the tap is turned off, so to speak. This is one of the main driving forces behind Alevo's battery development, which provides the means of storing excess energy to be reintegrated into the grid. On top of this, the key is to use a variety of sources spread over a wide area, including solar and wind, biogas, biomass and geothermal sources. This minimises reliance on one or two sources and mitigates the issue that these sources may produce energy only at certain points. So, the short answer is yes. The fact that renewables produce energy only at certain times can be overcome by providing the technological infrastructure for the grid to store as well as transmit energy.

Jostein Eikeland
CEO of Alevo

How can we combine various renewable energy systems to a create a constant source of energy? What technologies and infrastructures are necessary for the development of such a system?

One of the main focuses of attention needs to be overhauling the grid system to add the capacity to store the energy that is already being lost within its networks. Beyond this, it is increasingly important to develop and implement intelligent technologies and data analytics systems that enable us to track and manage patterns in energy usage in order to provide efficient but flexible power that matches demand throughout the day. Additionally, an electric grid system is perfectly capable of integrating renewable technologies if it is designed to do so. However, most grids at present are not built to accommodate these sources. In this regard, transforming the grid system to integrate and optimise the use of renewable energies will be a long-term project. This factor makes the importance of optimising the grid in its current form with data analytics and storage systems an even greater priority.

Jostein Eikeland
CEO of Alevo

Chapter 3

Biodiversity

Biodiversity is crucial to human survival. Not only does it provide us vital services which ensure ecosystems can remain healthy, but these services are also crucial in the functioning of human societies. Certain organisms allow us to produce our food, others ensure there is not too much CO_2 in the air and others ensure that ecosystems are preserved. In a biodiverse system, if one organism can no longer fulfil an ecosystem function, another will take its place.

In recent decades, habitat loss, often because of human activity and the effects of climate change have combined to threaten biodiversity where it once thrived. Among the areas most affected are the biodiversity hotspots, relatively small areas that hold a disproportionate amount of the world's biodiversity. Some animals have adapted to increasing human influence by changing their behaviour and feeding patterns to survive in urban areas. Nevertheless, those not able to adapt quickly enough to the Anthropocene are facing extinction.

Knowledge about the risks and threats posed by biodiversity loss has been growing with international institutions, NGOs and governments developing frameworks to deal with the preservation of biodiversity. These have included increasing the number of protected areas (which cannot be exploited) on land and sea, the sustainable use of natural resources and increased awareness about the benefits of biodiversity to our societies. The combined implementation of these policies should help play a role in our preservation of biodiversity.

How have human processes (the Anthropocene) impacted on the environment thus far? Are they reversible?

Our use of natural resources accelerated exponentially with the start of the industrial era, becoming unsustainable due to the population and economic development boom that began in the 1950s. Never before in the history of the planet, has one single species ever had such an important impact. After we successfully boosted food security by domesticating animals and plants and intensifying agriculture, we also ingeniously found a way to unlock the energy trapped in our planet's large fossil fuel reserves that fuelled our industrial revolution, intensification of agriculture and exponential population growth. More recently, unprecedented technological and infrastructural development has accelerated the global mobility of people and goods.

These achievements were not without consequences. It has taken a long time, but today, the undeniable evidence of the impact of our activities and the risk of a global ecosystem collapse is vividly clear, as are the catastrophic consequences for our own well-being. We have lost about a third of the world's forests, initially in the temperate world and then, more recently, in the tropics, where much of today's deforestation is driven by large-scale production of a few commodities like palm oil, sugar cane, timber, paper, soy and beef. This is driving the deforestation, degradation and fragmentation of natural habitats.

The combination of deforestation and of rising GHG emissions from the burning of fossil fuels has warmed up not only the atmosphere but also the oceans. In the last 200 years, oceans have absorbed around a third of the CO_2 produced by human activities and over 90% of the extra heat trapped by the rising concentrations of atmospheric GHG.

Scientists are warning that sea temperatures and acidification could bring the ocean ecosystem to collapse with catastrophic consequences. The ocean produces more than half the oxygen we breathe and ensures food security for hundreds of millions of people, particularly in poor coastal communities. Warming waters are affecting many marine species already. Even corals, although they are adapted to warm tropical waters, are dying because of abnormally warm water temperatures, a phenomenon called bleaching, where their beautiful colours turn white. We have lost half of world's tropical coral reefs in the last 30 years!

Unsustainable hunting is another short-term driver of wildlife extinction and decimation. Iconic species like tigers, elephants, rhinos and many other less charismatic ones are killed to supply the lucrative wildlife trade, much of it illegal. We are also catching fish faster than they can reproduce — 90% of the world's fisheries are either fully fished or overfished.

Dr. Marco Lambertini
Director-General of WWF International

Habitat loss remains a leading threat to biodiversity, and it is largely driven by our growing appetite for resources. Unsustainable fishing, logging, mining, agriculture and other activities are threatening the survival of an increasing number of species, such as the Pacific Bluefin tuna, the Chinese pufferfish, the American eel and the Chinese cobra. Climate change is adding to the stress on species and its impacts are set to grow. Experts warn that future global temperature rises could threaten up to one in six species under current policies.

The consequences of mismanaging our natural habitat are evident in the increasing rate of species extinction, which is estimated to be more than 1,000 times the natural rate. Today, we are witnessing the greatest extinction crisis since dinosaurs disappeared from the face of the Earth 65 million years ago. Unlike previous mass extinctions, this one is largely caused by humans.

While we cannot fully reverse the situation, we do have the power to make significant positive changes that can protect and regenerate the natural habitats that we depend on for our survival. The international community has agreed on a series of targets aimed at improving the health of the planet, including the SDGs, the Paris Agreement on Climate Change, and the Aichi Targets on Biodiversity. All these recognise the critical role that healthy ecosystems play in achieving sustainability.

The challenge now is to move from agreement to implementa-tion. This means reducing the pressures on biodiversity and implementing proactive measures to restore species and their habitats. One tool at our disposal is expanding the existing coverage of terrestrial, coastal and marine protected areas, such as national parks or marine reserves. Protected areas are proven cost-effective and sustainable natural solutions that can address a range of environmental and social needs on land and sea.

Another example of action is the Global Partnership on Forest Landscape Restoration, coordinated by the International Union for Conservation of Nature (IUCN). It was estimated in 2011 that there are two billion hectares available globally where opportunities for restoration may be found. Analysis suggests that restoring 350 million ha by 2030 can sequester significant amounts of CO_2, helping to reduce the impacts of climate change.

Inger Andersen
Director-General of the International Union for Conservation
of Nature (IUCN)

How are animals adapting to the effects of human-induced environmental change? How have the Anthropocene and its initiating processes affected animal behaviour?

Different species adapt in different ways. Many species of birds, foxes, raccoons and even bears (when allowed) found in cities around the world are becoming increasingly urbanised. Manatees have learned to escape the winter cold by congregating around power plant, taking advantage of the warm water run-off. Many insect and bird species are extending their range due to global warming — hot climate species appearing further north. As mosquitos appear further north, so too do the diseases they carry, such as dengue fever and the zika virus. Other species, needing the cold, are retreating higher into the mountains. As temperatures rise, some plant species are flowering earlier, some insects are breeding earlier. But many other species are suffering. The polar bear is not able to adapt well to shrinking sea ice. Thousands of species suffer from pollution — whales and fish are found with more and more harmful chemicals in their bodies. So are we.

Dr. Jane Goodall
Founder of the Jane Goodall Institute and UN Messenger of Peace

Some animal species have adapted their behaviour in order to be able to live in a world dominated by people. For example, urban foxes have a different diet, lifestyle and even a different morphology from that of their recent ancestors. This is a common pattern since there are many new ecological niches created by people, and the most adaptable animals have successfully evolved to exploit them. These are often species that we think of as pests because they become very abundant in activities that are specifically for people. However, the other side of the coin is that there are many other species that cannot adapt successfully, and these are the ones that we should be concerned about. Species that have particular lifestyles that are difficult to accommodate, such as the giant panda or large carnivores, are especially at risk. But there are a large number of other species as well that are threatened. The latest IUCN red list of threatened species includes 77,340 assessed species, of which 22,784 are threatened with extinction.[ix]

Prof. Georgina Mace
Professor of Biodiversity and Ecosystems
Director of the UCL Centre for Biodiversity
and Environment Research
University College London, UK

The planet has been evolving in and out of glacial and interglacial periods for millions of years and has experienced natural variability over its hundreds of millions of years of existence with high-order biological life, and during this time, we've had variability in species from plants to microorganisms to higher order mammals on the planet. However, the difference is that now, in the Anthropocene, the pace of change is unprecedented. In fact, the pace of change is so quick that species on Earth are not able to adapt to these changes as animals and plants have been doing naturally throughout our planet's history.

So, what we're seeing now is the die-back of forests, coral reefs collapsing under unnatural degrees of warming events causing bleaching, upwelling from oceans, changes in fish stocks moving very rapidly from one latitude to another, and it's happening so fast that science does not yet know, for example, whether the changes in halibut and cod stocks are occurring in ways where they will be stabilising in a new stable state or whether they are simply urgently positioning themselves in a new latitude and then potentially facing a collapse (and dying out). So, in this way, the pace is the key. We have seen change before, but never so fast. In fact, it is now so fast, we are in the sixth mass extinction of species on the planet, the first to be caused by another species, us humans.

Prof. Johan Rockström
Executive Director of the Stockholm Resilience Centre
Professor in Environmental Science
Stockholm University

Adaptation to environmental changes is the key to the way life has evolved on our planet. But the way Homo technologicus is today impacting on the planet's natural systems has left species struggling to adapt to the scale and pace of change. Extinction rates of vertebrates over the last 100 years are a 100 times higher than historic rates. WWF's Living Planet Index shows a 52% decline in wildlife populations since 1970, meaning that some species have disappeared forever, and that half of the world's wildlife population has been lost in less than a generation — species that have been around for millions of years.

Some species, particularly in the tropics, are very sensitive to habitat degradation, and habitat loss is the main driver of extinction and decline. The equation is frighteningly simple: a reduced natural habitat equals fewer wildlife. It's true that a small minority of species has adapted to live in man-made environments like cities and farmlands, but the majority have not.

In addition to habitat loss, the impact of climate change is also being felt not only amongst more mobile species like birds, fish and butterflies but also amongst turtles and cetaceans that are expanding north, birds are migrating earlier. Mountain and high altitude species that are adapted to cold environments are quickly running out of suitable habitat. Arctic species that depend on sea ice cover, like polar bears, beluga whales and bearded seals are beginning to run out of ice. It is estimated that climate change, based on current projections, will soon be the most powerful driver of species extinction globally.

We are seeing some examples of animals changing their territory or range in response to climate change. For example, butterflies have been documented shifting their range towards the poles and to higher altitudes. Changes in ocean temperature are altering the timing of key biological events such as plankton blooms and the spawning and migration of turtles, fish and invertebrates. However, some species may be unable to adapt, some may not have available habitats to move into, and changes in the timing of biological events can have severe consequences on other species and even for broader ecosystems.

Dr. Marco Lambertini
Director-General of WWF International

What makes biodiversity so integral to ecosystems and so vital to human processes?

There is no life without biodiversity. It is as simple as that. The survival of the people is dependent on oceans. For example, in the Pacific, in Tuvalu, and in many other small island states, the oceans are the basis of our livelihood. If you damage the oceans, there is no basis for survival. And increasingly, the islands dependent on the oceans, and on the system of the oceans, find themselves needing to protect the people affected as well. And we now know that the atmosphere, the air we breath is at great risk because of pollution and CO_2. In this sense, carbonisation is not only in the air, but also in the oceans. In situations like Tuvalu, we have a problem of acidification, of the carbonisation of the oceans, of coral reefs, of biodiversity, of rocks, of sand, all carbonised because of uncontrolled GHG in the atmosphere. So, we must address this: we have to both cut down the carbonisation and move to decarbonise our economies, particularly in industrialised countries.

H.E. Enele Sopoaga
Prime Minister of Tuvalu

In what ways do our societies benefit from and are somewhat dependent on ecosystem services?

Forests, for example, protect watersheds, provide clean drinking water, and prevent erosion. They also provide clean air and oxygen. They sequester CO_2 in trees and in forest soils, thus mitigating global warming. The great rainforests control global rainfall. Mangrove forests protect the land from storms — where mangroves are intact, the devastating effects of tsunamis are considerably reduced. Many ecosystems, especially tropical rainforests, provide food and medicinal plants on which many indigenous people depend. Nature provides mechanisms for pollination, on which a large percentage of our food depends. Bees are the main pollinators, but some plants are pollinated by birds and bats. In addition to the ecological services, ecosystems provide spiritual benefits and are often integrated in different cultures.

Dr. Jane Goodall
Founder of the Jane Goodall Foundation and UN Messenger of Peace

For most of our natural history, humankind has been depending on nature for food, materials, health and shelter. Although this is less obvious in our largely urbanised and globalised world, this is still the case.

Much of the food, timber, fibre and the medicine that we use in our everyday lives still comes directly from wild nature. Forests, lakes, rivers and mountains provide innumerable ecosystem services to our well-being, health, economy and even social stability. The oxygen we breathe and the clean water we drink need healthy ecosystems.

The water we use in our homes does not come from the tap but from mountains, forests, lakes and rivers. Even our agriculture and food security depend on pollination, climate stability, soil preservation, flood control and regular rainfall patterns that are all provided by natural systems and by biodiversity, the plants and animals that make them function.

Dr. Marco Lambertini
Director-General of WWF International

Despite the societal benefits biodiversity provides, the extinction rate has gone up to around 1,000–100,00 times the normal level in recent decades, according to some estimates.[x] This rapid rise in species extinction, unprecedented in 65 million years, has been termed 'the Sixth Mass Extinction', after the five previous points in Earth's history when extinctions had reached such a high level.[xi]

How are we responsible for the 'Sixth Mass Extinction'? Which of our collective actions in particular have increased the extinction rate to such an abnormal level?

The immense growth of the human population, coupled with increasing global levels of industrialisation and consumption, have played a major role in the unprecedented extinction rate of plant and animal species, often referred to as the sixth mass extinction. Collectively, our high reliance on fossil fuels — through mass industrialisation and individual consumption — has undoubtedly contributed to increased CO_2 emissions in the atmosphere, as well as pollution of our vital water sources.

Increasing urbanisation, with more than half the world now living in cities, is equal to higher demands for energy and material goods, which require more electricity to power production and lifestyle needs. This is still heavily reliant on the extraction of coal from the Earth with CO_2 and other harmful byproducts resulting in the degradation and loss of important life-sustaining ecosystems and habitats. These ecosystems also provide us with invaluable services through various natural processes. For example, wetlands provide water purification services for the environment, forests serve as the Earth's lungs by purifying the air and insects ensure thriving agricultural crops through their pollination services.

Theressa Frantz
Head of Environmental Programmes at WWF South Africa

What consequences does biodiversity loss have on ecosystems?

The life forms that make up an ecosystem are interconnected and dependent on each other in ways we do not yet fully understand. We do know that the decline or extinction of one species can trigger a chain reaction affecting the whole ecosystem. In 1999, overfishing led to a crash in herring and pollock populations in the north Pacific. This affected populations of sea lions and seals who feed on them, which, in turn, are an important prey of orcas. Orcas turned to other food, including sea otters. The 90% decline in the numbers of sea otters led to a massive increase in their favourite food, sea urchins. Sea urchins feed on kelp and kelp forests were soon devastated. And this affected the many species of life they support, including mussels, fish, ducks, gulls, bald eagles and the remaining sea otters, sea lions and orcas.

Dr. Jane Goodall
Founder of the Jane Goodall Foundation and UN
Messenger of Peace

What repercussions could biodiversity loss have on our societies and the processes they are dependent on?

Biodiversity underpins all life on Earth. Without species and ecosystems, there would be no oxygen-rich air to breathe, no food to eat, no medicine and little water to drink. There would be no human society at all. Biodiversity provides ecosystem goods and services that benefit humans and sustain our lives. These services all depend on the ecological processes of functioning ecosystems that are underpinned by biodiversity. The benefits of biodiversity have been the foundation of the well-being of all past human civilisations, while the degradation of ecosystems and depletion of natural resources have been root causes for the collapse of past civilisations.

The loss of biodiversity often reduces the productivity of ecosystems, thereby shrinking nature's basket of goods and services from which we draw. It destabilises ecosystems, weakens their ability to deal with natural disasters such as floods, droughts and hurricanes, and with human-caused stresses, such as pollution and climate change. Already, we are spending huge sums in response to flood and storm damages exacerbated by deforestation; climate change is expected to increase such damage.

Biodiversity loss also hurts us in other ways. Our cultural identity is deeply rooted in our biological environment. Plants and animals are symbols of our world, preserved in flags, coats of arms, songs, names of sport clubs, sculptures and other images that define us and our societies. We draw inspiration from just looking at nature's beauty and power.

Dr. Braulio Ferreira de Souza Dias
Executive Secretary of the Convention on Biological Diversity

Biodiversity provides important resources in support of humans: food, fibre, shelter and sometimes just flavour (bergamot orange in Earl Gray Tea) or scent. In other words, there is a great deal of direct consumption. Individual molecules from nature are used in medicine or in science, like the molecule from *Thermus aquaticus* which drives the polymerase chain reaction that has revolutionised diagnostic and forensic medicine and made the human genome project possible.

Biodiversity has also been shown not only to be the structural element of ecosystems but also to contribute in important ways to ecosystem functioning, ecosystem resilience to stress and to productivity and efficiency in resource use. In other words, any ecosystem service we value — such as the provision of reliable supplies of clean water (e.g., the New York City watershed), the pollination of crop plants, and more — erodes as biodiversity of ecosystems erode.

What is little appreciated is the value that biodiversity plays as the fundamental library for the life sciences because every species is a set of solutions to biological problems, any one of which could turn out to be of great value. Observations of particular species led to the discovery of antibiotics, and to the concept of vaccination. A recent discovery from a Nova Scotia soil fungus holds the promise of addressing antibiotic-resistant microbes (the so-called super bugs). A degraded planet serves no one.

Prof. Thomas Lovejoy
Professor at George Mason University, USA

How have human processes and activities been responsible for a great portion of the deforestation and habitat destruction which has contributed to biodiversity loss? Is there any way we can remedy this?

Human activities have impacted on biodiversity since time immemorial, but we are confronted with a doomsday scenario where the speed at which it is happening is a major source of concern. When humans conserve biodiversity, is it altruistic? I would say an emphatic NO, in as much as the survival of humankind depends on the conservation of our biodiversity. Biodiversity underpins life on earth. The ecosystem services that nature provides us are often understated and misunderstood. I often cite the figure of 1.4% of the entire land surface of this planet as providing humankind with over 30% of our needs.

We need to protect animal and plant habitats as much as we need to protect individual species. Just like us humans, plants and animals also like their comfort zones, and they too need their environment to survive and in return to ensure our survival — it is a symbiotic relationship that is now also being threatened by climate change.

H.E. Ameenah Gurib-Fakim
President of Mauritius

Climate change, biodiversity loss, deforestation and the degradation of the world's drylands, wetlands, mountains and oceans are inter-linked and cannot be addressed by a compartmentalised approach. While the loss of individual species catches our attention, it is the fragmentation, degradation and outright loss of forests, wetlands, coral reefs and other ecosystems that pose the gravest threat to biodiversity. Forests are home to much of the known terrestrial biodiversity, but about 45% of the Earth's original forests are now gone, cleared mostly during the past century. Forests are increasingly threatened as a result of deforestation, fragmentation, logging, hunting, fires, climate change and other stressors that can be linked to human activities. Their degradation threatens biodiversity by reducing habitat and the provision of ecological services.

Habitat loss through changes of land use, in particular the conversion of natural ecosystems to cropland and rangelands, continues to be the biggest direct cause of biodiversity loss. Already, more than half the Earth's 14 terrestrial biomes have seen between 20 and 50% of their total area converted to cropland and rangeland. Ecosystems can be managed to lessen the vulnerability of biodiversity to the negative impacts of climate change, to combat desertification and land degradation and to help people adapt to the adverse effects of climate change. Ecosystem-based approaches for adaptation can include sustainable management, conservation and restoration of ecosystems as part of an overall adaptation strategy that takes into account multiple social, economic and cultural co-benefits for indigenous peoples and local communities.

Dr. Braulio Ferreira de Souza Dias
Executive Secretary of the Convention on Biological Diversity

What types of policies can governments enact to preserve biodiversity and their encompassing ecosystems?

It requires a truly integrated approach. Progress in cleaning up our water and air must continue in the context of preserving critical habitat, particularly in areas where species are threatened. Coordinating these efforts will ensure that stressors are reduced across entire ecosystems. Comprehensive plans to encourage low impact development, manage stormwater, reduce toxics, limit carbon pollution and preserve riparian habitats will work together, yielding benefits beyond the sum of their parts. Investments must also be made to better understand the breadth of species in those ecosystems so that our management efforts can adapt and target those species at greatest risk.

Jay Inslee
Governor of Washington, USA

Our Vision 2021 paves ways for Bangladesh to graduate as a middle-income country by 2021 and our Vision 2041 envisions that Bangladesh will emerge as a developed country by 2041.

In order to realise the ambitious visions in our sustainable development pathway, we focus on the preservation of our ecosystems. Despite all the challenges that we face in terms of environment, ecology and climate change, our people have turned vulnerability to resilience. For instance, we have developed home-grown technologies, solutions, approaches and initiatives within our limited resources and means. Despite the fact that climate change and disaster heavily impact on our agriculture, we have attained self-sufficiency in food production. We developed many varieties of rice that are tolerant to floods, droughts or salinity. We have installed around 4.5 million solar household systems that have changed lives in poor households and off-grid areas of Bangladesh. Similarly, solar irrigation pumps, millions of modestly improved stoves and biogas plants across villages are having transformative impacts. We mobilised our own resources to establish a National Climate Change Fund. We pledge to further mainstream sustainable development and climate change across our development policies.

The FAO and the UN Champion of the Earth recognition have reaffirmed our resolve on combating climate change and on protecting the environment. It was truly an uphill task to maintain over 6% growth for over one decade against so many challenges and constraints — where as much as 2–3% of our precious developmental gain stands to be wiped out every year on account of climate change.

H.E. Sheikh Hasina
Prime Minister of Bangladesh
UN Champion of the Earth Award, 2015

WWF's One Planet perspective asks not only governments but also companies and individuals to take part in a major shift of our economic development model to achieve the following outcomes:

- Produce better and consume wisely. Reduce inputs and waste, manage resource sustainability, scale up energy efficiency and shift to renewable energy. Adopt low footprint lifestyles and promote sustainable products.
- Redirect financial flows. Invest in sustainable activities, value nature and account for the environmental and social costs of development and investment, support and reward low impact sustainable infrastructures and resource management.
- Preserve natural capital. Recognise the intrinsic and material values of nature, protect natural systems and their biodiversity and restore degraded habitats on land and at sea.
- Equitable resource governance. Share sustainably and equitably available natural resources, make fair and informed choices, measure success beyond GDP.

Dr. Marco Lambertini
Director-General of WWF International

What role does preserving biodiversity hotspots play in protecting biodiversity worldwide? How can we preserve biodiversity hotspots?

We urgently need to protect the most important places for biodiversity on land and in the oceans. Biodiversity hotspots are located mainly in the tropics, yet they are only one part of the jigsaw of critical areas that we need to protect. We must not forget that the biodiversity of all parts of the planet is important and that to improve its status, we must safeguard species, ecosystems and genetic diversity.

The IUCN is currently working to consolidate a global standard to identify sites that make a significant contribution to the global persistence of biodiversity. These sites — which we call key biodiversity areas — include terrestrial, freshwater and marine ecosystems. Governments, NGOs, the private sector and other groups can use this standard to identify national networks of internationally important sites for conservation.

Inger Andersen
Director-General of the International Union for Conservation
of Nature (IUCN)

Biodiversity hotspots are among the richest and most important ecosystems in the world. They are home to many vulnerable populations directly dependent on nature to survive. They must be protected. By one estimate, despite comprising only a few per cent of Earth's land surface, forests, wetlands and other ecosystems in hotspots account for about a third of the ecosystem services that vulnerable human populations depend on.

Around the world, 35 areas have been identified as hotspots. They support more than half the world's endemic plant species and nearly 43% of endemic bird, mammal, reptile and amphibian species. Only a small percentage of the total land area in biodiversity hotspots is presently protected. Effectively managed protected areas play a role in the conservation of the Earth's natural heritage. Through associated ecosystem services, protected areas also support the livelihoods of more than 1 billion people worldwide. To effectively conserve biodiversity, protected areas need to be located in the right places, be well governed and managed and be adequately planned.

In 2004, parties to the Convention made the most comprehensive and specific protected area commitments ever made by the international community in adopting the Programme of Work on Protected Areas (PoWPAs). The PoWPA enshrines the development of participatory, ecologically representative and effectively managed national and regional systems of protected areas, where necessary stretching happens across national boundaries. It is a framework for cooperation between governments, donors, NGOs and local communities. Without such collaboration, these programmes cannot be successful and sustainable over the long term. The Convention's Strategic Plan for Biodiversity 2011–2020 includes Aichi Biodiversity Target 11 (to protect by 2020 at least 17% of terrestrial and inland water and 10% of coastal and marine areas) which specifically focuses on protected areas and sets an ambitious agenda for the years ahead. In undertaking actions to achieve Aichi Target 11 and through the implementation of PoWPA, countries are helping to improve the coverage of biodiversity hotspots. As of 2015, 15.4% of the world's terrestrial surface and 8.4% of coastal and marine areas (up to 200 nautical miles) are under protection.

Dr. Braulio Ferreira de Souza Dias
Executive Secretary of the Convention on Biological Diversity

How can governments ensure that human activities do not harm biodiversity and their encompassing ecosystems?

The only way to ensure the protection of biodiversity and ecosystems is for governments to pass strong laws relating to the conservation of the environment. And these laws will need to be enforced, which will not only mean allocating sufficient funding but also stamping out corruption and resisting the huge pressure of corporate interests.

Dr. Jane Goodall
Founder of the Jane Goodall Institute and UN Messenger of Peace

Primary forests in biodiverse regions need to be preserved at all cost. These forests are the repository of countless life forms (ranging from bacteria and insects to fungi). Not much is known, for example, of the cloud forests or the diversity of bryophytes, and yet they regulate processes such as water cycles. Governments should enact appropriate enabling policies.

H.E. Ameenah Gurib-Fakim
President of Mauritius

This is a very complicated question, and I am not sure that this is necessarily the concern only of governments. Civil society institutions and social groups often have stronger motivations and effective systems for managing the biodiversity and ecosystems within their domain. The responsibility of governments probably lies with the larger scale and longer term causes and consequences and their actions should be to make sure that local actions can be effective, and to then develop laws, regulations, taxes and subsidies that encourage the right actions to take place.

Prof. Georgina Mace
Professor of Biodiversity and Ecosystems
Director of the UCL Centre for Biodiversity
and Environment Research
University College London, UK

We can do this by implementing our laws effectively. Looking at the Clean Water Act, for instance, which has the explicit objective 'to restore and maintain the chemical, physical and biological integrity of the Nation's Waters'. Setting environmental standards, permitting facilities that discharge pollutants into the environment, monitoring compliance with permit requirements and taking enforcement actions, as needed, are all part of our work to protect and restore ecological quality.

The Environmental Protection Agency's efforts to protect ecosystems also includes supporting scientific research. This is useful in understanding ecosystem services and in developing and evaluating innovative scientific and technological solutions that ensure clean, adequate and equitable supplies of water to protect human health and to protect and restore watersheds and aquatic ecosystems. Ecosystem services are the benefits that flow from nature to people, e.g., nature's contributions to the production of food and timber, life-support processes, such as water purification and coastal protection, life-fulfilling benefits, such as places to recreate, and the genetic diversity associated with healthy ecosystems.

Laura Vaught
Associate Administrator for the Office of Policy
Environmental Protection Agency, USA

Governments can play a major role in protecting and restoring biodiversity. Adopting and implementing policies and laws to stop habitat loss, control invasive species, reduce pollution and curtail the illegal trade in wildlife are just some examples of actions that need to be taken urgently. Other significant steps needed to halt the loss of biodiversity include removing environmentally harmful subsidies and implementing incentive schemes that reward the sustainable management of natural resources.

Investing in nature-based solutions to tackle some of the most pressing challenges of our time can also be very cost-effective. Nature-based solutions help safeguard the environment and halt biodiversity loss, while providing numerous economic and social benefits by improving quality of life, creating jobs and boosting innovation. These approaches include climate-smart agriculture (agro-forestry and soil conservation), integrated water resource management, coastal and marine management and sustainable forest management.

Inger Andersen
Director-General of the International Union for Conservation
of Nature (IUCN)

Governments need to take on the critical role of leadership, particularly by adopting legislation and other policies to ensure the sustainable use of natural resources, by undertaking conservation efforts, including the creation of protected areas, by restoring degraded ecosystems, by creating clear rules on use and access to genetic resources and by conserving and sustainably using biodiversity where they have direct control over natural resources. Awareness in the business sector, the general public and other sectors of society is key to the success of biodiversity policies. Governments should thus establish coherent, strategic and sustained communication efforts, strategies and campaigns to increase awareness of biodiversity and its values, and of ways to support its conservation and sustainable use.

There needs to be better targeting and integration of policies aimed at the sectors that have the largest adverse impacts on biodiversity, particularly agriculture. Governments should further develop integrated policies to address habitat loss and degradation. They should also have an effective process for engaging with sectoral stakeholders, indigenous peoples and local communities, landowners and civil society groups. Governments should also take steps to ensure that cross-sectoral policies, such as those on development, finance and planning, support the goals of the strategic plan for biodiversity[xii] and do not create negative incentives or results. They should ensure the enforcement of relevant regulations and laws. While governments should play a leadership role, other sectors of society need to be actively involved. After all, it is the choices and actions of billions of individuals that will determine whether or not biodiversity is conserved and used sustainably.

Dr. Braulio Ferreira de Souza Dias
Executive Secretary of the Convention on Biological Diversity

Prioritising the protection of local biodiversity combined with the development and sustainable use of our natural resources should be done in a rational and pragmatic manner that minimises the impact on the environment. Economic and social development must take into account the integrity of the environment's natural systems — thus forming the three mutually reinforcing pillars of sustainable development — in order to ensure that human health and well-being are also sustainable.

The sustainable use of our living resources has long been a mantra of conservation, and increasingly, of governments too. Governments have made international commitments through the ratification and signing of multilateral environmental agreements, such as the 1992 Convention for Biological Diversity. Most recently, on 25 September 2015, governments also made commitments to the 17 SDGs for 2030. Critically important to honouring these commitments is the embedding of targets into national laws, followed by the implementation and enforcement of such laws.

However, governments need to address the social and economic hardships faced by many users of these natural resources in order to ensure the ecological sustainability of our shared resources for current and future generations. As long as the inequality gap between rich and poor continues to grow, preventing the widespread access of sustainable alternatives, our natural resources and ecosystems will continue to be threatened by unsustainable levels of use.

Today, partnerships and innovation offer great potential to solve some of our serious challenges of access to clean water, clean air, renewable energy and to nutritious food for all. In this way, livelihoods and the fabric of society are inextricably linked to the health of our natural resources and ecosystems.

If we value our lives on Earth, then our ecosystems should be highly valued too, as we are dependent on and part of these natural systems. This challenge is too large for governments alone, so they need to be open to partnerships with businesses, non-governmental organisations and civil society, as the solutions are not only to be found in multilateral environmental agreements and national legislative frameworks but also amongst the people. All organisations are made up of individuals, after all, and each of us possesses the power of positive influence and choice — to think and act responsibly, conscious of our individual footprint and our collective impact.

Theressa Frantz
Head of Environmental Programmes at WWF South Africa

Why is it much more complicated to restore an ecosystem once it has been destroyed? Are the impacts our actions have had on the environment thus far reversible?

The ecosystems we have are the result of the stable environmental conditions over the millennia (like the inter-glacial equilibrium we've had for the past 12,000 years). So, for example, a rainforest becomes established as a result of suitable environmental climate conditions and the feedback that keeps them in place. So, in the case of the Amazon, it is the moisture feedback that self-generates rainfall and keeps moisture at such a high level, thanks to their dense canopy that keeps moist air under its green roof, that they become stabilised as rainforests.

Now, if you push such a system too far due to global warming and deforestation, you risk losing that feedback and it changes from a self-moisturing to a self-drying feedback, which pushes it irreversibly towards becoming a savannah, where dry air can flow freely and where rainfall is lower. Now, once it has tipped over into a savannah state, meaning that the feedback suddenly is no longer to generate rainfall but to generate droughts, that results in a new equilibrium. And once you get stuck in that equilibrium, the system cannot easily get back to rainforest. In fact, we don't even know how to get a savannah back to a rainforest, but we know that we can lose it very quickly from a rainforest, and we call this the 'hysteresis effect'. It's one thing to lose a system, but it's a much more uphill struggle to get it back in its former equilibrium, and we don't even know how to do that.

Prof. Johan Rockström
Executive Director of the Stockholm Resilience Centre
Professor in Environmental Science
Stockholm University

Not only is restoring ecosystems complex, it is also expensive. Therefore, maintaining intact ecosystems is more cost-effective in the long term. Nevertheless, where ecosystems have been destroyed, it may be impossible to restore them completely and to reproduce the exact same environmental conditions that existed in the intact ecosystems — both living (e.g., microorganisms and species) and non-living (e.g., soil nutrients, water and air). Understanding the threats to ecosystems is important in finding the appropriate solutions to reversing degradation.

Depending on the degree of ecosystem degradation or damage over time, it is possible to achieve restoration where degradation is moderate. Sadly, where creatures big and small have gone extinct in the wild due to the complete loss of their habitat, they may never be restored again, for example, the passenger pigeon, the dodo and the desert rat-kangaroo.

However, if critically endangered plant species can be artificially propagated, or if critically endangered animal species are able to breed in captivity, and if a suitable habitat is sourced, then it is possible to reverse imminent extinction by reseeding or restocking them in the wild. Critical to the success of this reseeding would be the planned protection of this population in the wild to allow it to then breed and thrive to a viable size. In addition, careful consideration would have to be given to demand reduction[xiii] of the species, to tackle threats, such as poachers, in order to be successful at rebuilding or restoring the resource.

Another example of restoration is the removal of invasive alien plant species from wetlands or riparian zones to restore water flow in indigenous ecosystems. There are many more examples that demonstrate where our impacts may be reversible or irreversible.

Theressa Frantz
Head of Environmental Programmes at WWF South Africa

How can we strengthen ecosystem resilience (to human pressures)?

There are some very simple actions that can be effective in increasing resilience, for example, (i) maintaining diversity at the level of genes, species and ecosystems, (ii) maintaining good quality habitats for species as well as landscape connectivity and (iii) maintaining well-functioning ecosystems for particular services such as carbon storage, water regulation or pollinator abundance. Reducing the rate of change and the intensity of human impacts can also help ecological systems to develop their own coping mechanisms.

Prof. Georgina Mace
Professor of Biodiversity and Ecosystems
Director of the UCL Centre for Biodiversity
and Environment Research
University College London, UK

Well, there's a whole battery of strategies, but the red thread aims at investing in and nurturing safeguards of diversity and flexibility. So, we want to encourage ecosystems that have multiple ecological functions, like, for example, a variety of different pollinators, a variety of different microorganisms, a variety of top predators. But if you lose one species due to disease or due to sudden variability, be it through natural or man-made causes, you normally have other species that can step in and take up that same ecological function. We need to avoid ending up with a monocultural ecosystem, which is the same with social systems: you don't want to put all your money in the same bank account or all your money in the same share on the stock market. So, ecosystems behave in the same way. Ecosystems teach us to nurture and to be ambassadors to safeguard diversity and flexibility.

Prof. Johan Rockström
Executive Director of the Stockholm Resilience Centre
Professor in Environmental Science
Stockholm University

Life on Earth has been through stress periods before. Think of meteorite impacts and glaciations. Most natural systems are able to recover if given the time and opportunity, but we need to provide the right conditions. To ensure nature's functionality and resilience, we need to conserve enough of it, enough natural habitats that are representative of the biological diversity of the planet. Today, we protect (and not that well) just 15% of our land and a mere 4% of our ocean.

Many scientists estimate that to keep the global ecosystem functional and productive, we need to conserve one-third of the planet's land and seas in a healthy natural state. This includes restoring degraded landscapes and seascapes and sustainably managing natural resources like forests, water and seafood. This simply means that to continue cutting trees, they must be allowed to regrow, to continue catching fish, they must be allowed to reproduce. The biggest challenge perhaps is to make smart plans for the use of land, deciding where to produce and where to protect, while at the same time maintaining a good balance between the two and the connectivity between natural spaces.

Dr. Marco Lambertini
Director-General of WWF International

What can be done to return the extinction rate to an ordinary level?

This is a huge challenge. In the short term, we need to reduce the risk of extinction that species face, which means halting habitat destruction and deforestation, reducing pollution, halting the spread of invasive species and putting an end to illegal wildlife trade. Governments have signed up to the Aichi targets, the 'big plan to save nature'. Now, they need to take action to reach these targets. We know that conservation action works, but there is much more that needs to be done, and greater investment is needed to both gain a better understanding of the current state of biodiversity and to implement conservation action.

The IUCN's goal is to assess 160,000 species by 2020 to make the IUCN red list of threatened species a more complete barometer of life. This will provide a stronger baseline to guide policy and conservation action. But halting biodiversity loss will also require some major changes in society. We need to learn how to use land, water, energy and raw materials more efficiently. We also need to rethink our consumption habits and transform our food systems to make them more sustainable. Restoring ecosystems so that they can continue to provide essential services, particularly in agricultural landscapes and reducing waste are essential steps on the road to a healthier planet.

Inger Andersen
Director-General of the International Union for
Conservation of Nature (IUCN)

An important role in creating environmental sustainability will be the preservation of biodiversity and of ecosystems. This means being able to continue doing as many as possible of our activities without harming the environment. It means ensuring that ecosystem losses we cannot prevent do not exacerbate climate change. And most of all, it means that human progress and advancement does not have to be at the expense of our surrounding environment.

Chapter 4

Nourishing Our Planet

Agriculture is unique in the sense that it is both one of the causes of and one of the sectors most at risk from climate change. The deforestation that results from agricultural expansion, the CO_2 released in the production and transportation of crops, and the methane emissions from livestock all contribute to climate change. Agriculture is also responsible for 70% of global water consumption.[xiv] But changes in weather patterns, increased droughts in some parts of the world, and the subsequent consequences to water availability all threaten food production.

In the face of these risks, more sustainable forms of agriculture are being developed and adopted around the world. These are almost unique in their incorporation of all three aspects of sustainability: environmental protection, human development and economic development.

Firstly, technology-sharing may allow the most efficient forms of agriculture to spread to parts of the world practicing less efficient agriculture. The resulting increase in efficiency and boost in yields may help ensure that less, if not no land, is deforested for agricultural expansion and that less water is used to grow crops.

Secondly, though many acknowledge that enough food is currently produced to feed everyone,[xv] hunger persists because of food spoiled on the way to markets, usually in developing countries, and because of food wastage in supermarkets and in homes, usually in developed countries. For the food spoilage problem, social programmes that enable food to be preserved before it is sold present ways to reduce waste, reduce hunger and lift people out of poverty. The infrastructures required for such programmes may also help boost economic growth and development. For the problem of food waste, the solution is harder. Legislation enacted in France in 2016 ensured that supermarkets must donate food that is not sold instead of throwing it away.[xvi] In the USA apps have been developed to allow food to get from those who do not want it to those who do.[xvii]

In this way, more sustainable forms of agriculture can, if correctly and effectively implemented, promote environmental protection, social inclusivity and economic development.

How is climate change likely to impact on the agricultural sector? How can the agricultural sector adapt to and mitigate its effects?

Climate change and increasing demands for food, water and energy from a growing population are two of the greatest challenges of the twenty-first century. Agriculture and smallholder farmers are central to both, and while smallholders are already battling against the impacts of climate change, they are amongst those who are most vulnerable to it. Rising temperatures signal more extreme weather events that will put lives and livelihoods at greater risk, increasing smallholders' vulnerability to drought, famine and disease. Mean temperatures in Africa will rise faster than the global average, exceed 2°C and may reach as high as 3–6°C greater than twentieth century levels. Agricultural losses in Africa will amount to up to 7% of GDP by 2100.

Climate change affects not only yields but also food quality and safety, and the reliability of its delivery to consumers. By 2050, hunger and child malnutrition could increase by as much as 20% as a result of climate change. However, smallholder farmers can be agents of change. When given the right options and incentives, they can drive sustainable agricultural development that builds resilience and reduces Greenhouse Gas (GHG) emissions. Across Africa, climate change could spur countries to invest in renewable energy technologies, create new markets for agricultural producers and build human and institutional capacities to support a knowledge economy based on innovation, R&D. To do this requires enabling policies and incentives for smallholder farmers to invest in environmental services, preserve biodiversity, sustainably manage natural resources such as land and water, and use energy efficiently.

Prof. Sir Gordon Conway
Head of Agriculture for Development
Imperial College London, UK

Hundreds of millions of farmers all over the world are already experiencing problems because of the changing climate. Currently, it is seen in the variability in the weather and unpredictable seasons, so farmers don't know when the rains are going to start or end, or whether they will be sufficient, from floods resulting from very heavy precipitation or the increased frequency of storms, and from increases in average temperature as well as an increase in days with temperature extremes. These weather events are making the lives of hundreds of millions of farmers much more difficult.

The change is not steady and incremental. Instead, it is manifested in the increased volatility of weather patterns and it is affecting the most vulnerable and marginalised farmers. There are half a billion small-scale food producers around the world, and they and their families constitute 2–2.5 billion of world's population. Hundreds of millions of these half-billion small farmers are already suffering and will suffer even more in the future.

The ones who suffer the most, and are at greatest risk, are the ones with the least assets, the smallest land holdings, the smallest fishing boats or the smallest number of livestock, or those, particularly women, who lack secure rights to land tenure and access to resources. It's often the women in these households who are particularly affected, which leads to increased poverty in the family and less food available to eat. This, in turn, means that farmers often have to leave their land and migrate in search of alternative employment. This is happening in the parts of the world that are marginal, like the Sahel and the Horn of Africa. It is also increasingly occurring in some areas that border the sea, where salinisation of land has increased.

It is happening now and it's going to get worse. Agricultural livelihoods, especially those of small-scale producers, need to be resilient in the face of shocks like increased adverse weather. This means support for the adaptation of farming systems, so they are less weather dependent, using varieties that are more hardy, whether in terms of both crops and livestock, and making better, more efficient use of water and other inputs. The adaptation of agriculture is already happening, but it needs a lot more support by farmer organisations, by extension services (farmer education) and by research to develop agricultural patterns that are better adapted to climate change.

There is increasing recognition that agriculture can mitigate the effects of climate change. Sustainable agriculture can reduce carbon in the atmosphere by increasing the capacity of the soil to trap and then to use carbon to create greater fertility. That's where reduced tillage of the soil helps: less oxygen comes into the soil, and the increased use of manure and compost agro-ecological techniques help maintain carbon in the soil. Sustainable agriculture also gives priority to the trapping of carbon from the atmosphere and into green trees and plants through photosynthesis. To take advantage of this potential, the amount of forestation should be increased — including in agricultural lands. Efforts should be made to reduce farmers' need to cut down trees because they see the need to increase their areas of land under cultivation.

In this way, agriculture can be part of the solution to climate change, as opposed to serving as a source of the problem. Finally, one can reduce the emissions in agriculture by changing practices, for example, raising cattle in different ways so that they are less likely to produce methane, reducing the amount of corn fed to beef animals, or alternating wet and dry rice paddy systems that produce less GHG. In various ways, agriculture has an important role to play. Agricultural activity should be adapted to changing climates, it can be modified to reduce the amounts of GHG emissions and it can be adjusted to increase the extent to which carbon is taken out of the atmosphere and stored.

Agriculture should be at the centre of all current conversations about climate change. It's not at the moment. Many groups are working hard during this COP with a view to ensure that by the time of the next COP in Marrakech, agriculture, agri-food systems and the work of farmers are much more at the centre of the discussion.

Dr. David Nabarro
UN Secretary-General's Special Representative
on Food Security and Nutrition
Special Adviser to the UN Secretary-General on the 2030
Agenda for Sustainable Development and Climate Change

How can we feed a growing population? What innovative methods and locations could be used to grow more food?

Increasing global food production by 60% to meet the demand for some 9.1 billion people by 2050 is doable. For different parts of the world, the required increase in food production could come from a combination of factors including land expansion, sustainable intensification through the greater and more efficient use of water resources, higher yielding varieties and increased use of fertilisers. There are still sufficient arable land and water resources to do all this, especially in Latin America and Africa. In Africa, for instance, less than half of the available arable land and only 4% of the available water resources are currently exploited. Obviously, we will need to make the investments required to develop these resources so as to not only bring more land into agricultural use but also significantly increase the extent of cultivated land under irrigation which, so far, is barely 6%. Beyond the potential for land expansion, the FAO estimates that 90% of the growth in food production globally and 80% in developing countries should come from higher yields and increased cropping intensity. In this regard, growth in food production in developed countries would rest mainly on new advances in science, agriculture research and innovation.

For developing countries, particularly in Africa, there is ample room for increasing crop yields, livestock and fisheries productivity, even with the existing technologies. In Africa, the yield gap is huge, the current yields of most crops are still below world averages and much below the levels that could be attained in the different agro-ecological zones.

Given adequate investments in agricultural R&D and appropriate macroeconomic and sectoral policies, we believe it is reasonable for Africa to aim at tripling its current level of food production by 2050, by at least doubling agricultural productivity (which is one of the 2025 targets of the CAADP-Malabo Declaration) and expanding cultivated land by 50%. This would be enough to feed Africa's growing population and leave a substantial surplus to supply the global food market.

H.E. Tumusiime Rhoda Peace
Commissioner for Agriculture and the Rural Economy
African Union

Advances in food productivity are nothing new. Developments in agriculture coincided with the industrial revolution and in the 1960s, the development and implementation of new techniques and crops to maximise productivity greatly increased yields in India and other developing countries in an advance known as the Green Revolution. As it often relied on intensive resource use (e.g., fertiliser and water) and on machinery, it had adverse environmental impacts such as the overuse of water and the run-off of fertiliser into rivers and ponds. These intensive techniques often harmed the surrounding environment, which is why many have argued that future advances in crop productivity should be sustainable. The Green Revolution of the 1960s was successful in increasing agricultural yields, but at the cost of the damaging and unsustainable side-effects of increased water consumption and fertiliser run-off.

How can we have another Green Revolution (the so-called 'Doubly Green' or 'Evergreen' Revolution) without similar side-effects?

One goal is to find ways to increase crop production and yields on land already under agriculture while reducing inputs and losses of nutrients, water and pesticides. Commonly called 'sustainable intensification', this approach is knowledge-intensive and requires carefully selecting and managing crop types based on climate, soil type, nutrients and application timing, sometimes with the use of soil-plant models and remote sensing of nutrient demand. Perhaps, the biggest challenge with such practices is that they are not always easy for farmers to use, so approaches that help engage farmers in developing, testing and then using them is critical. Numerous approaches are also being developed to use ecological approaches in agriculture — for example, conservation tillage, cover cropping[xviii] and multi-cropping — and these approaches can maintain agricultural production and under some conditions improve it. But again, getting these practices honed for specific locations and cropping systems, and then used by farmers, is hard.

Prof. Pamela Matson
Dean of the School of Earth, Energy & Environmental Studies
Stanford University, USA

The current farming model has served us well for a hundred years or more, including intensification during the Green Revolution of the 1960s and 1970s that kept food production in pace with population growth. But the context has radically changed. Our current food crisis — recurrent food price spikes, the existence of about 800 million chronically hungry people and the need to feed a growing, more prosperous population in the face of threats from climate change — is not a transient affair. Moreover, conventional intensification is not a viable solution if it comes at the expense of the environmental and social resources on which it depends. We need radical measures and new paradigms. I believe that one such paradigm which offers solutions is sustainable intensification. Sustainable intensification integrates practices and innovations from the fields of ecology, genetics and socioeconomics with the aim of building sustainable, equitable, productive and resilient ecosystems that improve the well-being of farms, farmers and families. It offers a practical pathway towards the goal of producing more food whilst ensuring the natural resource base on which agriculture depends is sustained, and indeed improved, for future generations.[xix]

Prof. Sir Gordon Conway
Head of Agriculture for Development
Imperial College London, UK

Why are localised solutions necessary to transition to more sustainable forms of agriculture? How can localised solutions be developed?

A one-size-fits-all solution will not deliver sustainable agricultural systems around the world for several reasons. Firstly, not all parts of the world are at the same level of technological advancement in agriculture. Developed countries and those who benefitted from the first generation of the Green Revolution have achieved considerable gains in productivity from the intensive use of improved varieties and chemical inputs, often at the cost of environmental damage that needs to be contained or reversed through increased efficiency in the use of resources and inputs. On the other hand, developing countries, particularly in Africa, have mainly relied on extensive production systems, using little or no external inputs and, in most cases, mining and degrading the natural resource base (especially land) of agricultural production. These countries need to upgrade to more modern and sustainable intensive production systems through the increased and efficient use of improved inputs and equipment that is compatible with the sustainable management of land and water resources, and of the environment. Secondly, solutions to transition to sustainable agriculture must be agro-ecologically specific, taking into account not only the current potential of different zones but also of their future prospects with regard to climate change. Thirdly, localised solutions need to take into account the differentiated capacities of farmers under diverse socioeconomic circumstances such as their scale of production, technological proficiency and financial capacities.

Agricultural science, technology and innovation systems play a central role in devising appropriate, sustainable agricultural solutions based on these regional, agro-ecological and socioeconomic specificities. Targeted policy and institutional provisions developed with the effective participation of all relevant stakeholders should help make widespread use of the localised technological solutions resulting from agricultural R&D.

H.E. Tumusiime Rhoda Peace
Commissioner for Agriculture and the Rural Economy
African Union

Why has agriculture in the developing world been relatively inefficient? How can we improve the efficiency and productivity of the agricultural sector in developing countries?

Before answering directly, I think we must ask how 'efficient' and 'inefficient' are being used in this question. Typically, the efficiency of agricultural production has been defined in terms of yields per hectare or production per hour of human labour. In those conventional terms, agriculture in industrialised countries has been relatively more efficient than agriculture in most developing countries. If, instead, we defined efficiency in terms of production per unit of fossil fuels, most developing country agriculture would be much more efficient because the input of fossil fuels is very low.

In conventional terms of production per unit of land or labour, developing country agriculture has been less efficient because of constraints in three interrelated categories:

- *Technology.* Technology includes crop and livestock genetics, soil management techniques like fertiliser, weed control methods, pest management, food storage and processing methods and mechanisation of agricultural operations.
- *Inputs.* Inputs include seed, fertiliser, herbicides, insecticides, hermetic storage containers, equipment and a wide range of other items used in agricultural production. Farmers don't need to understand the science behind the technology, they just need to know how to use the input.
- *Institutions.* Institutions include farmer or commodity organisations that advocate for agricultural interests, agricultural input supply chains, food value chains to the consumer, banks and other financial organisations, cadaster and other land tenure arrangements, legal systems that facilitate contracting, and research and extension organisations that create new technology and share it with the agricultural sector.

The efficiency of agriculture in developed countries can be substantially improved by addressing the constraints in these three areas. It should be noted that the exact mix of constraints is different for each country and region in the developing world, there is no 'one size fits all'.

The barriers to improving technology, input supply and institutions are often political and social. Even if resources can be found to do appropriate research and to extend improved techniques to farmers, entrenched political and social interests may limit their application. For example, in some countries, ownership of land is highly concentrated in the hands of a few families. If farmers were given more property rights in the land they cultivate, those few families would lose and consequently would probably oppose the change even if the overall society benefited.

As those entrenched social and political interests will probably change only slowly, new technology, input supply approaches and institutions must 'wire around' those interests and be effective in spite of the constraints. For example, in some countries in Africa, planting trees confers property rights to the person planting them even if they do not 'own' the land, consequently land owners often discourage renters from planting trees. This limits the use of agro-forestry techniques that might increase overall productivity and improve the environment. One technology that 'wires around' the concern about property rights caused by tree planting is to use strips of perennial grasses instead of trees to produce biomass and reduce soil erosion. Planting grasses typically does not confer the same type of property rights as tree planting.

Prof. Jess Lowenberg-DeBoer
Agricultural Economics
Purdue University, USA

To say that agriculture in the developing world has been inefficient is a bit strong. For instance, contrary to popular belief, agricultural production in Africa has increased steadily over the last 30 years. Its value has almost tripled at a growth rate that has exceeded the global average. Yet, we must admit that, overall, the performance of the agricultural sector has been far below its potential, for lessons we have learnt in Africa, but which also apply to other developing regions of the world. As acknowledged in the World Bank's 2008 World Development

Report, there has been a severe neglect of agriculture over several decades. A lack of consistency in the degree and direction of priority has resulted in severe underinvestments in and undercapitalisation of agriculture. This, in Africa, has translated into sustainable land and water management in few agricultural areas, the negligible use of improved inputs (especially fertiliser and seeds) and equipment, poor production and market infrastructure and utilities (roads, electricity and communications), weak agricultural R&D systems and the absence of a vibrant agro-industry and agri-business sector. The combined effects of these features have contributed to stagnating or declining agricultural productivity, weak backward and forward linkages between agriculture and other sectors, increased food insecurity, and natural resource and environmental degradation.

It is to address these challenges that the African Union's political leaders adopted the Comprehensive Africa Agriculture Development Programme (CAADP) in 2003. Ten years later, we realised that agricultural production had grown by 4% per year, but mainly from land expansion, an increase in livestock numbers and a bigger labour force, and little from improvement in productivity in the absence of a widespread adoption of modern farming as well as post-harvest technologies and techniques. In line with the 2014 African Union Malabo Summit Declaration, we need to address this challenge by investing in and creating the necessary policy and institutional conditions and support systems to facilitate:

- Sustainable and reliable production and access to quality and affordable inputs.
- Appropriate knowledge, information and skills supplied to users.
- Efficient and effective water management systems, especially through irrigation.
- Suitable, reliable and affordable mechanisation and energy supplies.
- Inclusive and responsible private sector investments in African Agriculture.

H.E. Tumusiime Rhoda Peace
Commissioner for Agriculture and the Rural Economy
African Union

As Africa is the area with the greatest untapped agricultural potential, how can we ensure that it fulfils its potential while remaining sustainable (and not overusing non-renewable resources)?

It is estimated that 50% of all uncultivated arable land in the world is in Africa. Yet, Africa remains a continent that is unable to feed itself. This is partly because people use rudimentary, age-old techniques of farming that are back-breaking, tedious and unrewarding. Very few scientific methods are used, resulting in low yields and, consequently, low profits. The youth are therefore not attracted to the land because incentives are low.

For Africa to achieve its full potential in food sustainability, new farming practices have to be adopted that will give added value to what is produced. Farms have to be modernised using science and technology in terms of fertiliser, fast-growing seed and machinery; farm managers must also have business acumen. Women should not be excluded from taking loans for farming and, for young people, going into farming must bring them rewards in innovative ways. With the threat of climate change so present these days, it is imperative that Africa adopts climate-smart agricultural practices that seek to adapt, mitigate and be resilient to the menace posed by the build-up of CO_2.

John Kufuor
Former President of Ghana (2001–2009)

How are changing food demands, especially in developing countries, likely to affect the climate-stressed agricultural sector?

As incomes increase worldwide, people demand a better quality diet. In most cases, this means more animal products. In many cases, it also includes more fruit and vegetables. They are no longer satisfied with the high carbohydrate diet that is typical of the poor in developing countries.

The impact of increasing animal production depends on how it is accomplished. Increasing intensive livestock production modelled on grain-intensive industrialised country systems may have negative environmental impacts if they are not managed properly. Grain-intensive systems typically used many kilograms of grain to produce one kilo of meat or other animal products. That means more energy, water and land use for that feedgrain. Intensive systems are often very concentrated, so the animal waste is also very concentrated in a small area, where it may have negative effects. Some animal production methods create methane gas, which has been linked to global warming.

One alternative to the grain-intensive industrialised country approach would be a more dispersed system of livestock production that is better integrated with crop production. Livestock systems could be devised to make more use of crop residues and byproducts, thereby reducing demands for additional energy, water and land for feed grain. With smaller livestock production units, animal waste is more dispersed and can more easily be recycled in cropping systems. Because more dispersed livestock production probably requires more labour, these smaller-scale livestock production units might be most easily adopted in developing countries where labour costs are still relatively low.

Another alternative would be to help people understand that the quality of their diet can be improved by making greater use of vegetable proteins, including beans, peas and other grain legumes. We see this happening already in some high-income communities in industrialised countries, where the highest social status diet is often a vegetarian or vegan diet. We also see it in countries like India, where religious and cultural practices limit the use of animal products. Greater use of vegetable-based proteins will require more research on production technology for grain, legumes, nuts and other vegetable protein sources, and on food science that produces palatable food from these vegetable sources.

Fruit and vegetables typically require more water, pesticide and management than grain production. This might strain water and other environmental systems. Greater use of water-saving technology such as drip irrigation and integrated pest management can help the world produce more fruit and vegetables with a limited water and environmental carrying capacity.

Prof. Jess Lowenberg-DeBoer
Professor of Agricultural Economics
Purdue University, USA

Though enough food is produced worldwide to feed everyone, it is not being evenly distributed and a lot of food is wasted on the way to markets and in homes. How can individual governments and the international community ensure that food is better distributed and that less food is wasted?

In most developing countries, a lot of wastage in food production happens at the farm gate. Firstly, farmers incur huge losses because they lack the means to store and husband their harvested crops. These crops, left at the mercy of the weather, decompose rapidly and go to waste. Secondly, middlemen, taking advantage of the situation, bargain for lower prices, which is a disincentive to the farmer and discourages them from producing as much in coming seasons. Thirdly, the road network linking the farm gate to the markets are in many parts unmotorable. This results in frequent breakdowns in vehicles carting foodstuffs, which then arrive at their destination in a poor condition. The perishable nature of the foodstuffs means that only a fraction are worthy of consumption to feed an ever-increasing urban population hungry for food. This leads to hikes in prices as there is not enough food to go around. Both the international community and individual governments need to (i) build storage facilities at the farm gate to help store harvested crops, especially those that can be released during the lean and dry season, (ii) build good, motorable roads between the farm gate and city centres, where there is a high demand for food crops, (iii) introduce improved, high-yielding and weather-resilient crops that would ensure rapid productivity as well as stand the test of time, (iv) add value through processing and preservation of crops and their packaging for distribution.

John Kufuor
Former President of Ghana (2001–2009)

Indeed, enough food is produced globally to feed everyone. But not all the food produced is used effectively. The FAO estimates that one-third of the edible food produced for human consumption is lost or wasted. Heavy food losses occur in developing countries because of poor post-harvest operations, while in the developed world, food is mainly wasted by consumers. In addition, there are serious gaps between the global availability of food and universal access to it. To follow Professor Amartya Sen's argument, while some people (especially in developed regions) have problems of excess food, severe failures deprive large groups of people (mainly in developing countries) from a supply of food that is adequate in quantity and quality, either through their own production or via the market. Hence, at both global and regional levels, supplying food-deficit areas and households by using pockets of surplus food production is less than optimal, owing to the weak purchasing power of poor households, poor market infrastructure and integration, and failures in market and trade structure and conduct.

To reduce food losses, governments and the international community should undertake appropriate measures to support and facilitate investments by farmers and private agribusiness actors in improved and more efficient post-harvest infrastructure, equipment and technologies for product handling, transport, storage and processing, especially in developing countries. In addition, targeted education and policy-led incentives should help consumers minimise food waste in affluent regions, societies and households. To improve food distribution globally, trade policies and regimes should be more open and fair. In developing countries, governments and the international community should invest in developing market infrastructure, utilities, and facilities such as roads, electricity, communications, commodity exchanges and market information systems. Yet, as markets serve only those with an adequate income and purchasing power, dedicated public interventions are required to develop effective social protection measures to secure and fulfil the right to food of the world's most vulnerable people. Brazil's successful zero-hunger initiative provides the world with a useful blueprint for this.

H.E. Tumusiime Rhoda Peace
Commissioner for Agriculture and the Rural Economy
African Union

Post-harvest loss can have a big effect on the useful output of African farms. Good warehousing is one way that post-harvest loss can be reduced. I experienced a good example of this in 2014 when I visited the AgroWays (U) grain warehouse in Uganda. AgroWays offers transport, cleaning, drying, grading and storage services to small-holder farmers at affordable prices. Farmers are encouraged to organise into associations with up to 60 farmers to collectively pro-duce 5 metric tons, the minimum required for pick-up by AgroWays at village aggregation centres. To prevent spoilage, rot and infesta-tion, the grain is retrieved within two days of harvest, and taken to the Jinja warehouse, where it is cleaned, dried and graded into either grade one or two maize, and stored in a fumigated warehouse. Farmers gain mainly from reducing post-harvest loss, but also through direct price negotiation with buyers. Representatives of farmer associations negotiate with prospective buyers. Once a price is agreed, the farmer associations are paid for the amounts of grade one or two maize they have deposited and wish to sell, minus the warehouse charges.

An important element of this system is that the farmers retain ownership of their grain. If they find they can get a better deal else-where, the farmer associations can take back the equivalent number of bags, pay the warehouse charges and sell them privately. The charges are clearly shown to the farmers before they deposit their grain. Expanding value chains may decrease food waste and involves the growth of national and regional trade in foodstuffs for the urban retail sector and major supermarket chains. The aim is to design value chains that deliver greater value to smallholder farmers, reduce their risks and increase their resilience.

Prof. Sir Gordon Conway
Head of Agriculture for Development
Imperial College London, UK

Food distribution is usually a question of income inequality. Wealthy people seldom go hungry. Income distribution is essentially a political question. Making access to adequate food a human right for all is often not supported by local elites. Access to food is now often used to motivate poor people to work at low wage jobs and to be politically docile. Well-fed low-income people may make different choices about how they spend their time and who they vote for than hungry people.

Food waste is a more tractable question, especially in the developing world, as estimates indicate that roughly 30% of food produced around the world does not get to consumers. In developing countries, that food loss is mostly in the harvesting, handling and storage stages. There are proven technologies for reducing the loss at those stages.

Prof. Jess Lowenberg-DeBoer
Professor of Agricultural Economics
Purdue University, USA

In what ways can the international community act to end chronic hunger and ensure food security? What types of policies would be effective in achieving these goals?

The current focus of agriculture, food security and hunger elimination is on encouraging policies that lead to smallholder farmers having greater resilience and an improved ability to produce and sustain not just crops that have mix of nutritional value, but also crops they can sell at a time when it suits them. When we encourage such policies, we are working on the core elements of food systems for the future.

The main requirement is to focus on smallholder farmers. As I explained earlier, there are more than half a billion of these farmers. They are necessary, not just for the availability of food, but also for employment in the future. They are key to the prosperity of rural areas. So, all our work on agri-food should not be limited to producing lots more food. Instead, it should aim to create viable livelihoods for smallholder farmers, who then become the primary source of food for the local-level food chains that feed most of the world's poor people.

Secondly, we need to concentrate on areas of the world which are experiencing long-term crisis because these are where most of the world's hungry people live. They are called "protracted food crises".

Over the course of 2015, the Committee on World Food Security developed new guidance on action needed to help communities withstand and eventually emerge from these protracted crisis situations. It is vital that systematic work on protracted crises becomes central to the way in which nations, civil society and other stakeholders work in areas of protracted crises that contribute to long-term food insecurity.

Thirdly, we need to concentrate on reducing the amount of food that is lost or wasted in food systems, which amounts to around 30% of all food, but up to 50% of perishable foods. With a relatively small introduction of incentives and technologies, as well as the right attitude, this food waste and loss can be reduced.

And finally, the real test of whether hunger is reducing is the extent to which all people can access the food they need when they need it. This means having in place functioning social protection programmes for poor people so that they are able to get access to food. Many of the world's poor people are also smallholder farmers, so it's really important to have social protection for them so that they can access food, particularly when times are bad. When such interventions are in place (as happened in Brazil with the social welfare programme, Bolsa Familia, as well as in Angola and in Vietnam), levels of hunger reduce and food security improves.

Dr. David Nabarro
UN Secretary-General's Special Representative
on Food Security and Nutrition
Special Adviser to the UN Secretary-General on the 2030
Agenda for Sustainable Development and Climate Change

How can we end chronic hunger without instigating another form of malnutrition (such as obesity or micronutrient insufficiency)?

Malnutrition is not simple to deal with. If people eat too much, particularly of the wrong foods, they become obese: they may also develop disease conditions that are associated with eating the wrong food. If, on the other hand, they eat too little, or if they've got a disease that prevents them from absorbing their food, they become undernourished. Initially, they become thin (or wasted) — in the longer term, the rate of physical growth and intellectual capability can be impaired (this is referred to as stunting).

Even if people ingest adequate energy-producing foods and — from the outside — they look well nourished, they may be deficient in certain nutrients like vitamin A or D, or iron. Iron deficiency is extremely common and leads to anaemia, particularly in women. Vitamin A deficiency leads to partial blindness and also to increased susceptibility to disease. Vitamin D deficiency leads to rickets. And there are other vitamin deficiencies as well. This micronutrient malnutrition is sometimes described as hidden malnutrition. Action to tackle malnutrition increasingly focuses on all types — undernutriton, overnutrition and micronutrient malnutrition.

Within the 2030 Agenda for Sustainable Development, world leaders set the target of ending hunger by 2030. Experiences to date indicate that this is feasible, but that it requires the recognition that nutrition is not just about the quantity of food people consume. It is also concerned with the extent to which people are able to eat the kinds of food that are good for their health, and whether they are well enough to use the nutrients from these foods (People who are sick — for example, with gastrointestinal disease — may be prevented from absorbing the nutrients that they need from food they have consumed). So, a focus on nutrition means a focus on diet, on health and on the time available in the home for feeding and caring for young children. Modern nutritional practices focus on the multiple determinants of malnutrition and give each of them the attention they need. Alternative approaches that focus on one or two causes alone are unlikely to result in lasting improvements for nutritionally at-risk populations.

Dr. David Nabarro
UN Secretary-General's Special Representative
on Food Security and Nutrition
Special Adviser to the UN Secretary-General on the 2030
Agenda for Sustainable Development and Climate Change

Education about the need for a balanced diet is essential, especially among the poor and vulnerable. In most parts of the developing world, food is scarce and usually one has very little choice of what one consumes. The craving to satisfy hunger means you eat whatever is put on the table, regardless of its nutritional content. What is worse is that sometimes mothers do not know that simple and inexpensive dietary combinations could make up a healthy, well-balanced and nutritious meal that could help safeguard the health of their child and ensure their longevity. This is especially critical in the first 1,000 days of a child's growth, where children's chances of survival are enhanced by what they eat or do not eat, or where their ability to function as healthy functioning beings is affected.

Eating healthy, nutritious meals also impacts positively on the economy of the nation as it saves on costs of medical care. Healthy citizens have less need to see doctors. This improves individuals' personal income levels as well as save the state from excessive spending on the health sector in favour of other deprived areas. The end result is a blossoming economy where more resources can be ploughed back into improved farming methods to produce more nutritious food which can benefit all citizens.

John Kufuor
Former President of Ghana (2001–2009)

How can we encourage the consumption of more nutritious foods?

It all starts with the individual, or in the case of children, those who care for them. If they understand what food is appropriate for a good life and good health, they in turn will start to demand that the food they buy is nutritious, safe and affordable. This means that attempts must be made to remedy situations where nutritious food is accessible but unsafe (and potentially causing disease) or where it is so expensive that poor people just cannot afford it. The diet that people can access should be nutritious, safe and affordable. This transformation of food systems has happened in many countries though poorer communities still face complex challenges with ensuring good nutrition for all. Hence, the need for people to speak out about food, health and nutrition — especially in small and growing children. There is also a need for people's representatives to focus on the importance of nutrition for both individual and community development: this means working closely with parliamentarians, civil society organisations and religious leaders. Once they focus on nutrition and stress the damage that malnutrition causes, governments, people's organisations and business enterprises are more likely to act for people's nutrition. Retailers see the value of ensuring that the food they sell is nutritious, safe and affordable.

Within the UN system, we encourage consumers, people's representatives and governments to come together and take responsibility for ensuring that food and health systems respond to people's nutritional needs everywhere. As there is increased emphasis on nutrition, those who produce and process food will become part of local, national and global movements for people to be able to enjoy good nutrition. The cost of this not happening is very high — for individuals and their societies, especially in years to come when the malnourished children of today become the productive adults of tomorrow. The opportunities are great and can be seized, for example, by governments checking that their policies enable all people to be in a position to access nutritious food. If farmers receive subsidies, they should be designed to reflect the nutritional interest of people: they should be incentives for production of nutritious, safe and affordable diets. This will be possible if policymakers everywhere take account of all people's needs to access foods that both prevent hunger and produce good health. It means linking together health, nutrition, food systems and agriculture, so the right kinds of incentives are built into the food systems on which poor people depend.

Dr. David Nabarro
UN Secretary-General's Special Representative
on Food Security and Nutrition
Special Adviser to the UN Secretary-General on the 2030
Agenda for Sustainable Development and Climate Change

GMOs have been presented as solutions to the world's food shortages. Do you believe their benefits outweigh their costs? Why?

Genetically Modified Organisms (GMOs) are not the solution to the world's shortages, but they are potentially one of the tools to support not only our need for more food but also the need for more nutritious food. It is not all a matter of producing more food, it is about producing more of the right food.

At Linking Environment And Farming (LEAF), we recognise the importance of modern biotechnology developments such as GMOs. The potential benefits to farmers and consumers need to be weighed against the alleged risks associated with growing these foodstuffs. Risk management is thus paramount to the decisions being made. LEAF will continue to monitor developments. We recognise that the vitamins in nutritionally enhanced foods show great potential. However, there are several areas that cannot be neglected. GMOs are not an alternative to good husbandry practices and integrated farm management and these systems must not be compromised. Rotations, safe use of inputs, cultivation choice, variety choice, good record-keeping and management systems are essential.

However, there are new developments in breeding and ever-changing advances in GMO technology, and at this stage of knowledge, LEAF supports the need for segregating and labelling GMOs throughout the food chain as well as at the point of sale to the final consumer. Indeed, LEAF believes that we need more open discussions with consumers on matters such as GMOs, food versus fuel and the trade-offs and synergies required in balancing our need for food and the need to protect the environment.

Caroline Drummond
CEO, LEAF UK

Yes. Genetic engineering has great potential to transform the agricultural sector. New plant varieties and animal breeds could deliver higher yields and better tolerance to climate conditions as well as the ability to adapt to changing climates, increasing drought, salinity and chemical toxicity. DNA technology allows new combinations of genes that are selected beforehand and, with skill and care, are precisely achieved. The process is faster than conventional hybridisation and genetic material sources are less restricted by geographical or biological boundaries, so plant breeders are no longer limited by the genetic variation in a traditional breeding programme. Some of the most valuable applications lie in the conferment of foodstuffs to resistance to bacterial and virus diseases and to insect pests, and there are many examples of its success.[xx]

Ingredients produced from genetically modified crops are found in thousands of products and consumed worldwide with no legitimate evidence of harm to human health or the environment. GM cultivars have been granted wide and growing acceptance amongst farmers globally. Between 1996 and 2014, the acreage devoted to genetically modified crops increased hundredfold from 1.7 million ha in 1996 to 181.5 million ha in 2014. There is a wide body of scientific evidence concluding that GM foods are safe to eat and do not pose environmental risks. Findings from the International Council for Science that analysed a selection of approximately 50 science-based reviews concluded that 'currently available genetically modified foods are safe to eat', and 'there is no evidence of any deleterious environmental effects having occurred from the trait/species combinations currently available'.[xxi] This sentiment is supported by findings by the FAO, the Royal Society, the British Medical Association, the EU Research Directorate, the OECD, and the Nuffield Council on Bioethics, amongst others.

Nonetheless, there are a number of challenges to adoption. These include underdeveloped national regulation and biosafety laws, the prohibition of GM crops within trading partner countries, a lack of capacity in developing new gene sequences in country, low public funding of biotech research and issues of intellectual property and technology ownership. Additionally, farmers may be reluctant to adopt GM varieties due to distrust of the technology among local consumers or perceived exploitation by transnational seed companies, despite the fact that development of new GM technologies in Africa is dominated by the public sector. For example, the African Agricultural Technology Foundation, an African-based and led organisation, is assisting national agricultural research organisations to test and develop new appropriate GM crops, using donated genes from organisations such as the International Wheat and Maize Improvement Center and international seed companies such as Monsanto.

Prof. Sir Gordon Conway
Head of Agriculture for Development
Imperial College London, UK

How do agricultural systems get their water? Why are these sources increasingly under strain?

The simple answer is that growing plants, and especially crops with high yields that dominate many agricultural systems (such as rice and maize), require substantial amounts of water to grow and to maximise yields. This water for crops and pastures comes in two forms: (i) 'green' water such as soil moisture and rainfall that, typically, does not impose trade-offs in terms of the quantity of water used and (ii) 'blue' water that is extracted from streams, rivers, lakes and groundwater sources, which may impose trade-offs for other water users and the environment in terms of both water quality and quantity.

Overall, agriculture accounts for about 70% of global (blue) water extractions, but more than 80% of the blue water consumed because growing plants use a higher proportion of the water extracted compared with the water used in electricity generation or for domestic purposes.

Under a business-as-usual scenario, by 2050, feeding a projected 2.4 billion more people with incomes higher than present levels could require 50% more blue water than is currently consumed. This is neither desirable nor feasible. An alternative approach to water use in agriculture is required. Governments can assist in many different ways and I highlight just three: (i) R&D into water productivity and especially low-cost, low-energy, low-maintenance irrigation methods, deficit irrigation[xxii] and crops that use less drop per crop, (ii) the removal of perverse subsidies (such as energy subsidies that promote overextraction of groundwater) that encourage the overuse of water and (iii) support for institutional changes and water reforms that ensure that farmers and others pay the full economic costs of the water they use, including the costs that they impose on others and on the environment.

Prof. Quentin Grafton
Professor of Economics at the Australian National University,
Australia
UNESCO Chair in Water Economics and Transboundary
Water Governance

In many parts of the world, agriculture relies on using water stored in aquifers. These underground water stores have filled over thousands if not tens of thousands of years as rainfall has progressively accumulated in these aquifers. They have filled over the course of millennia, but they are now being depleted at a comparatively unsustainable rate. Because more water is being extracted each year than is put back in through rainfall, the overall level of water stored in these aquifers has been falling. Parts of the world, such as the American Midwest and the Indian Punjab, may be facing empty aquifers over the coming decades if water is not sustainably managed. The emergence of precision agriculture may prove to be an effective solution.

How can precision agriculture maximise crop yields without increasing water consumption? What benefits would a precision agriculture revolution provide?

Precision agriculture has many definitions, most of which focus on the use of information and information technology to improve the productivity, profitability and sustainability of agriculture. Most precision agriculture makes use of electronic information technologies such as Global Positioning Systems (GPSs), geographical information systems, sensors mounted on satellites, airplanes, drones or ground-based equipment, and equipment designed to apply seed, fertiliser and other inputs to specific sites. In industrialised countries, precision agriculture technology is already being used to increase yields and economise on inputs. For instance, GPS guidance for seeders, pesticide sprayers and fertiliser applicators improve input effiency. Multi-variety seeders might be used to plant seeds with different genetics in different parts of large fields based on their microclimate and soil type. Variable rate fertiliser applicators might be used to avoid over-fertilising or underfertilising certain areas in large fields.

In some developing and middle-income countries, the precision agriculture technology designed in industrialised countries is already used in large-scale commercial agriculture. This includes countries like Brazil and South Africa. Very little precision agriculture technology is used for smallholder farming in the developing world. Precision agriculture technology from industrialised countries typically assumes that production occurs on large fields with substantial in-field variability and that production is mechanised. Smallholder farming is often on small fields and is not mechanised. The concepts of precision agriculture are potentially useful to smallholder farming, but the research has not been done to adapt precision agriculture to the smallholder setting.

Some ideas for adapting precision agriculture to smallholder agriculture in the developing world include:

- *Counter-top soil testing equipment in each fertiliser shop.* The motivation for this stems from the observation that smallholder farming field size is often smaller than in the developed world. For example, in the USA, the most common area unit for precision agriculture soil sampling is 1 ha (i.e., 2.5 acres), but most smallholder farm fields are smaller than this. It would be technically possible to use the same sensors being developed for in-field soil testing in a counter-top device. Smallholder farmers could bring soil samples from their fields to the fertiliser dealer, put the samples in the device and receive a fertiliser recommendation. This would help overcome one main problem with fertiliser application in the developing world, which is that farmers often do not know what fertilisers to apply and at what rate. A field-specific

recommendation would increase the probability that their investment in fertiliser would result in higher yields or profits.

- *Collection and distribution of weather, pest management and other
  information by cell phone.* Many farmers in the developing world now
  use cell phones. That opens the way for greatly improved use of
  information in their agricultural practices. In a few places, there are
  already attempts to deliver weather, prices and other information via
  those phones — either by SMS text or orally. It is possible to build
  on that by creating algorithms that use satellite and other sensor data
  to create individualised warnings that could alert farmers to severe
  weather, spreading pest infestations and other conditions. In addition, cell phones could be used to provide farm advisory services.

Prof. Jess Lowenberg-DeBoer
Professor of Agricultural Economics
Purdue University, USA

To us at LEAF, precision agriculture has added to the tools our farmers use in the adoption of more sustainable agriculture through integrated farm management. The capability of farmers to drill their seed
with accuracy and without overlap in the field and to optimise the
capability of their soil types has meant that individual plants survive
better, grow more uniformly and can be harvested more successfully.
This efficiency and attention to detail means farmers are able to grow
their crops more efficiently, utilising natural resources, such as soil and
water, in a way that does not put more pressure on the environment.

Furthermore, where irrigation is used, the adoption of precision
agriculture has led to the measurement of the right amounts of water
to be placed in the right areas, and this has meant that crops are
grown to their maximum potential without increasing water consumption. More still needs to be done, but precision agriculture helps
make available more detailed information, records and evidence for
farmers to do the right thing, the right way, and for the right reasons
and to grow their crops to their full potential.

Caroline Drummond
CEO, LEAF UK

Though agriculture is an important source for much of the food we eat, the ocean remains the primary source of food for hundreds of millions, if not billions, across the planet. In this way, fishing remains the livelihood and the source of income for many coastal communities around the world. But once again, as with the unsustainable use of water in underground aquifers, the rate at which fish are being caught exceeds the rate at which they reproduce in many parts of the world.[xxiii]

There exist two primary solutions which can stop this unsustainable degradation of fisheries. The first is to introduce a cap-and-trade system where, as with CO_2 emissions, a certain number of permits are issued, each allowing a certain number of fish to be caught. These permits can be traded or sold, but the overall number of fish caught remains the same. Thus, fishing can be capped at the optimal level to allow ocean fisheries to maintain their sizes.

The second solution has been to promote the use of aquaculture, aquatic farms aimed at raising fish for consumption. As ocean fisheries are increasingly strained to their maximum capacity, aquaculture has increasingly been used to respond to continually increasing demand for fish. Despite the health risks associated with the crowding of fish in such dense spaces, it has become a useful tool to prevent overfishing in the oceans.

How can governments control overfishing? Would a cap-and-trade permit system be effective?

Governments help set the rules of the game about how fishing occurs (when, with what fishing gear, and how and where it is done). In many places, these rules are improperly enforced or they provide perverse incentives for fishers to catch even more fish before someone else does.

A way to overcoming overfishing and to generating both profitable and sustainable fisheries is to focus management on fishers and their incentives and actions. Instead of top-down-based regulations, fishery regulators need to use bottom-up approaches that provide fishers with long-term incentives, rights and responsibilities for marine ecosystems. In addition, management targets and incentives must explicitly account for uncertainty and disturbances to fish populations. This should include an ecosystem focus and consideration of ways to promote the resilience of marine systems to bounce back following a negative shock.

Cap-and-trade mechanisms, called individual catch shares, already exist in fisheries and were pioneered at a national level in Iceland and New Zealand in the 1980s, but they have subsequently been applied in many other fisheries. There are not a panacea to all the challenges in fisheries, but if they are properly enforced and well-managed, they can generate an appropriate incentive for individuals to improve their returns and support long-term conservation outcomes.

Prof. Quentin Grafton
Professor of Economics at the Australian
National University, Australia
UNESCO Chair in Water Economics
and Transboundary Water Governance

What do you believe the world can learn from traditional communities when it comes to farming, fishing and protecting the environment?

As I sit at my desk to write this, I do not see the days shortening, the nights drawing in, I do not feel the rain on my face or the wind rearranging my hair, I do not appreciate the changing seasons, the arrival of the first swallows and the cuckoo. It is the farmers and fishermen who work and live with the environment, appreciate the seasons, recognise the signals of a storm coming in and the effect it will have on their harvest or where the fish are in the sea. Those traditional communities respect nature and there is much we can learn from them. In a modern society where food is plentiful, as we draw from the global marketplace, it is hard to fully appreciate the effort and care that farmers and fishermen put into striving to make a living and feeding our nations. The real solutions for food and farming of the future will need to come from new partnerships, and farmers and fishers need a place around the table as we look for new ways to feed our planet. We will need to learn from nature, exploiting the diversity of plants for nutrition, developing medicines, and strengthening the structures of buildings.

And there is more than just the appreciation of the environment and food, there is the opportunity and well-being associated with the sheer physical exercise inherent in the job of being a farmer or a fisherman. My husband is a farmer and I know that by 9 o'clock in the morning, he would have walked at least 9,000 steps, a distance many of us struggle to complete in a day. Nearly every day, he will have walked at least 22,000 steps! Farming and fishing are some of the most important industries in the world and there is much to be learned from their values, folklores and wisdom.

Caroline Drummond
CEO, LEAF UK

Chapter 5

Population, Health and Consumption

Traditional environmentalist views on population and consumption epitomise previous approaches to sustainability. They argue that our planet cannot sustain a population as large as ours and that we consume too much to the detriment of our environment. Such views sometimes go as far as to argue that our population size and consumption should be decreased, that we should make sacrifices if we wish to preserve the planet. Though high population growth and many of our consumption patterns have led to environment harm in the past, this chapter tries to demonstrate that transitioning towards more sustainable societies does not necessarily require radical and pervasive measures.

As the sustainable development agenda is pursued and as societies become healthier, wealthier and better educated, their population size stabilises and in many cases even decreases. Dealing with such novel demographic changes may become increasingly important to policymakers in the twenty-first century. As for consumption, the key, as Professor Braungart argues later in this chapter, is to change our consumption to render it beneficial rather than to simply cut back on harmful consumption.

In demonstrating that these issues can be resolved through positive societal changes, rather than through collective sacrifices, we can highlight the benefits of living in more sustainable societies.

Why is the world's population continuing to grow?

The main cause of high population growth is that birth rates have declined much more slowly than death rates. In most countries, birth rates start to fall down with a certain time lag after the decrease in death rates. Demographers call this the demographic transition. During this transition process, population growth is high. High fertility rates result in exponential growth, as high birth rates result in large new generations that will have many babies themselves, not only because they have high fertility rates but because every new generation is bigger than its predecessors.

Fifty years ago, many developed countries experienced high population growth, but as fertility levels have declined strongly during the last half-century, population growth has gone down. In many Asian countries, birth rates have declined strongly in recent years. As a consequence, the rate of population growth has gone down, but because the age structure of these population is still young, the population will continue to grow for some time. Due to its one-child policy in China, fertility declined very strongly in the 1980s. As a consequence, new generations are relatively small. This will result in a decline in the Chinese population within 15 years or so. In some African countries, fertility levels are still very high, as high as on average, a woman will have five or six children. This has resulted in very young populations that are likely to continue to grow until the end of this century, even after fertility rates decline strongly.

Dr. Joop de Beer
Head of the Department of Population Dynamics
Netherlands Interdisciplinary Demographic Institute

Is our planet "overpopulated"?

The word 'overpopulation' already includes a value judgement that should not naively be accepted. The fact is that the world population has been growing very rapidly, especially since the 1960s when modern medicine, better hygiene and better nutrition spread to the developing world, resulting in a rapid decline in death rates. Since birth rates are strongly embedded in traditional norms and religions, they continued to be very high in most of the affected countries where many more children survived. This resulted in high rates of population growth. Typically, a couple of decades after the death rates decline, so do birth rates. This has already happened in most of East Asia and Latin America. It is well underway in South Asia and just starting in sub-Saharan Africa. Depending on how rapidly the birth rates decline in these countries, the world population will either stop growing during the second half of the century or continue to grow well beyond 10 billion.

Prof. Wolfgang Lutz
Director of the Vienna Institute of Demography
at the Austrian Academy of Sciences
Founding Director of the Wittgenstein Centre for Demography
and Global Human Capital

Why is the world's population growth slowing? Why are fertility rates declining?

While the end of population growth is already being experienced by some countries such as in Japan (due to its very low fertility) or in Eastern Europe (due to a combination of low fertility and out-migration), much of East Asia and Europe is also expected to see a stabilisation or decline of population size over the coming decades. The highest levels of fertility can still be found in sub-Saharan Africa. This is because the process of demographic transition of declining mortality followed by declining fertility started later there and norms of large family are particularly strongly embedded in African cultures. But many countries there have started their fertility transitions, and within populations, there are big differences, primarily by the level of education of women. Hence, the future of fertility decline in Africa will largely depend on progress in educating young women, which will bring down their desired family size — they want fewer children who will have a better life — and empower them to pursue their wishes even against resistance from husbands or other social pressures. It will also be facilitated by family planning services that allow women access to modern contraception.

Prof. Wolfgang Lutz
Director of the Vienna Institute of Demography at the Austrian
Academy of Sciences
Founding Director of the Wittgenstein Centre for Demography
and Global Human Capital

In reality, while population numbers are continuing to grow, the rates of growth in numbers are slowing. Population growth is not, however, something like a stock market that can change enormously from day to day: it involves processes that are often inexorable and very long term. These processes will drive decelerating rates of growth until, ideally, these cause stationarity (when the number of births = the number of deaths), but more likely — over the long run — will eventually lead to sub-replacement fertility (where the number of deaths is greater than the number of births), and with that distorted structures due to ageing. In all probability, over the next few decades (perhaps even less than that), the world will see the end of one challenge — positive population growth. But, humans will then have to face a new one — the problems associated with sub-replacement fertility.

This is not hyperbole: sub-replacement fertility already exists, across the More Developed Countries (MDCs) like Japan (while the USA hovers over it), in huge countries like China, Brazil and Iran and in many other smaller countries. Moreover, it is just around the corner in many other countries, including in other big ones such as India, Indonesia, Bangladesh and Mexico. Replacement and sub-replacement do not immediately produce negative growth, but eventually that will become the world's long-term challenge. This is not to write off the phenomenon of rapid growth as insignificant, for it still occurs in much of sub-Saharan Africa. They face major problems of population growth, thwarted development and poverty, however that is defined. But in today's world, fast growth, such as we experienced over much of the world in the 1960s and 1970s, has become a minority experience.

The sustainability of the planet will be determined by a range of factors, only one of which is population. Globally, because of the decline in population numbers, the critical factor will not be crude population density or numbers of people, but instead will be social and economic density: how we use the planet and how humans allocate the planet's resources. Amartya Sen is correct when he talks about the unequal distribution of resources; in contrast with his considered view, ecologists who see population as a univariate threat are being simplistic about the determinants of the planet's challenges.

Of course, crude density will be a major factor in places such as Bangladesh, and this will be exacerbated by rises in sea levels and by wilder and more frequent variations in climate extremes — floods, droughts, tornadoes and irregular monsoons. Similarly, the encroachment of humans onto the biosphere, from competition between herders and wild animals, through to the despoliation of the most remote corners of the world — say the Antarctic — by CO_2 emissions, is a factor of social rather than crude density.[xxiv] Elsewhere, such as in the Jordan valley, pressures on water supplies pose a major problem, made far worse by refugee-driven population displacements.

In strictly demographic terms, in reducing population growth levels since they peaked, the world has achieved much over the last 60 years. The global community has contained rapid population growth — unevenly, it is true, but overall there has been a high degree of success.

To reach manageable levels of fertility, there has to be far more entrenched, sustained and sustainable overall development. This has to be multifaceted and at the grassroots level. There is no silver bullet. This is why I have been so critical of the simplistic target of Millennium Development Goal-1 (MDG-1): to increase the minimum income by $X/per day. In fact, real decreases in poverty and malnutrition will come about only if all MDG targets (or their successors) are worked on simultaneously. The silo approach of the MDGs, where powerful international agencies fenced off their contribution, made that difficult; but poverty and malnutrition are absolutely central to the other

MDGs, especially the three dealing with health. Moreover, the MDGs seem to have been made about things, the environment, dollars, health, all factors other than people — without seeing people at the centre of all development.

The main factor will be the continuation of improvements in child survivorship. High levels of childhood mortality are associated with high fertility. Very pleasingly, however, there has been an 'acceleration towards the MDG-4 target'[xxv]: to reduce child mortality (deaths under age 5) by two-thirds between 1990 and 2015, an indicator that is very sensitive to development levels. Furthermore, other factors are favourable. Above all, 87% of children are in school and more than 50% of the world's people are urban and industrial; proportionately fewer are in rural occupations. In Ethiopia from 1990 to 2000, fertility declined modestly from a Total Fertility Rate (TFR) of 6.4 to 5.9, but in Addis Ababa, the rates dropped from a medium level (3.1) to sub-replacement (1.9).[xxvi] Effective, low-cost family planning is also available throughout much of the world. However, I must stress that family planning is merely a mechanism: the determinants of fertility control are good child health, education, especially for girls, social and economic well-being and urbanisation, with child health as the highest ranking of these determinants.

We used to think of high fertility countries as being in vast blocks: Africa, Asia and Latin America–Caribbean were in this situation in the 1950s, then Asia, apart from a few poorer and landlocked countries and west Asian Arab countries, saw declines. The World Fertility Survey in the 1970s signalled that rapid change was underway in most of Latin America, then Southern Africa joined the longer running declines that had already occurred across parts of North Africa. Today, there is not a single block of countries where fertility is high across every country in the region.

In fact, replacement fertility, particularly sub-replacement, is going to be the next challenge that attempts to achieve sustainability will face from human populations. The MDCs are already well below replacement and this affects every aspect of their social, economic, cultural and sub-national policies. More importantly, this is also true for large swathes of the Less Developed Countries (LDCs): almost all of East Asia, China (TFR = 1.7), much of India, much of Catholic Latin America, including the giant Brazil, and a mix of other countries, such as Armenia, Iran and the United Arab Emirates, representing totally different religious and cultural traditions. And interestingly, in countries like Iran, exactly the same factor that has produced sub-replacement fertility in western Europe is operating: delayed first conceptions (timing). Historically, across the globe, many women had births in their later reproductive years, but they had already had more than one child, whereas today they will typically not have had any children yet, having delayed births for reasons of education and career. Family planning must thus shift to timing and spacing (intervals between births). Fortunately, with modern condoms and the pill, the technology exists to achieve this.

Looming replacement and sub-replacement problems in the not too distant future will require a total change in the way societies approach economic policy. Europe is already wrestling with this issue. But, it was, for example, a critical question in China, where the one-child policy has badly distorted reproductive patterns. Couples raced to produce a first son, if possible, so that the fertility rate at the mother's age of 20–24 years is still far higher than that at 30–34 years. In western Europe, the fertility rate at 30–34 far exceeds that at mother's age of 20–24. This distortion in the mother's age at first childbearing has flow-on effects for the whole of social organisation, such as the work–family interface. The typical young MDC mother of a first child of today is aged in her thirties; in the 1960s, she would have been in her early 1920s.

An age-structural transition first produces a decline in the proportions of young people, but at a time when ageing has not yet set in, thus decreasing the need for spending in social sectors such as education and yet not requiring an investment in housing, pensions and health for elderly people. Against this, at this phase, termed a 'window of opportunity' (the UN sets this at less than 30% of those aged 0–14 years, and 15+% of those aged 65+ years), there is disproportionate growth of people who are of working age, which is good, as it allows economic and social development, investment in productive sectors, institution-building and savings, both nationally and at the household level. The window ends when ageing sets in. Of course, dividends will be realised only when this 'window of opportunity' is well governed and managed. Experience across much of the world shows that the window may generate real development, the drivers being changes in the labour force (widening of human capital) and the deepening of human capital, which together lead to the third driver of development: savings.

Well-managed, the dividends can produce the infrastructure and institutions that allow a society to accommodate ageing better than would otherwise be the case.[xxvii] For sustainable development, studies show that societies may have access to vast resources that hitherto have been poorly documented. The results are particularly powerful when non-monetised transfers are taken into account (e.g., grand-parents caring for children after school, thus allowing parents to pursue paid employment, a factor that is included in conventional national accounts but not if it is in the informal sector).

Though this topic focuses on replacement, policy-makers focus more on the number of births in any given year, and how individuals progress through each successive age group, affecting the demand and supply of goods and services at each stage. These are momentum effects and can produce growth in a population for a while, even after sub-replacement has been reached. Eventually, of course, as the population ages, the proportions of the total who are at the age where there are higher risks of mortality also increases and then deaths will exceed births. This natural decrease in the population is a major issue in non-metropolitan areas in Mediterranean Europe. Moreover, momentum may play a further role in the size of these birth cohorts. The fertility rate per woman may decrease, but the larger cohorts born in the past who are reaching reproductive ages can still produce more births.

But reaching replacement will not produce an immediate slowing of world growth, not the least because of the momentum effects I have noted. The eventual hovering of the world population around exact replacement is an ideal that would make policy planning feasible and development sustainable and less subject to severe fluctuations. But as this will almost certainly occur unevenly across different populations, there will still be other variations, to which I turn.

There are two other profound distortions of population levels: migration and urbanisation, whether urbanisation within countries or intercountry (e.g., in sub-Saharan Africa towards South Africa), inter-regional or intercontinental movements, of which the refugee flows are merely the highest profile examples. In this, we should recall that 86% of refugee movements are within one country or to neighbouring ones, for example, to Lebanon from Syria.

Whether they are refugees or documented migrants, young adults form the largest group of migrants. The rural areas where they often come from lose their labour and reproductive capacity, but they become disproportionately represented in urban agglomerations in their own countries or elsewhere. This is also true of some countries today. In the past, when rural fertility was typically higher than urban fertility, rural losses of population, especially as the labour force got older, could be sustained — in fact, some young people may have been pushed out by the loss of work, particularly as the use of oxen for draught power and then mechanisation replaced the need for human labour. But eventually, out-migration erodes both the workforce and the reproductive potential of rural areas. They then go into decline, as has occurred for a number of decades in rural regions in Mediterranean Europe. I see advantages in vibrant concentrations of people in urban areas and have few romantic images of rural subsistence ways of life. However, the current fad in economics extolling the virtues of agglomeration glosses over the downsides both at the destination (the growing metropoles) and at the sources (e.g., the rural areas).

This means that the mechanisms are in place for huge exchanges of working-age populations that could, in part, replace the productivity lost as countries age and pass out of their windows of opportunity. According to media reports, some Germans see the inflows of young, often skilled, refugees replacing the workers retiring in Germany as a benefit. But this will occur at a moment without historical precedent: low rates of natural increase occurred in the past, usually for limited periods, when high fertility was offset by high rates of childhood mortality. Today, however, stationarity is being approached because of declines in fertility, not high rates of mortality. Yet, the way this will happen will be very uneven across the globe. Some regions, notably sub-Saharan Africa, will still face the 'continuing challenge of high growth', as John Cleland elegantly argues,[xxviii] becoming the incubators of mass migrations in normal years — spurred on by refugee flows resulting from conflict or environmental catastrophe.

Prof. Ian Pool
Professor Emeritus of Demography
University of Waikato, New Zealand

What trends are likely to affect future population growth?

Population growth rates are very unlikely to remain constant for the reasons described earlier. But depending on the speed of fertility decline, the world population will be between 7 and 13 billion by the end of this century. In the poorest countries, where population growth is still the highest in the world, a further increase of the population by a factor of three or four is particularly likely to pose very serious problems in terms of food security as well as the expansion of basic health and education services. Under conditions of climate change, these poor, uneducated and rapidly growing populations will be especially vulnerable to changing temperature and precipitation as well as natural disasters.

Prof. Wolfgang Lutz
Director of the Vienna Institute of Demography at the Austrian
Academy of Sciences
Founding Director of the Wittgenstein Centre for Demography
and Global Human Capital

There is a very strong relationship between the level of education of women and their fertility level. Women with more education have fewer children. They want fewer children and they find better ways to have the number of children they desire, as they make effective use of contraceptives and are less vulnerable to misinformation and cultural objections than less educated women. In most developing countries, the percentage of women with a high education is still very low. This is one main causes of high fertility rates. Since low levels of education of women are one main cause of both high fertility and poverty, better education opportunities for girls should have the highest priority.

Dr. Joop de Beer
Head of the Department of Population Dynamics
Netherlands Interdisciplinary Demographic Institute

How have high fertility rates affected poverty rates in developing countries? Is there a common solution?

Above all, high poverty rates have meant that two important determinants of fertility, improved infant survivorship and basic education, cannot be addressed directly in the countries involved. This is a tautology as both these determinants are indicators of poverty, as is inadequate income and malnutrition. The world has made great progress in health through low-cost public health programmes such as immunisation, so much so that an apocalyptic disease, smallpox, has been eliminated and polio almost so, as have some highly lethal childhood infectious disorders such as measles among poor children. But this does not eradicate the underlying problems: a child with dysentery or diarrhoea can be treated with penicillin and then return to the same insanitary environment to which she was previously exposed. Eventually, effective public health programmes must be bolstered by real development to overcome the underlying causes. The reduction of mortality from communicable disease, however, is accompanied by the greater diagnosed prevalence of non-communicable diseases such as diabetes. The causes of this are too complex to discuss here, but there seem to be two important determinants: (i) there is a link with increasing wealth, which has occurred in many societies — at least for some privileged groups, as income inequality has also grown, and (ii) differential levels of vulnerability. Non-communicable disease mortality is the overwhelming problem that the MDCs seek to address. In the LDCs (and even in the least developed ones), the burden of disease generated by non-communicable causes, and other factors, such as obesity, is associated with people who are better off, yet more refined data have produced unexpected results. For example, 'among India's 40 million individuals with diabetes, the most severely affected are the rural poor'.[xxix] The net result is that a 'double-burden of disease' has become apparent.

Prof. Ian Pool
Professor Emeritus of Demography
University of Waikato, New Zealand

What contributions does enhanced public health provide to sustainable development?

Health underpins everything we do. A healthy community is a prosperous one. Our goal of sustainable development cannot be fully realised without healthy men and women driving that sustainability forward.

The pervasive ailments of malaria, HIV/AIDS and tuberculosis have crippled the economies of many developing nations. When people are ill, it affects their daily lives in profound ways — they are unable to work or care for their families, and children's attendance in school is disrupted. Prioritising the health of all people will be instrumental in seeing countries prosper.

Take malaria, for example. A new analysis published in a report released in partnership with Bill Gates estimated that, if we succeed in eradicating malaria within the next 15–20 years, we can save 11 million lives, avert 4 billion infections, and return $2 trillion to the global economy.

Dr. Ray Chambers
UN Secretary-General's Special Envoy for Health
in Agenda 2030 and Malaria

What actions can governments take to boost public health in the context of sustainable development?

Political leadership and government commitment to meet the health needs of their citizens is vital to sustainable development. Our ambitions to rid the world of preventable diseases like malaria, HIV and tuberculosis cannot be accomplished without increased domestic funding for preventative health and treatment options. I applaud the leadership demonstrated by governments who have kept health high on their national agendas, scaled up their health interventions and implemented significant new policies to provide people with access to quality health care.

The African Leaders Malaria Alliance — a coalition of forty nine heads of state who jointly monitor progress against malaria on a scorecard, collectively bargain for the best commodity prices and hold each other accountable for outcomes — is a testament to what our collective forces can accomplish when we work in partnership towards a clear set of goals and fuelled by the will to persevere. It is this political leadership that saw the delivery of over one billion mosquito nets to Africa, in addition to the hundreds of millions of effective tests and treatments that contributed to the reduction of malaria-related deaths in children under five on the continent by nearly 70% since 2000.

Dr. Ray Chambers
UN Secretary-General's Special Envoy for Health
in Agenda 2030 *and Malaria*

How can public health programmes be financed, especially in parts of the world that are more vulnerable to preventable diseases?

We must pivot away from the traditional funding paradigms to which we have all become accustomed. As the financial landscape continues to evolve, we must tap into the growing economies of developing countries. There is great opportunity for these countries to become self-sustainable in addressing their citizens' health needs as their economies expand.

We also need new and bold investments going forward in areas in which the health returns are greatest. Global and national investors are seeking new types of investment that have a social impact. This is a trend unlike others I have seen in my decades of financial and business experience. We need to capitalise on this groundswell of enthusiasm and help direct it to where it can have the greatest impact.

And, finally, if the Ebola crisis has taught us anything, it is that we must strengthen global health systems, including robust teams of community health workers who can detect and respond immediately to emerging public health emergencies. These health systems cannot emerge on an *ad hoc* basis — they must have significant investment upfront and with continued financial support to stem future global health crises.

Dr. Ray Chambers
UN Secretary-General's Special Envoy for Health
in Agenda 2030 and Malaria

What policies have contributed to a stabilising fertility rate?

All over the developing world, better educated women want fewer children and find ways to have fewer children. Hence, universal primary and secondary education for all girls and boys — as just established by the sustainable development goals — is likely to result in lasting declines in fertility, especially if this is combined with the availability of reproductive health services.

Prof. Wolfgang Lutz
Director of the Vienna Institute of Demography at the Austrian
Academy of Sciences
Founding Director of the Wittgenstein Centre for Demography
and Global Human Capital

In most parts of the world, the traditional incentivising of family planning is probably no longer appropriate as the overwhelming majority of women and couples seem to favour some form of fertility regulation. To achieve this aim, they need to have services that enable this. At the very least, there must be an attempt to make effective modern methods of contraception available even in the most remote areas of a country, free of charge or at a minimal cost. The services available must also be appropriate to the needs of the population.

Many years ago at the Bucharest UN Population Conference (1974), there was a marked schism between the delegates from developing and those from developed countries, or more particularly, some of their donor agencies. The latter saw family planning, however it was achieved, as the single solution for development. By contrast, developing countries coined the phrase 'development is the best contraceptive'. History has proved them right. Attempts to promote the acceptance of family planning in the absence of real development — say in Ghana and Kenya — saw expensive programmes put in place. These often drew nurses and healthcare professionals away from more urgent tasks in the health services. In Ghana, for instance, a special cadre of family planning staff who were better paid than regular personnel were integrated in hospitals.[xxx]

Unfortunately and additionally, the 1980s and 1990s became lost decades for development, at least in Africa. This was because the Washington Consensus agencies dominated the development agenda and prioritised debt servicing. At the height of the ebola epidemic, these agencies and others voiced concern that the structural adjustment programmes had minimised the capacity of the affected countries' health systems to respond to this threat. The sectors most affected by the structural adjustments of the Washington Consensus were health, family planning and education, the three development sectors that the World Bank's own studies had shown to be the most effective.

What is needed is development overall, especially in social sectors, but less on the huge infrastructural vanity projects seen in the past. Above all, some modern version of maternal and child health should be given priority: however paradoxical it seems, it is a reality that the most effective means of reducing fertility is to improve child survivorship. This will, of course, increase total population numbers and the size of the child population. But, then fertility rates will decline. In fact, with world fertility rates declining, and this even holds true in the least developed countries, this trend is underway.

The shift towards replacement and below replacement population raises another set of problems for sustainable development. These include major new issues about how to maintain fertility around replacement, issues most MDCs are having to confront. Here, the experience of western Europe is a useful guide, especially if one compares Britain and France. Development is once again the key to success, but takes a different form. France has kept its TFR hovering around replacement and has done so by a wide range of policies that favour families and allow couples to transition between paid work and family commitments: maternity leave, preschool care, paediatric health care, school after care — and, as the national transfer accounts for France show, grandparents also help their children in child rearing. By contrast, the British TFR, which used to be almost the same as France's, has slipped, in part because of less developed social support systems. A professional or managerial woman aged 30 in France will already have had a first birth; a British woman will not.[xxxi]

Furthermore, to live sustainably, a first and urgent step is the better sharing of resources. The spectre of major deficits in water supplies is clearly the most urgent subset of this issue as major aquifers are siphoned off.

Secondly, however, I am concerned that there is a tendency by some environmentalist activists to place sustainability above people. The question is not so much protecting the natural environment — that is simplistic — but how to manage an accommodation between humans and the environment. People are everywhere, they have the capacity to despoil at an ever-increasing rate, and they are the major actors in the environment. Clearly, there can be no sustainability unless management systems are developed to forge this accommodation.

Prof. Ian Pool
Professor Emeritus of Demography
University of Waikato, New Zealand

Would there be any advantage to a stabilised fertility rate and population?

Changes in the population age structure rather than the growth rate can be expected to have an impact on economic growth. When the fertility rates decline below replacement level, there will be a period in which the share of the working-age population will increase (because the number of dependent children decreases). This has a positive effect on economic growth unless a considerable part of the workforce is unemployed. After some decades the share of the working-age population will start to decrease due to the relative increase in the proportion of older persons. This will have a downward effect on economic growth unless labour force participation increases (e.g., higher participation by women and a higher retirement age) or productivity increases (e.g., due to a better educated workforce). If fertility rates remain below replacement level for a considerable period, population size may decline unless there is a large inflow of immigrants. When the fertility rate has been constant for some time, the age structure becomes stable. Total GDP may decrease as population size declines, but as the age structure becomes stable, GDP per capita may continue to grow as long as productivity continues to grow. The decline in total population size and total GDP may have a positive effect on the environment and limit the depletion of natural resources, while the growth in GDP per capita has a positive effect on wealth.

Dr. Joop de Beer
Head of the Department of Population Dynamics
Netherlands Interdisciplinary Demographic Institute

How would a world with a sustainable population be different from our present one?

Further world population growth by another one to 2 billion people is a near certainty because fertility rates do not change overnight and because the current population age structure is very young, which implies that more and more women will enter reproductive age over the coming years. Yet, under sustainable development scenarios, global population growth is likely to peak around mid-century and then start to decline to even below the current level by 2100. At the same time, the educational composition of the entire world population during the second half of the century will probably resemble that of Europe and North America today, which implies a similar standard of living, health status and quality of institutions. However, to achieve this also requires a sustainability transition not only of the population but also of our economy, and in particular, of our energy system.

Prof. Wolfgang Lutz
Director of the Vienna Institute of Demography at the Austrian
Academy of Sciences
Founding Director of the Wittgenstein Centre for Demography
and Global Human Capital

How has population growth affected consumption?

Almost 300 years ago, people were worried about the health of human society. In addition to climate change, failures of government and the vagaries of religion (the ideology of the day), the French philosopher Voltaire mentioned population increase. Already, the multiplication of humans, like that of any other animal species, was affecting the balance of the natural world: cities were then growing beyond their means, other living creatures — plants and animals — were adversely affected, and consumption of resources seemed out of control.

We have still more to worry about today. The steep rise in human numbers since the beginning of the industrial revolution has transformed much of the land surface of the Earth. Like any other animals, we have specific needs. Forests have been destroyed, industrial agriculture has changed the chemistry of soils and cities, where more than half the human population now lives, have become vulnerable. Any changes in supply of food, water and energy or in the replacement of human labour by new technologies are made more dangerous by the multiplying human numbers.

What can we do about it? Our first requirement is to promote greater public understanding of the issues from teaching in schools and universities to politics and business. In considering action to follow, such as by limiting Greenhouse Gas (GHG) emissions, it is vital to demonstrate how such actions are in the interest of all concerned.

Direct proposals to limit population increase run into obvious difficulties. An indirect but more effective approach is to reinforce the status of women worldwide. At the same time, we must reduce the size of cities and improve public services in them. Throughout, respect for other creatures and organisms within the natural ecosystem, of which we are an infinitesimal part, must be restored. As has been well said, we have to treat the Earth as if we intended to stay.

Sir Crispin Tickell
Director of the Policy Foresight Programme at James Martin School
for the Twenty-first Century
Oxford University, UK

What is a planet's ecological footprint and why has it been argued that ours is excessive?

I think that concept is just a human projection, like when people talk of the life cycle of a product. Products are not alive, how can they have a life cycle? The planet is generating a lot of organisms who have in turn an ecological footprint, but how could you argue the planet per se has a footprint? If at all, it has a positive footprint because the planet is generating biodiversity. We have an abundance of energy input, the energy humans need is less than 0.001%.

People want to be climate-neutral? How strange. People think it is good to be neutral, but you can only be neutral when you don't exist. Trees are not climate-neutral, they are carbon-positive and climate-positive, and so the whole approach of footprint calculation is pretty simplistic. We should celebrate the footprint, look at a child and say, 'welcome to this planet' instead of saying 'Can you reduce your carbon footprint'?

We should see humans as an opportunity, not as a burden. Footprint calculations see humans as a burden which needs to be minimised. This focus on zero emissions and a zero footprint is pretty cynical. It implies standardising human development, which isn't fair. Human development is different in each country, each culture and each society: it's not dependent on a few parameters. What I'm talking is about diversity, changing our footprint for the better rather than minimising human damage.

Prof. Michael Braungart
Scientific CEO of EPEA Internationale Umweltforschung
Co-founder and Scientific Director of McDonough
Braungart Design Chemistry
Professor at Erasmus University Rotterdam, Netherlands

How can we minimise the waste produced by our societies?

Societies should conceptualise waste as a resource. This means eliminating waste by setting political targets for recycling and by focusing on new technologies and business models that help us waste less. The circular economy is a wonderfully positive vision of a society, in which resources are circulated and reused again and again instead of being incinerated or ending up in a landfill.

We all know that the current linear economic model is not sustainable.

The concept of the circular economy envisages decoupling growth from resource consumption and maximising the positive environmental, economic and social impacts. It envisages designing products so that they are easier to reuse or recycle like Timberland's Earthkeeper shoes. It aims to make sure that every ingredient of every product is biodegradable or fully recyclable. This is done in some chemicals companies that replace the fossil fuel inputs in their production methods. It aims to maximise the useful life of products by repairing or remanufacturing like Caterpillar's refurbish and reuse programme of parts. It encourages new business models that shift from selling products to selling services like the tyre company that offers a 'per kilometer' tyre leasing service. It aims to have no waste from production, but instead to make sure the waste is recovered as valuable resources: waste heat, slurry, nutrients, organic material, metal and salt. It envisages engaging your customers throughout the product life cycle instead of just during the few minutes that they make a purchase, and, ultimately, it's about gaining competitive advantage.

If we design our production and consumption using the principles of the circular economy, we will have more efficient companies and smarter consumption and we will make sure that there are resources enough for all of us, even with 3 billion more people joining the middle class in the coming decades.

Ida Auken
Danish Social Liberal MP
Former Danish Minister for the Environment (2011–2014)

Why has it been argued we cannot continue to consume energy at our present levels even if we switch to renewable sources?

Energy is merely a means to various ends. A major end towards which modern growth-based technological societies apply energy is in the acquisition, processing and transportation of all other resources. Abundant cheap energy has enabled us to overexploit fisheries, over-harvest tropical forests, degrade soils and landscapes, expand our cities (even where there are few local resources) and displace thousands of other species from their habitats.

Some forms of renewable energy, such as wind and solar, may help reduce CO_2 emissions, but without a change in the fundamental values of the global society and global economy, renewable substitutes for fossil energy will continue to fuel the fatal depletion of the Earth. The world community should abandon the growth imperative and plan for the cooperative transition to a smaller-scale steady-state economy, one that can operate indefinitely within the means of nature.

Prof. William Rees
Professor Emeritus and Former Director of the School of Community
and Regional Planning
University of British Columbia, Canada

What types of policies can governments enact to reduce perverse forms of overconsumption?

Governments can make the better choices more visible, such as through labelling schemes. They can use taxation as a tool to create better incentives to avoid overconsumption. And then they could make it easier to recycle and reuse, and incentivise efforts to minimise waste (like food waste). Finally, governments must urgently find out how to handle the new 'sharing paradigm' and go beyond the 'sharing economy'.

Connie Hedegaard
Former European Commissioner for Climate Action (2010–2014)
Former Danish Minister of Climate and Energy (2007–2009)
and of the Environment (2004–2007)

The first, crucial step in creating a more sustainable and resilient society will be the rapid achievement of a net zero emissions economy. This is essential in order to reduce the increasingly high probability and risks of catastrophic global warming. The steps required to achieve a zero net emissions economy include:

- Reducing energy demand through reduced consumption and increased energy efficiency.
- Replacing fossil-fuel-based energy supply with renewable energy.
- Significantly expanding low-carbon land use, agriculture and forestry.
- Strengthening social and ecological resilience.

A more sustainable and resilient society will also be characterised by a more equitable distribution of resources within and between generations, more democratic decision-making institutions and processes and an economic paradigm informed by a far stronger understanding of the impossibility of infinite growth in consumption on a finite planet.

Prof. John Wiseman
Deputy Director of the Melbourne Sustainable Society Institute
University of Melbourne, Australia

How can governments curb the overextraction of non-renewable resources?

Governments will not do this as long as they remain beholden to corporate interests (particularly in North America, where private capital has captured the electoral process) and do not perceive massive public support for the needed policy shifts. That said, in the event of a sea change in public intelligence and political will, governments could rapidly reform the tax system to (i) eliminate tax subsidies on oil and gas development, for example and (ii) better reflect true cost pricing (or 'full social cost pricing').

Any good economist will acknowledge that ecological 'externalities' (the hidden cost of pollution and resource depletion) reflect environmental subsidies and market inefficiency. Goods and services that are consequently priced below their true social cost will be overconsumed (Climate change as a result of excessive carbon pollution is perhaps the best-known example of such gross market failure). Adequate pollution charges, including carbon taxes and resource depletion taxes (with revenues dedicated to repairing ecological damage), are sure ways of raising the prices of these goods to the consumer, reducing consumption to efficient levels, and providing a source of government revenue to pay the administrative costs, repair environmental damage and invest in renewal. Pollution and resource depletion charges should be low initially but escalate predictably until the desired changes in industry and consumer behaviour have been achieved. The longer we wait, the steeper the needed escalation.

Prof. William Rees
Professor Emeritus and Former Director of the School of Community
and Regional Planning
University of British Columbia, Canada

Overextraction occurs when the rate of the use of resources exceeds what is desirable from a long-term socioeconomic perspective. The challenge with non-renewable extraction is to determine what should be the desirable rate of extraction because it depends on many factors and unknowns, some of which will not be resolved for decades to come. Many consider the rate of fossil fuel extraction to be too rapid because the costs of their combustion on future climate change is not fully accounted for by users or consumers. While imposing a carbon price on major carbon emitters may be desirable, the difficulty is that it might generate a green paradox whereby the expectation of higher carbon taxes into the future may encourage more rapid fossil fuel extraction today. Similarly, imposing export controls on some non-renewables may increase CO_2 emissions if resource users were to substitute to more carbon-intensive alternatives. Thus, careful attention must be given to the unintended consequences of government actions. Controls and policies should incorporate an understanding about how people respond to incentives if the desired goal of the policy is achieved by a change in the rate of resource extraction. Further, the benefits of current extraction needs to be used wisely and invested appropriately for a time when these resources may not be available.

Prof. Quentin Grafton
Professor of Economics at the Australian National University,
Australia
UNESCO Chair in Water Economics and Transboundary
Water Governance

One cannot have infinite material growth on a finite planet. We can have substantial (but not infinite) improvement in well-being (without the necessity of growth) by distributing wealth and income better and by acknowledging the non-marketed contributions of natural and social capital to our sustainable well-being.

We certainly need a more equitable distribution of material wealth and we need to live within our planetary boundaries. We need to shift to renewable energy and live on that energy budget. Some economies have become obese and could do with losing some material weight. Others still need to grow, but in a different way from that in the past — in a way that balances the growth of built, human, social and natural capital and provides genuine progress.

Prof. Robert Costanza
Professor and Chair in Public Policy
Australian National University, Australia

How can we get people to make the connection between their consumption patterns and behaviour and their harmful effects on the environment?

When you buy a TV set, it usually has around 4,360 different chemicals, but do you really want to have 4,360 chemicals or do you want to watch TV? I don't consume a TV set: I use it, it's a service. So, the company making the TV is responsible for managing the material, not the person using the TV. Similarly, I don't consume a washing machine, I just want to have clean clothes. This is why it's important to recognise real consumption, like food, detergent, tyres and shoe soles, things that get changed by being used: chemically, biologically, physically. When things get changed by being used, this is consumption. But we do not consume a washing machine, we only use it. So, this is why we need to differentiate between consumption products and service products. We are optimising the wrong things just to minimise our footprint. A car tyre now lasts twice as long as it did 30 years ago. Do you think the tyre is good for the environment? No, we have made the wrong things perfect. Thirty years ago, a rubber tyre would hit the road and stay there, now the rubber fine dust is more persistent in the environment and is so small it floats in the air, making it breathable by people and animals.

It's not a matter of consumption patterns, it's a matter of the design of products from the beginning. The design decides the environmental consequences. Why should we make people's lives more difficult just because the design of products is so primitive? We can learn to make a planet that can support all species, this is why it's not a triple bottom-line that is needed, as some argue, it's a triple top-line. We need to be good for the environment, not less bad such as established in the triple bottom-line. There are too many people to minimise our footprint, to be less bad, we need to learn to be good. Good for the economy, good for society and good for the environment as well, so we can support other species. For example, biodiversity in the city of Berlin is three times higher than in the agricultural land around Berlin. This shows we can live well and support other species.

Prof. Michael Braungart
Scientific CEO of EPEA Internationale Umweltforschung
Co-founder and Scientific Director of McDonough Braungart
Design Chemistry
Professor at Erasmus University Rotterdam, Netherlands

Can our consumption of goods be replaced by a consumption of services? How would that help reduce consumption?

Consumption is a necessary part of life. No one can live without consuming basic levels of food, clothing and shelter. Consumption, to at least survival levels, is necessary for existence and it is not subject to substitution by services (and most people with the financial means would not be satisfied with mere survival levels of consumption). The simple fact is that people will not replace the consumption of goods with the consumption of services until their material needs and wants are largely satisfied.

That said, much of the demand for goods, particularly in high-income countries, is artificially created by the advertising and public relations industries. These industries exploit people's personal insecurities and competitive instincts to encourage them to consume more than they need for a materially satisfying life. People are encouraged to define themselves in terms of the size of their houses and cars and their accumulation of consumer goods. Certainly, there is much room here to reduce material consumption while improving quality of life through increased consumption of services (e.g., the arts) and investment in social capital. This will, of course, require a shift in cultural values and the ways in which people acquire self-esteem and social status.

Regrettably, however, even such a dramatic change in cultural norms would not necessarily increase prospects for global sustainability. Even if there are 2 billion genuine overconsumers on Earth, there are more billions of people who underconsume. Raising the billions who live in poverty to material adequacy — as is morally justified — would greatly increase demand for energy and material. This would easily overwhelm any positive effects of reduced demand by the wealthy resulting from a shift to the consumption of services.

What complicates matters is that this is already a world in overshoot — total consumption and pollution exceed the regenerative and waste assimilation capacities of the ecosphere. Given the moral justification for growth in consumption by the poor, it will take a great deal more than a shift to consuming services by the rich to reduce the human eco-footprint. As already implied, what the world needs is a sea change in consumer expectations and behaviour, leading to substantial absolute reductions in global energy and material throughput (bearing in mind that even services require energy and material). Such a consumer revolution is unlikely to happen voluntarily (which is itself a clarion call for government intervention in our collective interest, including taxation to reflect true cost pricing).

Prof. William Rees
Professor Emeritus and Former Director of the School of Community
and Regional Planning
University of British Columbia, Canada

As an example, a baby uses about 5,000 diapers and because of the ageing population, the volume of adult diapers in a country like Germany is higher than that of baby diapers. So, if you use cellulose-based tube absorbers (which can store the water) in diapers instead of polyacrylates (which are currently used), you can easily use them to grow 150 trees in Egypt or Tunisia. So even a baby can have a positive influence just in the diapers it uses.

When humans were hunting and gathering, our planet could sustain about 5 million people. When we learnt to do traditional agriculture, our planet could sustain about 500 million people. When we learnt to farm using traditional industrialised agriculture, our planet could sustain about 5 billion people. And we are definitely beyond that limit because industrialised agriculture is destroying the soil and isn't good for people. And it doesn't help to try and make our system more efficient. It's not a matter of reducing consumption, it's a matter of beneficial consumption. In seeing a cherry tree in the spring, we do not focus on what it has consumed. No, we are proud to see this tree and everything that it does is beneficial. The tree's not engaging in harmful consumption, it's engaging in beneficial consumption that supports other species.

What this means is that we are optimising the wrong things instead of first asking what the right thing is. What is healthy nutrition? But it's more about healthy consumption than about productivity. We don't look at nature and focus on its consumption. No, we ask how nature can be beneficial to others. Why should we be less smart than the other species on this planet?

Prof. Michael Braungart
Scientific CEO of EPEA Internationale Umweltforschung
Co-founder and Scientific Director of McDonough
Braungart Design Chemistry
Professor at Erasmus University Rotterdam, Netherlands

What are cradle to cradle products? How can they help reduce our consumption?

Cradle to cradle products are designed from the beginning to support biological systems (biosphere) or technical systems (technosphere). But when people talk about cradle to cradle products, they mean a world without waste. When you talk about zero waste, you're still thinking that in a mindset of 'waste'. Now, in cradle to cradle, everything is a nutrient for something else. But we need to make sure that we are seeing the glass as half full, not as half empty.

So, mostly what we need is to design things differently. When you produce a washing machine, you are no longer selling a washing machine which uses 150 different kinds of cheap plastics. Instead, there are washing machines now that have only three types of plastics which can basically be used forever. We aim to reinvent everything in the biosphere and the technosphere, and this has been amazingly economically successful because it's a matter of quality. A cheap product creates waste. We are not aiming at ethical responsibility because people forget to behave ethically the moment they are under stress. In a traffic jam, people often want to switch lanes to be a little faster, even if by doing so, they cause a bigger traffic jam for the people behind them, but they don't care because they're stressed. Similarly, sustainable design should not be an ethical matter. So it's not about business responsibility, it's only about innovation, it's about quality, maybe it's about beauty because nothing is beautiful when it's toxic.

But there will always be consumption products, like food or shoe soles, because consumption means that they are used up by being used. They are chemically and physically altered. I'm not interested in reducing overall consumption: instead, I want to engage in healthy consumption as other species do. I am interested in upcycling, not the circular economy, I want to learn, not stay the same. I am interested in reinventing things, I don't want to have the same stuff forever. Therefore, cradle to cradle is an innovation engine, but we need to be fast or a lot of our local industry will disappear. Nowadays, it makes sense to print a magazine or a book in China and ship it into London the next day. But, instead of using 50 different chemicals when printed locally, it now contains 90 different chemicals. The difference is that the book is now half as expensive, but we pay with exposure to more chemicals and doing the high-tech recycling of highly contaminated paper. So, if we stick to optimising the wrong things, we just make them perfectly wrong.

There is also the big problem of romanticising nature. Phrases like 'What did we do to Mother Earth?!' carry implications because there is no Mother Earth. The strongest carcinogens are still natural chemicals. The most toxic chemicals are still natural. Nature doesn't need us when we are older than thirty years. So, we can learn from nature.

Nature needs cancer to adjust the gene pool, but what mother would give her child cancer? So, nature is not our mother, and romanticising nature creates our biggest problems. Nature is our teacher, our partner, not our mother. We do not need to be emotional about it.

Nearly all people want to be good if you give them the chance. And this is why we should stop telling people to minimise their footprint because that makes them angry and greedy. But when people feel safe, when they feel accepted, they come and live a far more humble lifestyle, not because somebody tells them to, but because they're happy to share. Even the poorest of the poor are always frankly in sharing when they feel safe and accepted. That's what I'm talking about.

Prof. Michael Braungart
Scientific CEO of EPEA Internationale Umweltforschung
Co-founder and Scientific Director of McDonough Braungart
Design Chemistry
Professor at Erasmus University Rotterdam, Netherlands

Chapter 6

Protecting the Global Commons

The term sustainability has been used to describe the increasing complexity of the political, economic and social causes and solutions linked to climate change. As climate change has no single cause or solution, adapting to and mitigating it will require a broad and widespread cooperation between governments, international institutions, NGOs, corporations, cities and citizens. The causes and effects linked to climate change are global, therefore, any attempt to solve it must also be done at the global level. This is especially so because if there were no general agreement by all countries on how to manage CO_2 emissions and mitigate climate change, they would have no incentive to act on their own.

This was the problem described by Garrett Hardin in 1968 when he explained why common-pool resources were being overused. He argued that when everyone can access a resource at no cost (like the oceans for fishing, or the atmosphere for polluting), participants have no incentives to reduce their use of the resources on their own.[xxxii] This was what led to overfishing in the ocean and the accumulation of CO_2 in the atmosphere.

How can common-pool resources like the oceans, the atmosphere and the poles be conserved? What types of structures or institutions would facilitate their management?

Nature does not recognise human frontiers and so managing shared resources requires strong multilateral cooperation and initiatives. We have many of these already that are doing excellent work in protecting these resources. Indeed, it is said that the Montreal Protocol, which was established in 1987 to repair and protect the ozone layer, is probably the most successful international agreement ever signed. Through subsequent coordinated action, the Protocol brought the ozone layer back from the precipice of degradation in the greatest planetary repair job in history.

We will need to ramp up these efforts across the board. Our oceans, in particular, are massively overfished and polluted with an enormous amount of plastic. Coral reef bleaching is a major problem. Solving these issues requires intergovernmental cooperation, founded on a shared appreciation of the value of these ecosystems. We can have multilateral frameworks to support and manage these efforts, but ultimately countries will need to enforce domestic mechanisms to ensure compliance with goals they've set out at the international level.

Achim Steiner
Director of the Oxford Martin School, University of Oxford, UK
Former Executive Director of the UN
Environment Programme (2006–2016)

I think it's clear there's no single solution for managing common-pool resources, otherwise we probably would have found it by now. In fact, we've been having this debate for decades. For example, the Antarctic Treaty system was established in the 1950s and yet there are still several pieces of the puzzle missing.

The first piece is a clear understanding of the mechanisms that have led to unsustainable use of these resources. In our most recent work here at the European Environment Agency, we've been taking a much more systemic perspective on this. If you want to manage resources in a sustainable way, you have to understand the unsustainable nature of the current pressures on them. These are linked to our systems of production and consumption, so gathering knowledge about the drivers of unsustainability — for example, our energy, food, and transport and mobility systems — and the impacts they have on the state of the environment is absolutely crucial.

An increasing number of international agreements refer to these pressures. For example, the Paris agreement has a very clear link to all these systems and implies significant changes to them with its call to move towards decarbonisation.

Second, while it's all very well to understand what's wrong, we also need institutions that are equipped to combat the problems. I think it's quite clear that strong global institutions, with the world's governments and states on board, is one important element. To that end, the Paris agreement represents a major step forward, as it has increased the number of states that have, or are designing, climate policies, from some 35 to about 185.

But while recognition and understanding of the problem, and getting so many countries on board are important, it's still not enough. We also need more efficient and effective institutions. What is currently lacking is a global mechanism for compliance and sanctions, and this is where we can learn from areas that do have such effective mechanisms in place. The World Trade Organization is a case in point. It is a global institution and, although membership is not universal, it has a clear mechanism of arbitration, compliance and sanctioning. Gradually, members come to understand that they must take their commitments seriously and that, collectively at least, they can be named and shamed, and will face sanctions in the form of compliance mechanisms if they don't behave according to the rules.

The third element is that we're not going to succeed if we focus only on nation states. We know that the concept of sovereignty is, to some extent, being eroded. A lot of the systems that are fundamental to our society are not limited by territory and do not only concern public authorities, both of which are defining characteristics of the nation-state. They are global in nature, or at least transboundary, so we will need to focus on institutions that capture the global production and value chains of the systems. That means a greater involvement of key economic actors.

In addition to these elements, it's clear that sustainability starts at home, by which I mean we will need to involve all levels of decision-making, from the lowest — the personal, family or household level — all the way through to the global level. We need to be able to connect the principles for the successful management of common-pool resources to these different levels, especially the levels with which people identify and where they feel that they have agency and can have an impact on the situation. This is very close to the ideas of Elinor Ostrom, who won the Nobel Prize on common-pool resource management. Her important insight was to emphasise an institutional mechanism that operated at the appropriate, often more local level.

This approach hints at the complexity of managing common-pool resources sustainably and getting different actors to commit. It connects knowledge through a more systemic approach, where actors at different levels, not just national level, will have to work together. If you look at the major impacts of climate change, air pollution and resource depletion around the world, you see they are clearly forcing politicians to engage more openly in transboundary and global policy work as well as in their national commitments. And if you look at the pressures on emerging economies like China and India, and on food systems due to climate change in East Africa, it is clear that these translate into a need for stronger political action.

Dr. Hans Bruyninckx
Executive Director of the European Environment Agency

What roles do citizen oversight and participation play in protecting the global commons and in transitioning to an environmentally sustainable world?

We are all responsible and must be part of the solution! All of us need to respond to a common threat to humanity and to Planet Earth.

Dr. Gro Harlem Brundtland
Former Prime Minister of Norway (1986–1989; 1990–1996)
Director-General of the World Health Organization (1998–2003)

Across various policy areas, it's well documented that citizen engagement and involvement is important because you tap into local understanding and knowledge that you do not necessarily have in a national planning bureau or a university research lab.

It is essential to connect to the creativity and commitment present in society. It is also important because, ultimately, it will be a big challenge to change people's habits. Don't get me wrong, I do not belong to the group of thinkers who want to individualise responsibility for climate change and environmental degradation. I am not saying that it is just a matter of consumers making the right choices and that this will change everything because I don't think that is the case.

I'm talking more about citizens feeling connected to a larger cause, feeling a responsibility to discuss the problem, to discuss options for solutions, and to see themselves as part of the solution. We have very good examples of this. A lot of sustainable urban innovations are deeply embedded in citizen engagement. A lot of innovations in sustainable agriculture are based not on big agri-business, but on local communities of engaged farmers. Much of the renewable energy movement comes from collectives that, unlike big businesses, are citizen-owned whether through cooperatives, individual ownership or local organisations.

If we talk about changing systems of production and consumption, we are talking about social change. So it would be ridiculous to think that we can have social change without involving society in the most fundamental way.

Dr. Hans Bruyninckx
Executive Director of the European Environment Agency

What is the role of international institutions and international cooperation in solving the environmental crisis?

Faced with serious global environmental challenges that include climate change, air pollution and massive levels of soil erosion, the world needs to advance the widest possible cooperation by all countries and relevant stakeholders. International institutions, in particular, have a crucial role to play, as does international cooperation more broadly.

International institutions such as the UN can establish global strategies and norms for managing and conserving the global environment through the adoption of multilateral environmental regimes. This has been evident over the past 50 years during which new strategies, plans and multilateral environmental agreements emerged from conferences in Stockholm (1972), Rio (1992 and 2012) and, more recently, in New York with the 2030 Agenda. These outcomes over time inform and complement national laws, plans and programmes.

The 2030 Agenda for Sustainable Development and its 17 SDGs emphasise the interlinkages and integration between environmental, social, institutional and economic aspects of development. It signals a move away from addressing issues in silos and favours a coherent and balanced approach through integrated policy responses. The term 'environmental crisis' covers many topics — from man-made to natural disasters, from short-term events to long-term ecological changes and from a local to a global scale. History has shown that handling these in isolation leads to fragmented and imperfect responses.

Common to all these challenges is the need for an institutional response that addresses the interlinked nature of the problems. Institutions that enable integrated planning, early warning and comprehensive responses are critical. This is particularly the case when international institutions provided human, institutional and technical assistance to developing countries through financial support, technology transfer and capacity building.

Here, member states have established environmental funds such as the Global Environmental Facility and the Green Climate Fund (GCF) which support environmental sustainability programmes in developing countries. UN agencies such as the UN Environment Programme (UNEP), the UN Development Programme or, indeed, UN Habitat, play important roles at the national level. Other international actors such as multilateral development banks have an increasingly important role to play in supporting the transition to low-carbon climate-resilient economies. Many of these actors are supported by international cooperation in the form of Official Development

Assistance (ODA)[xxxiii] but recently they have also begun to draw on other sources of finance to boost their ability to respond to the environmental needs of developing countries.

Another role that international institutions such as the UN can play is in convening key actors to discuss crucial environmental issues. Here, the UN can engage with business and civil society to encourage them to align their activities with sustainable development objectives and to lend their expertise and reach to global efforts to protect the environment.

H.E. Mogens Lykketoft
President of the UN General Assembly (2015–2016)

When it comes to agreements on issues such as climate change, it is international institutions like the UN that provide the facility for governments to come together, discuss and agree what they want to do. Without international institutions, where would countries go to discuss and agree? Secondly, international institutions of different kinds have different capacities not only to support member states but also to support civil society organisations and subnational organisations with technical support, technical cooperation, data and financial support. All kinds of different institutions exist to help countries address environmental problems. The UNEP develops normative ideas, while organisations like the Global Environment Facility (GEF) or the World Bank have funding available for countries to address sustainable development. So, all in all, there are many international institutions and organisations that collectively support countries. And to implement the Paris Agreement we will need very strong international cooperation. And this is what will be facilitated, coordinated and organised — though some of it will happen bilaterally between individual countries — by international organisations of different kinds. So, the answer is that they're absolutely necessary.

Janos Pasztor
Director of the Carnegie Climate Geoengineering Governance Project
Former UN Assistant Secretary-General for Climate Change
Issues (2015–2016)

What has impeded effective international climate legislation and agreements from being passed and implemented?

The major element is the question of what is meant by 'common but differentiated responsibilities'? among Annex-1 (developed) countries and non-Annex 1 (developing) countries. In the Kyoto Protocol, Annex 1 countries made commitments that were intended to be binding, while the non-Annex 1 countries did not. This produced an impossible result because if it's binding for me but not for you, it's going to be very difficult to sell this kind of agreement to my citizens in my country. This is also what happened at the Copenhagen climate conference in 2009. I had the privilege of being present in Copenhagen at the very moment when President Obama said, 'I can't go back to my country with this kind of agreement' because of the way responsibilities were divided between the Annex 1 and non-Annex 1 countries.

Ricardo Lagos
Former President of Chile (2000–2006)

The science is already there, and it is telling leaders, especially the youth leaders of the world that our planet is already being threatened because of what past generations have done. Young generations must say to their leaders: 'Look, you have polluted our world, you must decide now to clean it and to give money to the people who have been damaged and harmed by climate change to help them adapt. You need to help them develop technologies that can develop their infrastructures and renewable energies, to help them build schools and educate their children and to provide health for their people'.

So, we must address this and move to decarbonise our economies, particularly in industrialised countries. They must take the lead in doing this because they are the biggest polluters and they have polluted the atmosphere over the long history of industrialisation. They must stand up to their duties, to their obligations to clean up the mess they made to our atmosphere. It's so unfortunate that they have not done their part. Instead, they are calling developing countries, even small island developing countries like Tuvalu, to do their part when they themselves have done nothing to clean the atmosphere. This is totally unjust and I urge the leaders of industrialised countries to do the right thing before calling on other countries who have contributed nothing to global warming to cut their style of life.

H.E. Enele Sopoaga
Prime Minister of Tuvalu

The main reason for this is, I guess, because you have weak victims and strong perpetrators. Any climate change negotiation process at the international level operates through the UN and its Framework Convention on Climate Change where nation-states negotiate with each other. Historically, the large emitters have been the rich countries that in general have felt themselves to be less vulnerable to the impacts of climate change either because of their wealth and their ability to afford resilience if they needed to, or because they were in a part of the world where the impacts were perhaps less dramatic or even in some cases had a positive influence. For example, in northern Europe, agriculture benefits from relative increases in global temperature because productivity improves. In one of the most sensitive sectors, a bit of global warming is good for Europe. But, on the other hand, the countries and regions that seem to be the most vulnerable are also those that emit the least, the poor countries that are also intrinsically more vulnerable. Thus, the negotiations are between unequal partners. On the one hand are the rich and the less vulnerable countries that potentially have a lot to lose, or so they might think, by completely revolutionising their energy systems and the costs of the change required. On the other hand, there is a large number of comparatively poor countries who are emitting less and who are more vulnerable.

And in that sort of negotiation the strong and the powerful who have most to lose are most difficult to change. And yet, it is amazing that we have this treaty in 1992 where rich and powerful countries begin to understand that they need to radically reduce their greenhouse gas emissions. And rapidly growing countries like India and

China, who themselves have become major emitters and feel themselves extremely vulnerable to climate change, have also become much more part of the argument. The political balance at the international level has changed and there is now an interesting political context in which countries are much more likely now to implement some kind of agreement on emissions control, even though it continues to be difficult. Moreover, there has been tremendous technological and economic development in new energy technologies, which, like solar and wind power, are now economically competitive in many parts of the world, unlike 10 or 20 years ago. So there is now a portfolio of viable alternatives. China and India have impressive renewable energy policies. Countries like Germany, Denmark and Spain also have aggressive policies to develop and spread these renewable energy technologies. People are much less sceptical about the possibility of using low-carbon energy systems and solar power. It also makes economic sense, so it seems more feasible politically at the international level because there is a greater convergence of interests. I think the situation looks much more promising than it did 10 years ago.

Prof. Frans Berkhout
Executive Dean of the Faculty of Social Science and Public Policy
King's College London, UK

Can we solve our environmental crisis without the participation of all nations? How can we convince and compel countries to participate in and comply with an international climate agreement?

All nations will subscribe to the Paris agreement — the Durban mandate is very clear about this, and we believe that countries are negotiating to sign on, not to stay out of this new agreement. Countries cannot be compelled to join — that would not make sense. It is the deep recognition of the negative consequences of climate change and the increased understanding of the benefits of climate action — numerous benefits beyond the atmospheric benefits — that will ultimately bring countries to do more than they currently want to do.

The visibility of action by all that the international agreement brings is an important step towards this learning. The EU believes that new agreements should contain a compliance system that helps ensure that all countries do what they promise.

Carole Dieschbourg
Environment Minister of Luxembourg

In our interdependent world, all major economies need to pursue a more sustainable growth path. In order to achieve this, it is paramount that some developed economies show that decoupling[xxxiv] is possible. Showcase good examples. Develop and disseminate new technologies. How to compel countries to participate? Maybe a bit more naming and shaming is needed.

Connie Hedegaard
Former European Commissioner for Climate Action (2010–2014)
Former Danish Minister of Climate and Energy (2007–2009)
and of the Environment (2004–2007)

What type of common ground can be found among members of the international community when negotiating an international climate agreement?

Building consensus has been the main effort over years. Increasingly, more countries are now aware they need to work together. There is now hope that broad consensus about action plans, different for each country and region, can lead to the necessary results.

Dr. Gro Harlem Brundtland
Former Prime Minister of Norway (1986–1989; 1990–1996)
Director-General of the World Health Organization (1998–2003)

This has already been achieved through the UNFCCC process under the heading of common but differentiated responsibilities for each state. In general, this means that the developed and rapidly developing economies provide finance and know-how to facilitate the transition to low-carbon economies and the adaptation measures required in developing countries, while all countries have a responsibility to mitigate their emissions. As a leading example, the British government established an International Climate Fund of £3.9 billion in 2011, which has been spent, and the fund has now been re-financed at £5.5 billion. The Paris agreement in itself signals a new beginning as all nations work together on the challenges.

Prof. Sir David King
Foreign Secretary's Special Representative for Climate Change
Emeritus Professor in Physical Chemistry at the
University of Cambridge
Chairman of the Future Cities Catapult
Former Chief Scientific Adviser to the British Government
(2000–2007)

The recently adopted UN SDGs are an important step to implement environment and climate protection goals in a worldwide partnership. They are also setting trends for future world climate negotiations. The most important pillars must be fostering renewable energy, energy efficiency and resource saving. Today, we have most technologies at our disposal to achieve this and Austria demonstrates how this is possible. Austria's environmental technology is among the world's best. Such know-how and innovations must be used to a much greater extent globally.

Andrä Rupprechter
Austrian Federal Minister of Agriculture, Forests, Environment,
and Water Management

To truly resolve the environmental crisis there is a need for participation by all countries, effective environmental protection laws in each, the incorporation of natural cycles in the economy and the valuation of natural capital. Finally, agreements must also incorporate the different local, regional and global dimensions of environmental issues. To resolve the climate crisis, all countries must reduce their CO_2 emissions, especially the 10 countries mentioned in Ref. xxxv that hold the bulk of the world's coal reserves and that must agree to keep them in the ground. But as the climate is already changing, we must also adapt, and therefore help each other, and this means everyone must participate and contribute. How to convince them? By mobilising their citizens when they become exasperated by their governments' inaction.

Brice Lalonde
Executive Coordinator of the UN Conference on Sustainable
Development (Rio + 20; 2012)
Former French Ambassador on climate change
negotiations (2007–2010)
Former French Minister for the Environment (1988–1992)

How can we recognise an effective international climate agreement? What would ensue from its implementation?

It will be effective if all participate. We need to encourage a 5-year ambition mechanism ensuring that all countries' commitments get stronger over time, ensuring we can achieve the long-term target. We need a long-term goal: the target for emission increases to remain below 2°C must be operationalised to send a strong signal to the world that high carbon development is over. We need strong systems to monitor, review and verify that the commitments are carried out, and a compliance system to ensure that commitments are implemented. The new China and France statement also mentions the importance of low-carbon plans for 2050[xxxvi] — we support the importance of such plans to avoid locking in high emissions by building the wrong infrastructure (for instance, power stations) that often remain active for 30–40 years once they have been built. Long-term planning can help avoid that.

Carole Dieschbourg
Luxembourg Environment Minister

The agreement reached in Paris is simply the beginning of a new process. The key is that the agreement contains a paragraph that refers to reviewing the progress on mitigation over the coming years, so that the commitments made by each country in December 2015 can be re-evaluated and tightened up to meet the prior UN agreement that the global average temperature should not exceed a temperature rise of 2°C above pre-industrial levels.

Prof. Sir David King
Foreign Secretary's Special Representative for Climate Change
Emeritus Professor in Physical Chemistry at the University
of Cambridge
Chairman of the Future Cities Catapult
Former Chief Scientific Adviser to the British Government
(2000–2007)

For the first time, nations have agreed to abandon the distinction between Annex 1 and non-Annex 1 countries. And therefore, the question now is how every country is going to make its own commitments, which are binding at both national and international levels. Problem: even all the commitments up to date are still far away from the target of the emission reductions needed if we are to avoid catastrophic consequences on our planet. Our planet will survive, but what is at stake is whether the conditions would be suitable for human life. And this means that after the Paris agreement, and after 2020, the question will be: how are we going to be able to speed up our own commitments? When there are nine billion people in 2050, the average emission per person cannot rise above about 2 tons per person per year. And we all know that today that CO_2 emissions per person per year are about twenty tons in the USA, about ten to twelve tons in the most important European countries, about eight to nine in Russia, about about five to six in Latin American countries, five in China, two in India. The problem in China, India, Latin American countries and in some other emerging countries is that we want to keep growing, and the question is how growth is possible and at the same time how emissions can be reduced: that is the challenge.

Ricardo Lagos
Former President of Chile (2000–2006)

It will allow us to combat poverty, to provide universal access to drinkable water, to reduce the health risks of unclean water or of industrial pollution and to transition towards a more sustainable energy system. So the benefits of the Paris agreement are enormous, especially compared with the economic and human costs of these risks, if we can ever decipher them.

Hakima El Haite
Minister for the Environment of Morocco

How can the international community adapt to be able to respond and be resilient to the increasingly frequent climate shocks of the Anthropocene?

The climate is already changing in ways that we can see and measure. So, the first thing that the international community collectively needs to do is to make sure there is access to better data and information about what is happening. Some specialised agencies of the United Nations like the World Meteorological Organization (WMO) have been specifically set up to give countries early warning systems, in general about weather patterns. There are also others like the Food and Agricultural Organization (FAO) and the World Health Organization (WHO), which focus on an agricultural or health perspective. But I think that number one issue is that we need better data and we need to be able to access it because sometimes the data exists but access is not available. So this is again where international organisations are helpful.

The second point is that once you know the data, you have to act on it. And what we're increasingly hoping for is that instead of simply reacting to disasters and emergencies, which will always happen, one increasingly applies more resilient approaches to development. Resilience, in this context, means being resilient to changes in climate. Thus, any new development project, for example, should be checked against climate change. Some people use the word 'climate proofing' for making sure that new development projects take into account the fact that the climate is changing and will be changing for the life span of the project in question. These are things that we can do to make sure that development becomes more resilient to environmental shocks and also to other shocks, as the climate is just one of the many environmental challenges that we face.

Janos Pasztor
Director of the Carnegie Climate Geoengineering Governance Project
Former UN Assistant Secretary-General for Climate Change Issues
(2015–2016)

Public policy-makers and people in many sectors are aware that climate change is happening and that it will have impacts right across the economy. They have done a lot of research in the last twenty years to understand what these impacts are and indeed what kinds of responses are possible in each individual sector. The most interesting aspect of this at the moment is the systemic risk issue, which we don't really understand very well. For instance, the risk climate change poses to global food supplies is a systemic one. And this is not a question of specific impacts in a specific region. We know that the grain we use to bake our bread, the vegetables that we consume and the meat that we eat are global commodities provided through global supply chains, and we know that those supply chains can become disrupted in increasingly unpredictable ways. But what happens if two of the large grain baskets of the world fail at the same time because of droughts or for some other reasons (e.g., some kind of climate-related pest)? You suddenly then have quite massive disruptions with global repercussions because suddenly grain prices could double, triple or quadruple with all sorts of economic and political effects as a result. So, I think what people are particularly interested in understanding now is the nature of these systemic risks and whether the international community can cope with them.

Prof. Frans Berkhout
Executive Dean of the Faculty of Social Science and Public Policy
King's College London, UK

Becoming more humane is needed to transition to a more sustainable planet. Some of the effects of climate change are now inevitable, even if we were able to restrict temperatures rises to 2°C. But because we are aware of these risks, those must vulnerable to them should be helped to adapt to them and to recover when climate shocks do occur.

As the rise in sea level and temperatures will affect an increasing number of people, this will begin to affect the habitability and economic potential of some areas. As islands disappear and as some areas become too arid for agriculture, the international community will inevitably face an increasing number of climate displaced people trying to escape these effects. Being able to meet their needs and respect their human rights to dignity needs to be a priority in the coming decades.

How can the international community respond to the needs of climate displaced people?

The global community is grossly unprepared for a situation where adaptation fails and people are displaced due to climate change. There is a continuum between the mitigation of emissions, adaptation and loss and damage. If reductions in emission are inadequate there is more need for adaptation and it is more likely there will be loss and damage when communities are pushed beyond their capacity to adapt.

The first thing the international community must do is to ensure that reductions in emission are greater. Then, it is imperative that adequate resources are available to ensure that meaningful adaptation action can be taken. People do not want to leave the homes of their ancestors as a result to human-induced climate change, but preventing this will require unprecedented levels of support. A recent report by the UNEP indicates that the global cost of adaptation could be as much as $200 or $300 billion per year by 2050. The rich countries that are responsible for the emissions that have caused this crisis must help to protect the culture, heritage and identity of the most vulnerable communities and countries.

Under existing international law, there is no protection of people forced to leave their homeland and flee across a border. This requires urgent attention. People must be allowed to migrate with dignity.

The issue of internal displacement must not be overlooked either. States facing climate-related displacement within their borders require significant financial support and technical expertise to develop solutions that provide for the rights of those affected. In this regard, the Peninsula Principles provide a normative framework, based on human rights, to address the rights of internally displaced people.[xxxvii]

The Nansen Initiative, a state-led, bottom-up consultative process intended to identify effective practices and build consensus on key principles in relation to people displaced in the context of disasters and climate change, concluded at the end of 2015. The Nansen Agenda for the Protection of Cross-Border Displaced Persons in the Context of Disasters and Climate Change was released in October 2015 and offers a list of best practices and recommendations for dealing with cross-border climate and disaster displacement.

Mary Robinson
President of the Mary Robinson Foundation for Climate Justice
Former President of Ireland (1990–1997)
Former UN High Commissioner for Human Rights (1997–2002)

One of the many ways states fund their sustainable development programmes is through ODA. This is official aid by wealthier nations to assist developing ones in funding specific programmes and in adapting to and mitigating climate change. This, in addition to private financing (e.g., through NGOs and corporations), has helped nations seeking to develop in an environmentally friendly way. The Paris agreement has set a goal of $100 billion to be mobilised every year by 2020 to help states fulfil their climate and environment-related development goals.[xxxviii]

How can countries find the money to fund their sustainable development programmes? Are there alternatives to ODA?

The key is to make *all* investments sustainable — including private investment. There is no way we can make the necessary — speedy — transition using only ODA financing. However, ODA and public money should be used to leverage private investments and to pay for the additional risk in choosing the more sustainable solutions over the cheapest traditional ones. A good place to start is also to price externalities — that is, reflecting the true, long-term costs in the way we price initiatives — and to stop subsidising fossil fuels.

Connie Hedegaard
Former European Commissioner for Climate Action (2010–2014)
Former Danish Minister of Climate and Energy (2007–2009)
and of the Environment (2004–2007)

Implementing ambitious sustainable development programmes will require countries to tap into a varied set of financial resources — public and private, domestic and international. It is not so much that we need alternatives to ODA but that we need additional finance to supplement it.

Here, we can start with public finance, which remains centrally important to achieving the SDGs. There is a great need to strengthen our ability globally and domestically to increase the tax take, while also increasing the effectiveness of public spending. Many developing countries, for example, need to improve their tax collection systems in order to increase their ability to spend money on public projects, particularly as economies grow. Fighting domestic corruption as well as money laundering is also crucial. Here, capacity building can help create more effective and accountable tax systems and administrations in developing countries.

At the same time, there is a great need to improve international tax cooperation so that companies pay their fair share of tax in the country where they produce. It is unacceptable for developing countries to be deprived of their share of taxes as multinational companies based in the global north repatriate their taxes via tax havens. And it is equally unacceptable that ordinary citizens around the world are required to endure austerity while large companies pay less and less tax. This issue, as illustrated by the Lux Leaks case,[xxxix] affects and involves both developing and 'rich' countries. Taxation systems have yet to adjust to the interconnected world that we live in and reforms are needed in this area.

Clearly, public finance alone will not be enough to end poverty and realise the transition to a low-carbon, climate-resilient economy. Contrary to the common perception, there is no shortage of additional resources in our world. The challenge, however, is to redirect existing financial flows along a more sustainable path, as current financing and investment patterns do not support the common goals for sustainable development outlined in the 2030 Agenda.

Concrete initiatives that would help could be to abolish harmful subsidies, such as those on fossil fuels, or to introduce eco-taxes that shift the tax burden from labour and move it to environmentally harmful activities. Many countries have experience in that. Also, the banking sector could refrain from investing in or lending money to sectors that accelerate climate change. Already, private companies and public authorities are withdrawing from carbon intensive areas and the idea of divestment is quickly spreading worldwide.

More generally, the private sector should be included in funding SDGs and many companies, foundations and other private stakeholders are willing to do so. However, private sector involvement in financing SDGs has to go hand in hand with high standards for transparency and accountability. Companies should align their business practices to the SDGs. The right mix of incentives and regulations is crucial here.

If all these resources are efficiently explored and implemented, the reliance on ODA could presumably be reduced. For the time being, however, ODA remains a very important source of funding for many developing countries, especially the least developed countries. ODA goes to areas where it is usually more difficult to attract private money (e.g., education) and to those countries that find it more difficult to attract investment. Thus, ODA will continue to be a catalyst in mobilising further resources.

H.E. Mogens Lykketoft
President of the UN General Assembly (2015–2016)

How can developing countries be assisted to overcome poverty without exacerbating environmental harm?

In the early 1990s, some economists at the World Bank argued that environmental degradation was inevitable in the early stages of economic growth but would eventually decline as countries became richer. These assumptions are being refuted by a new generation of developing country leaders. Rather than sitting on their hands asking for a free pass to pollute until their countries' poverty has been overcome, many are already taking ownership of our planet's environmental crises. They are charting new paths to end poverty and hunger without breaking our planet's natural boundaries.

China's interventionist industrial policies mean that coal use has almost certainly now peaked. Together with India, the two countries plan to install around 1300 Gw of renewable energy by 2030 — greater than all installed power capacity in the USA today.

As poor countries embark on these new development paths that are markedly different from those of their OECD counterparts it is vital that the voices of people in poverty are heard in shaping their countries' futures. It is only by empowering citizens that governments can ensure these are just transitions towards more equal as well as more sustainable societies.

Winnie Byanyima
Executive Director of Oxfam International

This is an extremely complicated matter for which there is no single remedy. It requires a sustainable development approach; one that integrates the social, economic and environmental challenges faced by poor people in developing countries. This speaks very much to the issue of inequity in many developing countries. A 2014 Oxfam report[xl] suggests that more than half all South Africans are at risk of hunger. The report also notes that the poor have limited or no access to nutritious food, which affects their health and well-being as well as their dignity, especially when people are obliged to beg for food.

Access to food, clean water, sanitation and energy (including firewood) are some of the most basic human rights and needs. If these basic human rights and survival needs are not being met, then it becomes increasingly challenging to motivate the 27 million South

Africans at risk of hunger to care about and value the environment. Unless we begin to address these challenges in a meaningful way by meeting their basic needs and providing them with access to basic services, the challenges of varied environmentally harmful actions like pollution, the poaching of various species and the unsustainable use of trees for firewood, are very likely to continue.

Developing incentives and empowering poverty-stricken communities to take ownership in driving group clean ups, repurposing and recycling 'waste materials' and undertaking community vegetable gardening are just some of the positive initiatives that demonstrate the opportunities and benefits of a healthy environment to a local community.

Access to land and water, coupled with basic training in sustainable land use practices are important enabling factors for community vegetable gardens or even small-scale cattle farming. If produced in sufficient quantities, fresh produce could not only be available to locals at affordable prices, eliminating costly transport and waste, but their surplus could be sold to other markets. Access to other vital services such as health care, education, safety and security and employment are also critical socioeconomic matters that need to be addressed holistically for an improved environmental outlook.

The other side of the developing country coin is the growing middle class engaging in conspicuous consumption and waste. It cannot be ignored and needs to be addressed pragmatically to mitigate its harmful environmental impacts. Admittedly, the above examples may present a very simplified approach to a very complex question, but this should illustrate the complexity of environmental challenges in developing countries.

Ultimately, with education comes awareness, which in time leads to understanding, and subsequently, through community involvement and action, an empowered sense of ownership is developed to ensure responsible choices and localised solutions to support both the planet and the people.

Theressa Frantz
Head of Environmental Programmes at WWF South Africa

Could helping developing countries pay the initial costs related to renewable energy projects incentivise them to switch to a more sustainable and environmentally friendly source of energy? Could this be effective in mitigating the effects of climate change?

Well, much of this cost will have to be met by domestic resources, meaning the money that countries spend on their development, But it's also a question of doing development a little differently. The international community has made funds available through different institutions to cover different aspects of what needs to be done. One of them is the GCF, whose specific purpose is to help developing countries adapt to and mitigate climate change. The GCF is fairly new but it is now operational and has an initial capitalisation of $10 billion for 2 years, and they have started approving projects.[xli] There is also the GEF, the World Bank, regional banks and other international financial institutions. So, a whole set of institutions can either provide grants or loans to help countries face these situations.

Janos Pasztor
Director of the Carnegie Climate Geoengineering Governance Project
UN Assistant Secretary-General for Climate Change Issues
(2015–2016)

In the long run, it certainly can. Poor and developing countries are very low emitters anyway, so they're putting really trivial amount of CO_2 in the atmosphere. So in the short run, helping them reduce or mitigate their own CO_2 emissions will not have a great effect on global numbers. The main activity has to be in the big emitters, and that means China, the USA, Europe and India. But over the long term it is a challenge to encourage these countries to follow development paths that are low carbon, so that they don't follow the same trajectory in their energy systems that you've seen in other countries as they industrialised and became mature, high-income economies.

One of the big questions is what alternative growth pathways there are for some of these countries, which will grow rapidly in the future. Now, in energy terms and therefore in emissions terms, no country is the same, so British industrialisation starting in the early nineteenth century was completely different from Japanese industrialisation, for example. But in general what has happened in these countries is that they've had resource-intensive growth pathways. You see this in China as well. They tend to be driven by fossil fuels, often initially coal, and the question is whether you can imagine and then implement growth pathways in large parts of Africa, particularly in resource poor parts, that involve using renewable technologies from early on. This is still an open question but a lot of research is taking place to see whether you could make that happen.

Prof. Frans Berkhout
Executive Dean of the Faculty of Social Science and Public Policy
King's College London, UK

There is little doubt that financial support for developing countries to transition will be an important part of an overall deal. However, the most important thing rich countries could do is to rapidly reduce the cost of clean technologies so that it is in the economic self-interest of developing countries to adopt them without further assistance.

Prof. Cameron Hepburn
Professor of Environmental Economics
University of Oxford, UK

Chapter 7

Sustainable Cities

In the same way as international cooperation is important in transitioning towards a more sustainable planet, localised action through city governments is also crucial. As over half of the world's population currently lives in cities, the way cities are designed and organised is key to promoting more sustainable societies. In cases where national governments are too slow to respond to climate change, city governments can enact laws to adapt to and mitigate its effects. They can act as experiments to test the efficacies of laws which, if successful, can be enacted at regional and national levels.

In many cases, city governments have also made the link between promoting more environmentally friendly and sustainable modes of transport, energy and waste with greater citizen well-being. Cities that are less polluted and cleaner, that promote sustainable means of transport, and that have a greater environmental presence through urban parks are both more attractive places to live in and better able to adapt to and mitigate the effects of climate change.

But cities remain a large cause of climate change as they account for 60–80% of energy consumption and for up to 70% of Greenhouse Gas (GHG) emissions.[xlii] As the number of people living in urban areas continues to grow, assessing cities' increasing vulnerability to the effects of climate change and developing adaptation strategies will be essential in promoting sustainable urban development.

How can major cities, which are usually located on coasts or near rivers, adapt to be resilient to increasingly frequent and intense extreme weather-related events?

The evidence that climate change has led to significant changes in the frequency and severity of storms leading to riparian or coastal flooding is unclear and intensely debated. What is beyond doubt is the huge increase in wind and water damage from such events over the past half-century. This is mostly a result of economic development and location. There has been a burst in the construction of expensive buildings in silly places, such as on flood plains and coastal barrier islands. Cities can adapt to this situation by careful zoning to avoid building on fragile coastlines or flood plains. Managed retreat from these sites is a sensible portion, although a politically difficult one. What compensation, if any, should be available to those who lose their land and property in this way? Cities can also defend iconic coastal development by constructing hard sea defences, such as the proposed update to the Thames Barrier, although the infrastructural costs of these measures will be very high. Finally, there is the emerging field of 'aquatecture': the design and construction of floating buildings, inspired by the floating towns and villages of Southeast Asia.

Prof. Steve Rayner
James Martin Professor of Science and Civilization
Director of the Institute for Science, Innovation and Society
University of Oxford, UK

Urbanisation concentrates risk in cities and each has unique vulnerabilities. The best strategies for developing resilience will vary from city to city, driven by local or regional assessments of hazards and risks. Cities across the world are exploring innovative and inclusive strategies to address their vulnerabilities, while sharing knowledge that helps other cities identify and adapt resiliency strategies to address their specific needs.

In cities such as Curitiba, Brazil and Douala, Cameroon, resilience has been identified as the need to improve basic infrastructure and services in the poorest areas of the city. Curitiba's Vila Audi-União, an informal settlement in Curitiba, faces the constant threat of flooding because of its proximity to the Iguaçu River. The local government is therefore providing more resilient housing, along with large municipal tanks for storing rainwater, to alleviate risks. Similarly, the poorest areas of Douala are most at risk from flooding, which has prompted the city to develop a plan to improve drainage and housing in informal settlements. These basic measures will go a long way to reduce the risks faced by citizens and the most vulnerable among them.

Almada, Portugal, is using low-cost green infrastructure in the form of vegetable gardens. These are designed to absorb the water run-off in the floodplain during storms, in addition to mitigating the urban heat island effect,[xliii] contributing to Almada's food security and improving the urban water cycle.

In response to major floods in 2013, Boulder, CO, USA began developing a programme called 'Creating district scale safe havens to support community resilience'. Safe havens are self-sustaining and self-contained resilience centres that can operate during emergencies. This means that, unlike previous shelters, they do not require additional power hook ups, sewer off-takes, communications infrastructure and food and water management systems to effectively operate during a disaster. In the long term, Boulder plans to develop a network of safe havens; in the short term, it is aiming to bring three pilot installations online by 2020.

While each city is unique, there is significant potential for cities to transfer knowledge about adaptations to shared hazards. City-to-city partnerships of all types promote knowledge exchange, strengthen the capacity of local leaders and expose cities to networking and funding opportunities, accelerating their resilience efforts. For example, members of national networks such as Capitais Brasileiras 27 (CB27) in Brazil, which unites the capitals of Brazil's federal states, and the Association of Local Authorities of Tanzania are learning together through regular meetings and networking. The International Council for Local Environmental Initiatives (ICLEIs) facilitates these kinds of connections through its resilient cities congress series — the global platform for urban resilience and climate change adaptation.

Gino Van Begin
Secretary-General of ICLEI-Local Governments for Sustainability

Why do cities emit fewer CO2 emissions per capita than non-urban areas? How can we amplify this effect?

Cities that are densely settled have public transportation systems and walkable neighbourhoods produce fewer CO_2 emissions per capita because they have less reliance on fossil fuel fed vehicles that produce a good portion of the world's greenhouse gases. In addition, they tend to have buildings that offer opportunities for energy savings through a variety of means including district heating/cooling plans that take advantage of economies of scale, building codes that call for energy efficiency in lighting, HVAC (types of fuels used for heating), operable window and so forth. City governments have the capacity to develop and implement sustainability plans and legislation to enforce the efficiency that produces this effect.

Prof. Eugenie Birch
Lawrence C. Nussdorf Professor of Urban Research
Co-director of the Penn Institute for Urban Research
University of Pennsylvania, USA

Using public transport and denser housing are two of the main reasons. Comprehensive public transport systems help move people away from single-occupant cars, dramatically reducing CO_2 emissions. More compact housing is more energy-efficient, requiring less heating and reducing energy use.

It is not so much a question of amplifying this effect as it is of ensuring that, as cities grow, they are designed with CO_2 emissions in mind. Many cities in the developing world in particular will experience dramatic growth over the coming decades. It is vital to ensure that these cities grow in the most efficient way. That means investing in public transport systems, encouraging biking and walking, avoiding urban sprawl, building energy-efficient housing, developing local food systems, building sustainable local economies and making renewable energy the norm.

To develop in this way, cities need finance for their sustainability initiatives. The big challenge for our urban world is ensuring that developing cities and countries where new cities are being built have sufficient funding so that they can be truly sustainable with dramatically reduced CO_2 emissions.

Gino Van Begin
Secretary-General of ICLEI-Local Governments for Sustainability

Why are cities and local governments well placed to act and mitigate the effects climate change?

Currently, over half of the human population lives in cities. By 2050, 66% of the population will be living in cities.[xliv] Thus, the role of mayors and governors of cities and local governments in combatting climate change is very important.

Park Won-soon
Mayor of Seoul, South Korea

Cities cover only 2% of earth's surface, but over half the world's population live in them, and cities generate 75–80% of the world's GHG emissions.[xlv] It is action in cities that provides us with the greatest opportunity for deep cuts. It is clear that forward-thinking businesses see climate leadership not only as a matter of necessity but as a source of competitive advantage.

Clover Moore
Lord Mayor of Sydney, Australia

How can cities transition to a cleaner and more sustainable energy supply (dependent on renewable resources)?

The Economy of Climate Change, published by the Commission on Climate and the Economy, which I had the honour to be part of, demonstrated that in the area of energy, mitigation and cities, it is possible to make investments that are rewarding both in terms of climate and profit. For example, today there are two cities, Atlanta and Barcelona, that have the same population size of 5.3 million people and a similar per capita income. Nevertheless, because of the way Atlanta and Barcelona are organised, and because of the important role geography plays, Atlanta emits *several times more* CO_2 than Barcelona.[xlvi] Why is that? Because one uses public transport and one uses private transport. Because one, Barcelona, is much more dense simply because it is contained by mountains and the ocean, so its land area is very small and therefore its building density is much greater than in Atlanta. And so, in the coming decades, many cities will have to grow, as migration from rural to urban settings continues, particularly in the developing world. What kind of city would you like to live in? One like Barcelona or one like Atlanta?[xlvii] The right investments will have to be made in our cities because we have to learn from the lessons of the past.

Ricardo Lagos
Former President of Chile (2000–2006)

In Copenhagen, our goal is that by 2025, we will be the world's first CO_2-neutral capital. It sounds a little bit optimistic, but Copenhagen has already come a long way as we have managed to reduce our CO_2 emissions by more than 50% since 1995. We are positive that we — and other cities — can go all the way.

From our experience, the key to a successful green transition primarily lies in two things. First of all, to become a more sustainable city, intelligent urban planning is essential. One of the main reasons for our success is our political determination to incorporate more sustainable solutions in every aspect of urban planning — from heating districts and wind turbines to harbour baths and bicycle infrastructure.

Secondly, initiatives like our green solutions cannot be accomplished by a city council alone. In order to succeed, it requires a great deal of cross-sector cooperation with businesses, scientists and citizens. We need partnerships with knowledge institutions and businesses to develop and invest in innovative sustainable solutions. And to be able to incorporate all these green solutions, we have to involve the Copenhageners, so we make it easy for them to choose to bike to work, to recycle their garbage or to buy a share in a windmill.

Frank Jensen
Lord Mayor of Copenhagen, Denmark

How can cities encourage and promote the use of more sustainable means of transport?

Subway or railway systems are better than cars in terms of CO_2 emissions. And walking and riding bikes are even better than railway systems. It is a great trend for city managers to have more pedestrian-friendly cities. Establishing reliance on bike systems is an essential part for cities to become more sustainable. I am advocating using BMWs: Bus, Metro and Walking. BMW is very much important.

Park Won-soon
Mayor of Seoul, South Korea

First of all, cities should be deploying smart, sustainable and multimodal transport networks. For instance, they have to develop bike and car sharing, tramways or water transport, responding to citizens' demands for new means of transport to respect the environment. These means of transport must, of course, be affordable and inclusive. This is what we have recently implemented in Paris with the self-service bike rental Velib and the electric car rental service Autolib. As of October 2015, Paris has 14,320 Velib bikes and 2,900 Autolib cars. Moreover, the city offers €400 to help anyone willing to change their polluting vehicle for a greener means of transportation.

In 2015, Paris doubled the amount of bike lanes available and offered another 10,000 bike-dedicated parking spots to its citizens. In September 2015, Paris organised its first Car-Free Day during which car traffic decreased by 42% in the city centre. On the other hand, bike rentals skyrocketed: more than 144,000 bikes were rented that day, which is 35% more than usual. This was a great success for the city and shows how willing citizens are to change their habits.

Cities must also mobilise citizens and car manufacturers to adopt more responsible behaviour. For example, Paris has made a strong commitment to reduce the number of diesel vehicles allowed in the city.

Anne Hidalgo
Mayor of Paris, France

Sydney is constructing a 200 km cycle network with 55 km of separated cycleways. To date, we have created 12.5 km of separated cycleways, 60 km of shared paths and 40 km of other infrastructure. The number of bike trips has doubled in the past 3 years.

With more people living and working in the city, real solutions to make the city streets work more efficiently for everyone are required. Light rail, buses, walking and cycling are all part of the solutions to keep Sydney moving. The total number of people riding in and around the City of Sydney for work and recreation has soared to 132% in the 4 years leading up to 2015. The City is also investing $220 million in the state government's George Street light rail project, and has actively encouraged car-sharing — we now have over 25,000 members sharing approximately 2% of on-street spaces.

Clover Moore
Lord Mayor of Sydney, Australia

How can we reconcile an increasingly urbanised world with an increasingly urgent need to understand our dependence on nature? How can cities be designed to emulate nature rather than to disfigure it?

The simple point is that 86% of New Zealanders live in cities, yet across the whole country even our city dwellers have the best access to nature of everyone across the globe. Wellington has an ample urban beachfront, an urban forest, a wildlife sanctuary and substantive tramping tracks, all within the easy reach of the city centre. Our concerted effort dating back over 100 years to maintain a green belt in the form of the Wellington Town Belt has preserved substantial urban forests. This natural infrastructure allows us easy access to nature at any hour of the day, whether walking through the bush on a break from work or finishing up the day with a mountain bike ride home. We also have Zealandia within the city limits — one of the globe's only urban wildlife sanctuaries that has successfully led to a resurgence in numerous bird species that were previously scarce at best. There are tangible psychological benefits from having a close connection with nature, and Wellington's goal of being a 'city set in nature' is one of its highest priorities as a result. We perform very highly in quality of life measures, and we believe this is partially due to our excellent connection with nature.

It is important to take inspiration from these advantages, though, as preservation is not the only option. Reclamation can help redesign a city to emulate nature — look at Seoul's efforts to reclaim its city's natural look and feel through the Sky Garden reclamation of an old motorway and the Cheonggyecheon stream urban park. Much of the inspiration from this movement towards reclamation also stems from New York's efforts to create the High Line park on a former elevated railway line. Seattle's ambitious plan to underground a waterfront highway and create a waterfront park has even greater potential to reinvent the city's interactions with natural environment. These active reclamations of urban nature can reinvent the natural feel of even the most urbanised environments. Cities can use tools like green belts, high quality parks and compact development to remain in touch with nature without losing the benefits of agglomeration that make cities such powerful economic engines.

Celia Wade-Brown
Mayor of Wellington, New Zealand

How can buildings be designed (or redesigned) to be more efficient, to consume less energy and to reduce the carbon footprint of cities?

There are many ways buildings can be designed or redesigned to consume less energy. These techniques range from their siting (e.g., near public transportation hubs) or their orientation (to take advantage of Sun) to their internal construction, especially their systems lighting, heating, air conditioning and internal circulation. They can be designed with windows that open, so that natural air can be used to cool or ventilate them. They can be designed with skip-stop elevators so that people can walk a little to the different floors that are close to one another.

Prof. Eugenie Birch
Lawrence C. Nussdorf Professor of Urban Research
Co-director of the Penn Institute for Urban Research
University of Pennsylvania, USA

Most of the buildings standing today will still be with us in 100 years. Population contractions over time, especially of those in working age groups, are likely to fuel the need to redesign and find efficiencies rather than design new buildings. The population threat is not going unanswered in Wellington, which aims to become one of the globe's most attractive places for talented people to live. We are doing this through economic development and curating our compelling natural and social assets. However, globally, many cities will have to find different solutions to tackle this problem as their populations change. While elements like passive solar heating and building to green building standards offer opportunities for new builds, it is finding efficiencies for existing buildings that offers the greatest potential over the immediate and moderate term. This is why Wellington has started its smart building challenge to find efficiencies in existing buildings.

The core tenet of the smart buildings challenge is that to make buildings more efficient, the emissions of existing buildings must be measured. Smart meters and new technology have the potential to create powerful and easy ways of measuring energy and identifying problem areas, and this is probably the only universally applicable action that can be taken on every building, whether residential and commercial. Currently, building owners pay for some of the energy bills and occupants pay for others, and there is little incentive to invest in major capital works. More efficient boilers, rooftop solar and LED lighting throughout office buildings have a major potential to increase the energy efficiency of buildings. Similarly, the use of solar hot water, solar with battery storage in homes and, as the grid becomes more renewable, the electrification of heating and cooking have the opportunity to provide meaningful reductions in the overall footprint of buildings and cities.

Celia Wade-Brown
Mayor of Wellington, New Zealand

How can cities find the money to finance their transition towards less carbon-emitting and more sustainable infrastructures?

Environmental policies must be part of cities' priorities. Cities need to work together, implement common green strategies and use their financial resources more efficiently. In March 2015, Paris and other major European cities got together to coordinate their public procurements to promote common green investments. For example, Paris, Rome and Brussels resolved to mutualise their investments in waste-collection vehicles. Locally, Paris recently set up a participatory budget survey allowing citizens to vote for their favourite city planning projects. Carbon-reducing projects, such as increasing bike lanes, pedestrian areas and city revegetation received huge support from the inhabitants and will have been implemented by the end of 2016.

Cities need to collaborate not only with central and regional governments but also with international institutions and the private sector (e.g., banks and public or private investors) to fund their carbon-reduction plans. Indeed, recent reports and studies have shown that sustainability and energy transition are becoming more and more attractive to investors: according to Bloomberg New Energy Finance and the UNEP, new investments in clean energy increased by 17% in 2014 to $270 billion.[xlviii]

Anne Hidalgo
Mayor of Paris, France

Financing the transition to a low-carbon society is a complex challenge from the perspective of the city. With the anticipated contractions of working populations in much of the developed world, including New Zealand, it is key to keep in mind the stressors that would result from dramatic rises in property taxes. Wellington intends to attack the problem of an ageing population and a contracting working population head-on through economic growth initiatives and efforts to make it a place where talented individuals want to live. That said, it is important to keep in mind that increases in tax are not ideal. As property taxes are the primary method of financing local government in New Zealand, it is necessary to seek new levers for growth that will expand the overall revenue base to create more opportunity, more economic activity and, indirectly, more tax revenue for the city. In pursuing this dual track of seeking population and economic growth, the city both addresses its fiscal responsibilities and creates the fiscal flexibility to build a low-carbon future.

This isn't to say that tax is the only potential source of funding for low-carbon infrastructure. Reallocating funding to low-carbon modes of transport and promoting energy efficiency in the city operations offer opportunities to fund a low-carbon future without spending a single additional dollar. In the New Zealand case, participating in our emissions trading scheme to create forestry units also offers the opportunity for another carbon-related revenue stream that could be activated to fund low-carbon futures. The short answer is that there are plenty of opportunities, even outside the necessary efforts to create new economic opportunity that drives tax revenue increases, to create funding streams for a low-carbon future. This is true regardless of the context.

Celia Wade-Brown
Mayor of Wellington, New Zealand

Many of my mayoral colleagues might think that even though they have the political will to go green, it will be a huge challenge to fund the transition towards a more sustainable city. In Copenhagen, we have found that going green pays off.

First of all, there are huge economical advantages for local businesses in creating a strong demand for their sustainable products. The OECD and the London School of Economics have identified Copenhagen as a global leader in creating growth and jobs for the clean tech sector.[xlix] The 500 clean tech companies and about 30,000 people working in the clean tech sector in Copenhagen have seen a huge rise in productivity and exports, and the growth in the clean tech sector is substantially higher than in other sectors in Copenhagen and Denmark.

The returns of going green can be measured in terms of more than just a healthier climate, improved health and better quality of life. Building up a bicycle infrastructure, for example, does more than just reduce CO_2 emissions and air pollution. It also leads to more people taking their bikes to work, which in turn leads to improved individual health and lower medical costs. And it is estimated that more than a half the investment into improving the energy efficiency of public buildings will be repaid through lower energy costs by 2025. In short, going green pays off — no doubt about that.

Frank Jensen
Lord Mayor of Copenhagen, Denmark

The City of Sydney is committed to helping the community and businesses to respond to the challenges of climate change. More than 90% of Sydneysiders have told us they wanted action on climate change and through our careful planning and investment we are making significant progress.

The City has recently signed our fourth Environmental Upgrade Agreement (EUA) — an innovative funding agreement between a building owner, a finance provider and the council to unlock barriers to sustainability investments in buildings. Under an EUA, a finance provider lends funds to a building owner for specific upgrades and the loan is repaid through a local council charge on the land.

Financing an upgrade using an EUA delivers many benefits to building owners and tenants that are not generally achievable through traditional commercial finance. Upgrading using self-finance or traditional commercial finance usually results in the tenant receiving most of the benefits of utility savings, not the building owner. The building owner has no means of recovering these benefits outside lease negotiations. The EUA mechanism overcomes this by allowing building owners to share the costs of the environmental upgrade with their tenants through existing lease provisions or by specific agreement.

Other innovative financing mechanisms through which funding can be realised include climate bonds, which are like standard bonds but are issued in order to raise finance for climate change and environmental projects. Action on climate change can benefit the bottom line by reducing energy, waste and water use through efficiency programmes with modest initial investments. Programmes like CitySwitch and the City's better buildings partnership are greening our urban environment and making savings for businesses.

Better building partnership members have saved $25 million in electricity costs a year and reduced their emissions by 35% since 2006 — well ahead of the target to cut emissions 70% by 2030.

A retrofit programme of forty five of the city's buildings has cut the city's electricity use by about 6.6 million kWh a year — enough to supply about 1,000 households annually — and saved an estimated $1.1 million a year in power bills. In 2007, we became the first carbon-neutral local government in Australia and have since reduced our own greenhouse emissions by 21%. Emissions across our local government area have fallen by 12% amid strong economic growth.

Clover Moore
Lord Mayor of Sydney, Australia

What are the features of good governance in sustainable and resilient cities?

When it comes to sustainability and tackling climate change, you need to be ambitious. Too many national and municipal leaders have set the bar too low. Someone has to be the first in everything, and the world will not change unless leaders all over the world — presidents, ministers and mayors — have high ambitions.

Also, good governance means being able to build the foundation for fruitful partnerships across sectors and to make sure citizens, private businesses and politicians support the city to develop into a greener version of itself.

Frank Jensen
Lord Mayor of Copenhagen, Denmark

One thing that the most sustainable cities share is bold leadership. If we look at mayors of ICLEI member cities like George Ferguson in Bristol (the European Green Capital 2015), Mario Lacerda in Minas Gerais, Karin Wanngård in Stockholm and Gregor Robertson in Vancouver, we see that these figures are driving change in their cities through their commitment to sustainability. They are taking strategic decisions that support a long-term strategy to become more sustainable.

For example, both Stockholm and Vancouver have set ambitious targets. Stockholm is aiming to be fossil-fuel-free by 2050. To achieve this, the city has produced a detailed roadmap, with measures that include the gradual phasing out of all fossil-fuel-powered public and private heating, the introduction of smart energy grids, the generation of solar power and an urban mobility strategy to facilitate travel by bike and public transport and on foot.

Vancouver is aiming to become the greenest city in the world by 2020. To reach this goal, it is aiming to double the number of green jobs over 2010 levels by 2020, increase citywide and neighbourhood food assets by a minimum of 50% over 2010 levels and plant 150,000 additional trees in the city between 2010 and 2020. The city has also committed to obtaining 100% of its energy from renewable sources by 2050. The '100% Renewable Energy' movement is growing around the world, and it is the kind of ambitious yet tangible goal that citizens can understand and actively support.

Along with setting targets, sustainable cities also engage their citizens. A prime example of this is the carbon literacy programme in

Manchester. The project enables citizens to have one day's worth of climate change education, covering climate science, context and opportunities for action. Through this, the city equips its citizens with the tools and knowledge they need to act on climate change within their communities.

Another crucial element of good governance is vertical integration. This means that different levels of government — from national or federal to state or provincial to other subnational or local levels — regularly exchange, plan and coordinate activities that relate to planning, implementation and reporting. Sustainable cities are working with the other levels of government to ensure that their measurements of emissions and policies to reduce emissions are aligned, avoiding duplication or conflict.

Finally, good leaders recognise the importance of transparency. That is why over 600 cities are reporting their climate change actions to the carbon *n* Climate Registry. This platform allows cities to report the impact of their climate-related activities and to make themselves accountable to their citizens and to the global community.

Gino Van Begin
Secretary-General of ICLEI-Local Governments for Sustainability

How can cities be designed to be pleasant and to improve their inhabitants' well-being?

As I see it, sustainability and liveability go hand in hand. Incorporating sustainable solutions in urban planning is the way to improve the well-being of the inhabitants. In Copenhagen, for instance, we incorporate green solutions such as bike infrastructure, green roofs, harbour baths and wind power in our urban planning. As a result of this, we have fresh air and green urban areas, and we can swim in our harbour — something that was out of the question just 15 years ago. And 45% of Copenhageners ride their bike to work or school every day.

It is nearly impossible to create green solutions that do not improve citizens' health or well-being in some way. That being said, it is as crucial to involve the citizens themselves in designing a city and its green solutions as it is to include all aspects and exploit all opportunities that the urban space and its users represent. After all, citizens, not politicians, are the experts when it comes to using the urban spaces and green solutions in their everyday lives.

Frank Jensen
Lord Mayor of Copenhagen, Denmark

To design liveable cities and improve people's well-being, cities must focus on some important sustainable factors: environmental policies, the availability of infrastructure, education and culture, safety and, of course, social inclusion.

Over the years, Paris has launched some ambitious urban projects to make several parts of the city more sustainable, attractive, and inclusive (such as Paris Nord-Est in the north-east of Paris, Paris Rive Gauche project on the left bank of the Seine around the Austerlitz station and the urban Clichy-Batignolles neighbourhood). Implementing the Paris climate plan, we have created new pleasant public places and renovated green spaces, allowing biodiversity and nature to be introduced in the heart of Paris.

Sustainable transport is one of the roots of liveable cities, not only for inhabitants but also for commuters and visitors. In Paris, the Car-Free Day led to a 20–40% decrease of GHG emission rates in the city centre and attracted a huge amount of support from Parisians on social media: 10,000 tweets, 2,300 Instagram pictures and 20,000 followers on the Facebook event page.

Moreover, to make cities more liveable and inclusive, places dedicated to sport, leisure and cultural activities must be available throughout cities, especially in areas with special needs. This is the mission of most of our departments and the citizens of Paris have high expectations for further implementation of greener solutions in their city.

Anne Hidalgo
Mayor of Paris, France

Ultimately, we believe you need to design cities to be like Wellington — compact, set in nature, vibrant and well-supported with varied transport infrastructure. Because of its compact plan, the city offers easy opportunities to get around, including walking and cycling, and economic vibrancy through agglomeration. Because it is set in nature, the city promotes health and outdoor activity. Because of the vibrancy of its strong café cultures and nightlife, we have the best possible social environment for well-being. Because it offers various types of transport infrastructure, the city enables rich and varied lifestyles. Pleasantness is a band with many supporting players, and the missing instruments are evident when the band starts to play.

Celia Wade-Brown
Mayor of Wellington, New Zealand

Cities can be, and in many instances, already are, designed in many ways to make them attractive to their inhabitants' health, safety and well-being. To achieve this goal, a city must have an effective planning system in place that is responsive to socio-economic changes whether it be growth or decline. Such a planning system deals with the city's spatial arrangements (land use, circulation, provision of public space) and makes decisions in a timely, participatory and transparent fashion. First and foremost, the planning system must assure that the city's land uses meet its citizens' needs. It must have well serviced land for housing, an effective and energy efficient transportation system, room for economic production and public space for streets, sidewalks, parks, plazas and open spaces for pedestrian and vehicular circulation, recreation for all ages, informal and social convenings and sometimes to support livelihoods. Ideally, the spatial arrangements encourage mixing of these uses and encourage walking to various places, allowing people to live, work and play in close proximity. Finally, and most important, cities' planning systems need to be connected to their regions' systems in order to promote balanced territorial development within regions and to national urban policies that accomplish the same ends at a larger scale.

Take New York City as an example. It has very high use of public transit, relatively strong regulations on energy consumption for buildings, well-designed public space and zoning that encourages mixed uses. Its per capita GHG emissions are a fraction of what they are in the rest of the USA. Portland, Oregon, is another example that has contained sprawl with urban growth boundaries and now has a compact form which has contributed to making the city more walkable and reduced its consumption of GHG.

Prof. Eugenie Birch
Lawrence C. Nussdorf Professor of Urban Research
Co-director of the Penn Institute for Urban Research
University of Pennsylvania, USA

Cities must look beyond GDP as the primary indicator for development and choose instead to prioritise health and happiness for all. For example, ICLEI member city Thimphu, Bhutan has adopted a Gross National Happiness (GNH) index to measure its progress as a city. The four pillars of the GNH are sustainable socioeconomic development, the preservation of culture and tradition, respect for nature and good governance. Every policy is assessed on these four indicators.

One path towards healthy and happy communities is Eco-Mobility — travel using integrated, socially inclusive and environmentally friendly transport options, including walking, cycling and public transport. By enabling citizens and organisations to access goods, services and information in a sustainable manner, EcoMobility improves their quality of life, increases their travel choices and promotes social cohesion.

Many ICLEI member cities pursue EcoMobility strategies. Copenhagen, for instance, has become one the most bicycle-friendly cities in the world. As Morten Kabell has pointed out, Copenhagen's citizens choose to bike not necessarily because they are passionate about sustainability but because the local government has made biking the most convenient way of moving around the city.[1]

It is also important for cities to provide adequate green space for citizens. That is why, for example, Fortaleza, Brazil is constructing the

Rachel de Quieroz Park across 14 districts of the city. The population density in these districts is high and the environment is often degraded. The park, which extends for over 10 km and covers 137 ha, will change the landscape of the city, providing a landmark green space for leisure and relaxation.

Sometimes, it is the things we often take for granted that can have a significant impact on the well-being of citizens. Currently, only 15% of the city of Ebolowa in Cameroon benefits from public lighting. The lighting is concentrated in the main thoroughfares, leaving many public spaces, squares, intersections and roads unlit. To mitigate the consequential risk of traffic accidents and violence, and the negative impact on economic activities and tourism, Ebolowa aims to install 1,000 photovoltaic solar streetlights as part of its solar lighting project. Using solar energy mitigates emissions, while the project as a whole could change the picture of citywide energy access and equity.

Gino Van Begin
Secretary-General of ICLEI-Local Governments for Sustainability

Why are socially inclusive cities more likely to be economically productive?

The most successful global cities across the world today are characterised by high levels of social well-being, not just high national incomes. They are cities that put people first. Enlightened global city governments are meeting urban challenges proactively by using strategies to strengthen cities' social fabric and liveability. They are tackling critical issues like rising inequality, poverty and human right abuses so that everyone thrives. Improving collective well-being brings a wealth of benefits to our city. A strong inclusive society is increasingly recognised as integral to a strong economy and a healthy natural environment.

This is an issue not only for governments, but also for businesses and the wider community. We all benefit from being a part of, and playing our part in, building a socially sustainable City of Sydney. Societies which are socially inclusive value and enable the contributions of all citizens to economic growth and productivity.

Clover Moore
Lord Mayor of Sydney, Australia

Chapter 8

Sustainable Governance

Sustainable governance can be said to be environmentally friendly, socially inclusive, transparent and accountable.

This means that governments should seek to further their aims (to promote public welfare) in ways that preserve the environment. For example, investments in green technologies stimulate the economy and create jobs without damaging the environment.

Social inclusivity means that development and economic growth should benefit all sectors of society, and that governments should seek to promote the welfare of all its citizens rather than individual groups. In many ways, this means empowering previously disadvantaged groups, such as women, minorities, those living in poverty and indigenous groups. Apart from the obvious benefit of equality, the logic behind this is simple: the more people are empowered to act in ways that can benefit society, the more will do so.

But social inclusivity can often be achieved only if the government is transparent and accountable to its citizens. If citizens can communicate their discontent about fossil fuels or about inequality to their governments, the latter are more likely to implement changes. Thus, governments that empower their citizens, promote environmentally friendly ways of development and encourage the emergence of civil society organisations are more likely to improve their citizens' welfare.

What types of policies would be effective in facilitating the establishment of socially inclusive societies?

The wealth of the world's richest 62 people has risen by 45% in the 5 years since 2010 — that's an increase of more than half a trillion dollars ($542 billion) to $1.76 trillion. Meanwhile, the wealth of the bottom half of the world's population fell by just over a trillion dollars in the same period — a drop of 38%. Power and privilege is being used to skew the economic system to increase the gap between the richest and the rest.

This can, however, change with policies that work in the public interest of all the world's citizens — not just for the few. Inequality is not inevitable. When implemented fairly and progressively, tax, for example, is an investment with a high return and not a personal or business loss. When we pay taxes we expect something back from the state; it strengthens the relationship and accountability between us and our governments. It also pays for what private finance shouldn't: our needs for health care, education and social security. Growing economic inequality is bad for us all. If it is left unaddressed we could see more social unrest across the world, a brake on economic growth and all the work that has been done in the last quarter-century on poverty halted — or potentially reversed.

Winnie Byanyima
Executive Director of Oxfam International

It is my belief that the attainment of a truly inclusive society requires a holistic approach by all, including politicians, policy-makers, institutions, enterprises and civil society. A society with a wide divide in the educational sector is a society split along social and economic lines. We cannot say that we have a democratic society when there is no equitable access to the basic tools of democracy and to the fruits of the economy. Research confirms that the least successful students mostly come from the lower socioeconomic strata, whose status is perpetuated by a cycle of unemployment, poverty and further lack of skills. They live in a state of material deprivation, social exclusion and poor physical, emotional and mental health and well-being. Therefore, effective education policies that reach everyone are imperative.

Likewise, if we truly want societies to be inclusive, women have to participate in drafting policies and taking decisions. Only when there is a stronger presence of competent women in managerial posts will the decisions taken respect the interests, realities and, above all, the rights of a wide spectrum of people. Policies that support women in their daily lives need their greater involvement, resulting in a more inclusive society. Policies have to be put in place to strengthen women's participation in the economy, to support their enterprise and management and to develop vocational training to facilitate their participation in the labour force.

The studies carried out by my Foundation for the Well-being of Society show that precarious working conditions and poverty are among the biggest hurdles to lifelong learning and social mobility. Members of the community, local researchers and numerous documents, both local and international, remind us that poverty is still knocking at the door of our societies. Policies that tackle poverty at its roots and at a national, regional and international level should be at the heart of our concern.

I also believe in the power of civil society as valid agents of change, even in policy building. Civil society works with our communities, and their experiential and professional wisdom are indispensable to the well-being of society. This is why they need to be heeded and given the space and opportunity to contribute their ideas.

H.E. Marie Louise Coleiro Preca
President of Malta

How can we foster social trust and cohesion in our effort to transition towards more sustainable societies?

We can foster social trust and cohesion between the general public and the Government of Canada by conducting activities that are based on genuine openness, real transparency and meaningful engagement. We must listen to citizens when developing policy, and acknowledge mistakes when we make them. They expect us to be honest, open and sincere in our efforts to serve the public interest.

In terms of sustainable development, social trust will be particularly important as our country works to transition to a low-carbon and climate-resilient economy. Meaningful dialogue with provinces, territories, Canadians and Indigenous peoples will be particularly important as we work together on plans for a clean environment and a sustainable economy. As a government, we have committed to being open, honest and accountable to our citizens; these commitments will continue to be important as we work together towards the creation of a more sustainable society.

Catherine McKenna
Minister of Environment and Climate Change of Canada

Why is female empowerment and the implementation of gender equality essential in establishing a sustainable world?

Women constitute more than half the world's population. Their active role and contribution is vital for the successful development of sustainable societies. Gender equality is not only a human rights issue, but also a smart investment and a smart way to use all the resources and human capital available to us. It is smart economics. One plus one can always make more and better than one alone. Natural resources are being overused, human capital has not been.

The Millennium Development Goals proved to be a success in many ways, but now we are launching the implementation phase of a new and more universal and comprehensive set of goals, the SDGs. Gender equality and women's empowerment is high on that agenda. One main aspect is women's health, which will also be promoted by the high-level advisory group for every woman, every child and the global strategy for women's, children's and adolescents' health, which were recently launched by UN Secretary-General Ban Ki-moon.

Women's role as producers is very important as they produce most of the food. In Africa, women farmers produce some 80%, while in Asia, it is 60%. In developed countries, they manage the house-holds' daily purchases and their water and energy consumption. Women need to be involved, informed, educated and empowered to support more sustainable consumption and production.

We have two very encouraging recent examples. The SDGs were adopted by the UN in September 2015. Among these goals, gender equality stands alone, but it is also integrated in the other goals, such as those combatting climate change or changing consumption and production patterns. Another example is the recent Paris Agreement on Climate Change in December 2015. This agreement is a very powerful instrument for promoting sustainable development as it covers the most important economic, social and environmental dimensions. It has guiding provisions for all climate action, with gender equality and the empowerment of women among the most important. Women's role will be indispensable both in adaptation and mitigation. Women should have access to all decision-making on climate issues and resources, technology and knowledge to make their full contribution.

Tarja Halonen
Former President of Finland (2000–2012)

How can governments maximise their citizens' happiness? Why should that matter in the establishment of a more sustainable society?

Since coming to the Presidency, I have had several occasions to share in the joy of other people. This first-hand experience has made me realise that people's happiness and well-being must be the *raison d'être* of all we do. Together with my Foundation for the Well-being of Society and a number of international partners, we are in the process of establishing an Institute for Peace and Well-being. We will be researching, motivating and inspiring cultures of peace and well-being, exploring best practices and finding the most efficient and effective systems of knowledge sharing. Through the institute, we plan to engage with diverse communities from various parts of the world, learning about the ways these communities can achieve well-being as active citizens, effectively accessing and enjoying their rights.

I believe that if we make sure that citizens have every opportunity to participate and enjoy their rights, they can live happy, fulfilling lives, which in turn creates a more sustainable society. People who are fully engaged and happy are unlikely to be radicalised, do not seek out conflict or violence, even within their own homes, and do not search for alternate means of fulfilment. Instead, they seek peaceful existence with their fellow human persons; enjoy their own well-being and the well-being of others, and support those who are vulnerable, so they too may have the opportunity to live a decent life.

With this in mind, I truly believe that peace and well-being are two pillars that will determine our future, the future of our children and ultimately, the future of our planet.

H.E. Marie Louise Coleiro Preca
President of Malta

The lack of effective consideration of the needs of future generations is a great flaw of our political institutions. Many of the policies governments have enacted in the past and continue to enact in the present may adversely affect future generations and their ability to preserve our planet. Thus, some have argued that institutions should be established at the national and international level to ensure that the needs of unborn generations are voiced and considered when enacting new laws.

How can we take the interests of future generations into account when making policy decisions? How can they be represented in the policy-making process?

We are facing numerous challenges in the present that will impinge on the well-being of future generations. Growing inequality, extreme poverty and the threat of climate change should lead us to consider the nature of the world that we leave behind for generations yet to come. Sustainable development, if it is to be realised, must find a way of balancing the interests of future generations with the needs of the present. There is also a geographical dimension to intergenerational equity. The needs of future generations in the wealthy Global North must not be put before immediate needs of poor communities in the Global South.

My Foundation commissioned research to better understand how the concept of intergenerational equity might be operationalised within international processes, particularly within the post-2015 development agenda and the new climate agreement. The research assessed potential mechanisms to enhance intergenerational equity based on their effectiveness, political feasibility and moral legitimacy. What it found was that a range of actions are required at an international level to apply the principle of intergenerational equity in practice.

One strong recommendation emerging from the research was for a Commission on Future Generations to be established by the UN in the context of the implementation and review of the post-2015 development agenda. A commission is preferable to a commissioner, as a broader, regionally representative membership may enhance the likelihood that present-day contexts for poorer countries are taken into account in assessing long-term risk. The idea was first proposed by Edith Brown Weiss in 1989 though, to date, it has not been realised.

Mary Robinson
President of the Mary Robinson Foundation for Climate Justice
Former President of Ireland (1990–1997)
Former UN High Commissioner for Human Rights (1997–2002)

How can we combat the institutional short-termism that has impeded our ability to adequately respond to the environmental crisis thus far?

Societies, like individuals, can get trapped in patterns of behaviour that provide short-term rewards but are detrimental and unsustainable in the long run. These patterns of behaviour can be thought of as societal addictions or social traps. For example, our current societal failure to adequately deal with climate change is due to our addiction to fossil fuels and a growth-at-all-costs economic model. We can learn from therapies that have been shown to be successful at overcoming addictions at the level of the individual. In particular, Motivational Interviewing (MI) is one of the most effective therapies for treating substance addictions. It is based on engaging addicts in a positive discussion of their goals, motives and futures. The effectiveness of MI in the treatment of individuals with addictions suggests an analogy of using extended Scenario Planning (SP) in the treatment of societal addictions. SP can be used to involve public opinion surveys and forums engaging the entire community in a discussion about goals and possible futures. Effective therapy for societal addictions may be possible to overcome humanity's current addiction to growth at all costs and to help create a sustainable and desirable future.

Prof. Robert Costanza
Professor and Chair in Public Policy
Australian National University, Australia

How will current forms of governance need to adapt to better deal with the current environmental crisis and with the effects of climate change?

Today, the concept of the nation-state as a political entity, free to take decisions and act independently of other nation-states, faces increasing challenges. We are finally realising that interdependence amongst nations is much stronger than independence and offers opportunities to advance faster in the pursuit of our sustainable development goals. This is the case when addressing climate change and other global commons. By now it should also be obvious that only by nations working together can we achieve the progress we need to make in the time we have left to dramatically reduce CO_2 emissions.

José María Figueres
President and Chairman of the Carbon War Room
Former President of Costa Rica (1994–1998)

Good governance and the rule of law are important elements of the economic, political, social and institutional aspects of sustainable development. Governance is also increasingly seen as a top priority development issue by the people. Good governance is important in itself, but it should also be seen in connection with human rights, democracy and the rule of law. The effective and sustainable management of available resources is also part of good governance. When you have rich capital in natural and human resources, you should not over-exceed their renewable capacities to achieve short-sighted growth, but instead you should grow your capital so that it will be a renewable asset.

Governance needs to be transparent and inclusive. Governments need data and foresight to prepare longer term strategies. Though we need resources and investment to manage climate change, the payback will also be considerable. The more committed and holistic our approach is with regard to climate change or sustainable development more broadly, the more we will gain. Policies and actions will have to be geared and look towards the future, not just short electoral cycles.

Tarja Halonen
Former President of Finland (2000–2012)

What are the social repercussions of good governance? How can we promote good governance?

There is no single definition of good governance, and the term is used with flexibility. In general, however, good governance describes the quality of the way in which public institutions conduct public affairs and manage public resources. There is broad agreement on some of the main elements of the concept, which include the rule of law, participation, equity, transparency, effectiveness and accountability.

Numerous international agreements have recognised that good governance is fundamental to realising human rights and achieving sustainable development — most recently the 2030 Agenda for Sustainable Development. Good governance underpins many aspects of the agenda, from the seventeen SDGs themselves to the framework to support implementation, called the Addis Ababa action agenda, and the entire process for reviewing progress over the next 15 years.

The main elements of good governance are most prominently captured in goal sixteen, to 'promote peaceful and inclusive societies for sustainable development, provide access to justice for all and build effective, accountable and inclusive institutions at all levels'.[li] They are also found at the heart of many other goals such as on advancing gender equality, ensuring access to water and sanitation and promoting sustainable consumption and production.

For the goals to be reached, good governance will be required at all levels. It is central to improving the quality of policy-making, including by protecting civil society and promoting citizen participation to bring about more democratic governance. It is critical to mobilising the public and private finance needed from both domestic and international sources to advance social development or build sustainable infrastructure and clean energy. And it is essential to bringing about the main transformations promised: an end to poverty; a shift to low-carbon climate-resilient economies, major reductions in inequalities and more peaceful societies.

H.E. Mogens Lykketoft
President of the UN General Assembly (2015–2016)

To me, good governance is exercising political power in such a way that the people you represent are empowered and their lives uplifted. In this instance, the social repercussions should be self-evident. When people's rights are realised, they will live healthier and more fulfilled lives underpinned by freedom, justice and dignity.

A particularly important trait of good governance, as I see it, is that the fulfilment of the rights of people in one country does not undermine the rights of people in another part of the world. Climate change is one example of how this can happen. The industrial revolution and subsequent fossil-fuel-powered economic growth in industrialised countries has allowed a small part of the world's population to realise their right to development. Yet, as a result of these fossil fuel emissions, today the changing climate system is undermining the rights of those people made vulnerable by poverty, social standing and underdevelopment. This is an injustice. For many years, leaders in the industrialised countries did not know their development was unsustainable, but now everybody does. Good governance would avert dangerous climate change by taking the action necessary to stabilise warming as far below 2°C as possible. Now is the time for world leaders to demonstrate that they are capable of such governance.

Mary Robinson
President of the Mary Robinson Foundation for Climate Justice
Former President of Ireland (1990–1997)
Former UN High Commissioner for Human Rights (1997–2002)

How can governance structures take account of the environment's value and ensure its protection in practice?

Governments can encourage the greater use of public transport instead of cars, and other greener ways of travel. They play a role in integrating all the SDGs and in converging them towards the unified objective of preserving human dignity and human beings, to protect them from floods, rising sea levels and other threats. And international institutions also play a role in setting the goals related to climate change and sustainable development and in preserving human dignity.

Hakima El Haite
Minister for the Environment of Morocco

Environmental action can be taken at all levels, but we look to governments to enshrine the environmental agenda in policy. Environmental governance at the domestic level is a main element in ensuring our natural wealth is conserved and utilised sustainably. There are numerous initiatives that study how to capture the value of ecosystem services, which demonstrate to governments the real economic benefits of a healthy environment. The economics of ecosystems and biodiversity project, for example, was born at the G8 in

2007 with the express purpose of informing economic and social policy on the hidden values of ecosystems. And UNEP's ProEcoServ project found almost US$1 billion worth of value in these services in only four countries. Incorporating this value into policy decisions allows for a more comprehensive and ultimately better governance system for the environment.

Global governance of the environment will continue to rely on multilateral foundations to ensure that sustainability is at the forefront of policy worldwide. These include agreements, such as those on biodiversity, chemicals and oceans that affect shared resources.

The UN Environment Assembly (UNEA), the second meeting of which was held in 2016, is an important platform for promoting the environmental agenda and managing these agreements. UNEA boasts universal membership, which means that governments can take decisions and pass resolutions here that mandate the action needed for implementation of the sustainable development agenda. This Parliament for the Environment will continue to be a critical arena to share, debate and encourage effective environmental governance initiatives on a global scale.

Achim Steiner
Director of the Oxford Martin School, University of Oxford, UK
Former Executive Director of the UN Environment Programme
(2006–2016)

Some ideologies say that nature cannot be valued. But, in practice, if this is so, we can't incorporate ecosystem services in our economic accounting. Whether it be bees pollinating or water being used for industrial or human consumption, nature has a value. Our recent tsunamis have shown, for example, that coastal wetlands were key in mitigating the impact of the tsunami in the Coquimbo Region. So, we have a strong agenda in estimating the benefits of ecosystem services and also in environmental accounting. And we've introduced green taxes that incorporate the price of pollution in our transport and energy sectors. Finally, we're creating a biodiversity and protected area service that ensures central and coordinated actions are undertaken to protect our biodiversity. Environmental protection needs to be introduced in our economy through these taxes, and through the institutional framework that fosters it.

Michelle Bachelet
President of Chile

Economic growth and employment must go hand in hand with activities to protect the environment and our climate. For politics, this means promoting eco-innovations, fostering the use of renewable energy and energy efficiency measures and implementing sustainability in buildings, mobility, nutrition, production, tourism and agriculture. The Austrian Environment Ministry implements important and internationally recognised projects by means of its climate protection initiative *klimaaktiv*, domestic environmental support, energy turnaround and the action plan for renewable raw materials.

Andrä Rupprechter
Austrian Federal Minister of Agriculture, Forests, Environment,
and Water Management

Increasingly, governance of such habitats must include the local people whose livelihoods depend on that particular biodiversity. They should be entrusted with safeguarding these treasures just as they have been their custodians. Documenting traditional practices is also key, as these practices have ensured survival since time immemorial. Documentation ensures 'prior art' (the use of traditional management systems) in the course of future exploration of the various forms of biodiversity.

H.E. Ameenah Gurib-Fakim
President of Mauritius

There is the inherent need to preserve the world's natural heritage for our future generations. The sooner leaders and policy-makers realise this fact, the sooner we can start to care for our planet and halt its destruction. After the signing of the historic outcome of the 2015 UN Climate Change Conference in Paris by 195 nations, we hope that action will be taken to combat climate change and that nations will invest in a low-carbon, resilient and sustainable future. In order to move from words to action, appropriate financial commitments have to be made, particularly to provide adequate support to developing countries and those most vulnerable to consequences of climate change. There also needs to be international cooperation by cities and regions, businesses and civil society, if we are to affect any notable change.

However, we need to achieve similar agreements in other areas of the environment, if we are to ensure a sustainable world, including clean water and sanitation, and sustainable cities and communities. We need to create institutional mechanisms for cooperation between public administration, private and community sectors.

H.E. Marie Louise Coleiro Preca
President of Malta

I think that, to a certain extent, we have been building these types of institutions and tools over the last 50 years. From a European perspective, we've seen many benefits and success stories from over 40 years of European environmental policy-making, but we now need to go one step further by truly taking account of the environment's value and incorporating the real costs of harming it into financial markets.

At the EEA, we cooperate with Eurostat and other European partners to gain a better understanding of the concepts of 'natural capital' and 'ecosystem services'. This is not necessarily to give them market value immediately because that would suggest that if somebody is willing to pay the price, they can further use, consume and degrade the environment as they like, and that's not the point. The point is to have a more solid understanding of natural capital across Europe. For the moment, we are lacking that information, despite a variety of studies and experiments in the field. Furthermore, we don't have an accounting system for it, which makes it very difficult for traditional policy-makers to assess options or to understand the environmental consequences of their legislation.

So, in terms of government institutions, we have to change to a system where economic calculations at the state level incorporate human, natural and financial capital if we want to move towards more fundamental sustainability.

Dr. Hans Bruyninckx
Executive Director of the European Environment Agency

How can governments empower citizens to act on issues relating to climate change and sustainable development?

Citizens have a central role to play in actions on climate change and in making sustainable development a reality. Through information dissemination, policies and incentives, governments can empower citizens to act on climate change and sustainability issues in their personal lives by making them aware of ways to shrink our individual ecological footprints and removing disincentives to adopting these practices. This can include the adoption by individual Canadians of alternative forms of transportation and of clean technologies and renewable clean energy sources to reduce emissions of greenhouse gases and other pollutants as well as recycling and reusing to reduce resource consumption.

Furthermore, governments can incent and provide opportunities for individuals to accelerate shifts toward sustainable development — such as enabling innovative research, social or environmental activism, high impact entrepreneurship and business development, or leveraging cross-sector partnerships. Ensuring the work lives of citizens are able to fully contribute to sustainable development is an important role of government.

Also, effective public participation is a basic principle of responsible government in a parliamentary democracy which allows government to benefit from the experience and expertise of society at large, leading to more informed decisions. Towards this end, governments can empower citizens by widely promoting these opportunities to make Canadians aware of how they can participate in and inform government decision-making processes.

H.E. Justin Trudeau
Prime Minister of Canada

Governments have the primary responsibility of achieving sustainable development, including by addressing climate change. They do this by establishing the appropriate laws, norms, policies and programmes as well as incentives to encourage others to invest in green and low-carbon economies.

In today's interconnected world, however, actors such as large corporations, the financial industry, civil society and others exert considerable influence over the lives of ordinary people. This broad range of stakeholders must also take substantial action to reach our common goal of sustainable development and they must be considered in government and global policy responses to climate change and sustainable development challenges. In particular, given their ability to hold governments to account and to make policy more attuned to the needs of the vulnerable, it is of utmost importance that citizens and local communities become active agents for change at all levels.

There is a need, therefore, to increase citizens' capacity to engage in genuine participation and to create new spaces to build their awareness of sustainable development, including on how to address climate change. Governments can empower their citizens to take action through

- Disseminating information on all aspects of climate change and sustainable development, and the encouragement of public debates on relevant issues.
- Designing campaigns that sensitise children with relevant educational programmes at all levels in order to raise awareness and consciousness of climatic change risks.
- Making rules, regulations and a broad enabling environment that protects the freedom of assembly, expression and association that are critical to facilitating a vibrant civil society.
- Giving space and support for civil society participation in the decision-making processes on issues related to sustainability, both at the national (by establishing norms and legislation) and the international levels (by negotiating agreements and other outcomes).
- Providing targeted activities to empower people and communities to support more sustainable consumption patterns including incentives for recycling and the efficient use of energy.

- Supporting local governments and authorities close to the daily lives of citizens and those who can play an important role in educating the public on their sustainable responsibilities.
- Taking steps to strengthen the preparedness and resilience capabilities of the most vulnerable communities and people so as to minimise the effect of climate change on them.

H.E. Mogens Lykketoft
President of the UN General Assembly (2015–2016)

Like many issues involving broad social change, American citizens appear to be ahead of their elected officials in recognising the need for climate action. Leaders implementing the hard policies needed to shift to the clean energy economy should engage diverse perspectives in the public debate. People come to the climate issue for different reasons, and leaders can empower citizens by providing platforms for diverse spokespersons to build the case for change. Most importantly, they can direct the energy of diverse voices, once inspired, into the political process, giving these voices access to the decision-making machinery of modern politics.

Jay Inslee
Governor of Washington, USA

Civil society and the private sector are important partners for governments in implementing sustainable development. They will have to encourage the whole population in this work not only as beneficiaries but also as active agents. Consumers need to be made aware of and informed (e.g., by education and product labelling). Sustainable behaviour should be supported by regulations and pricing. Sustainable products and production should be guided by standards and norms (like the sulphur content of gasoline, energy certificates for buildings and emission standards). Sustainable choices can be encouraged by pricing. This can be supported by moving from the taxation of labour to the taxation of overused natural resources and the production of pollution. Harmful subsidies should be removed gradually.

Tarja Halonen
Former President of Finland (2000–2012)

Climate change is just not another challenge. It poses existential threats to the lives and livelihoods of people in Bangladesh and others around the world. We are adjusting our policies and practices in order to minimise the adverse impacts of climate change and to see how we can opt for a low-carbon growth path or for greener development in economic activities. Adaptation is the priority of Bangladesh. With our limited resources, we have been trying to our best to adapt to the negative impacts of climate change.

Whether we talk about climate change or about wider sustainable development, one starting point is a nationwide robust information, education and communication network that is contextualised and community-focused. At the same time, we will have to ensure that our policies and actions are people-centred and inclusive and that they address all forms of inequalities. This will apply to economic policies and must be complemented by our actions in the social domain. In respect of our wider national aspirations and our efforts to build pluralistic and inclusive societies, we also try to focus on vulnerable populations (e.g., people in coastal regions, small-scale and marginal farmers and women) to ensure they have access to productive resources and support measures and services. If we use this approach, as we have seen in other parts of the world, then the people at the bottom will automatically take care of themselves. That is how we can truly accomplish the empowerment of people.

Our Bangladesh Climate Change Strategy & Action Plan has been made in consultation with vulnerable people, civil society and others. Bangladesh is the very first of all developing countries to have made such a plan. To ensure sustainable development, the Bangladesh government has integrated environmental protection and climate change issues in all development planning and policy formulation. We have launched mega-plan programmes to train our youth to meet our present and future needs, in which sustainable development and climate change have been important components.

H.E. Sheikh Hasina
Prime Minister of Bangladesh

What is the role of NGOs in informing the public about the effects of their actions and in mobilising them to enact change?

By the time a consumer is asked to make a choice about sustainability, it's too late. Our power as consumers is vastly overstated, if not an outright illusion. Voters are asked to choose between candidates with economic platforms built on unsustainable growth. We, as consumers or voters, are almost invariably asked to select between fundamentally unsustainable options. Civil society has an urgent role to play in organising consumers and pressuring business and government to shift this paradigm: making it easy — inevitable — for people to participate in a sustainable economy. Offer us only sustainable options. Anything less results in pointless tinkering around the edges. While there is no question that consumer actions can be an important signal, the onus for change is on the corporations and governments to enable sustainable consumer choices.

A tiny minority of hardheaded individuals — usually with access to land — can create sustainable livelihoods for themselves, but most people would have to make their own products, fuel, food and so on in order to live their values. But sustainable options should be available to the consumer by default. Public pressure is essential to enabling this paradigm shift, despite ample evidence that sustainable companies almost always perform better. At the same time, civil society must set out a vision for a more equal economic system that is not predicated on infinite unsustainable growth. We are living so far beyond the planet's ability to sustain us that we cannot afford to postpone these very fundamental discussions any further. Either that or we need to invent another planet or two.

Stephanie Brancaforte
Global Campaign Leader on Climate & Energy at Greenpeace

How can governments encourage the development of sustainable or green technologies?

All actors in society have important roles to play in increasing investments in sustainable technologies. Governments, for their part, can ensure the right incentives are in place to encourage business to increase their investments, seek opportunities to innovate, and deliver sustainable products to market. On the demand side, carbon pricing and the phase out of inefficient fossil fuel subsidies can level the playing field and allow a transition to a sustainable economy. On the supply side, we can ensure the right tax incentives are in place to reward innovative investments and companies that take the necessary risks to develop new technologies.

Governments, by virtue of their economic size, can also help create demand and improve the market case for clean technology firms by increasing their procurement of clean technologies, for example, in its buildings and vehicle fleet. Also, governments can make direct investments in the development and deployment of clean technology through programs such as Sustainable Development Technologies Canada, and these actions can work in partnership with the private sector to enhance the availability of venture capital for clean technologies. A good balance between supporting the development of new technologies and creating the right market conditions is key to ensuring success for sustainable technologies.

Working with international partners is also important. For example, Canada has announced our participation in Mission Innovation, which brings together 20 countries and some of the world's best-known entrepreneurs — including Bill Gates, Richard Branson and Jeff Bezos — to push, promote clean technology like never before. The goal is to double government investment in clean energy research and development and to spur private-sector investments in clean technology over the next 5 years. This is an opportunity to reinvigorate energy innovation and accelerate transformative clean energy technology solutions.

H.E. Justin Trudeau
Prime Minister of Canada

The two core roles of governments are in supporting the fundamental research and development of new, cleaner technologies and ensuring that those producing pollution pay for the damages it causes. Governments have found it difficult to sensibly design policies to support new clean technologies, but there is now a great deal of evidence about how to do this better and our team at Oxford is working with governments to improve upon past efforts.

Prof. Cameron Hepburn
Professor of Environmental Economics
University of Oxford, UK

The single most important policy is to get prices right, as this establishes the price signals needed to create a demand for green technologies. For example, charges on CO_2 emissions will provide across-the-board incentives to develop lower cost technologies for saving energy and using low CO_2 emission fuels.

But getting prices right may not be enough because of additional market barriers. For example, innovators may be unable to capture the spillover benefits of new technologies to other firms that might copy the new technology or use knowledge about it to further their own research programmes. Large advanced countries and the EU support basic research at universities and laboratories, and it makes sense for these efforts to focus on technologies with a long-term potential, such as carbon capture and storage, energy storage, smart grids, energy efficiency and infrastructure for electric vehicles. Incentives may also be needed to promote applied R&D in firms, for example, by giving prizes for major technological breakthroughs and adequate safeguards for intellectual property. And there might be a case for further incentives to promote the deployment of new green technologies.

Nevertheless, it is important to bear in mind that incentives need to be carefully designed to avoid undesired and unintended side-effects and contain financial costs (e.g., through scaling deployment subsidies appropriately and phasing them out as technologies mature).

Vitor Gaspar
Director of the Fiscal Affairs Department at the International
Monetary Fund
Former Finance Minister of Portugal (2011–2013)

Chapter 9

Towards a Sustainable Economy

While many people view mitigating climate change as a moral imperative or as a humanitarian necessity, others see it as an economic problem. Economists argue that because polluting is free, from the viewpoint of the polluter, the cost is external to them. For example, if polluters release CO_2 into the atmosphere or waste into a river, it costs them nothing to do so and many of the subsequent consequences of their actions will be external to them. Thus, if polluting the environment costs you nothing, there is nothing incentivising you to stop.

Economists argue that internalising the cost, or making polluters pay for the environmental damage they cause, is essential to reducing CO_2 emissions and to promoting innovative ways to reduce waste. This can be done with policies such as taxing CO_2 emissions and pricing environmental services (i.e., the economic benefits the environment provides by simply functioning). These make polluting more costly and thus, polluters are much less likely to pollute as freely. And though such measures may be viewed as new and added costs, they simply make polluters pay for the damage they were already causing.

How can we ensure that fossil-fuel-dependent private corporations are not able to use their influence to delay the transition to a sustainable economy?

Global warming presents a real challenge for fossil fuel companies. Like tobacco companies, who discovered their products were killing people, fossil fuel companies discover their products could destroy our planet. Good companies will understand this; they realise that over time, their unsustainable activities will be run down; they will stop investment in finding unneeded reserves and they may even invest in new renewable sources of energy. Incidentally, if they plan now, these companies have time to transition.

But the worst companies encourage us to turn a blind eye and they even use their lobbying to undermine the global agreements we need to get this problem under control. These companies are not only acting against the public interest, they are acting against their shareholders' interests. At the Paris climate conference, for example, a petition signed by $25 trillion worth of investors called for a climate agreement, and they did so because that is the only way that the long-term future of our savings can be secured (our savings will not be safe if the environment is not sustainable). So companies that wilfully ignore these messages are in breach of their duty to their owners as well as abusing society more generally.

Good investment managers are now pushing to prevent such destructive corporate lobbying. We, as savers, should be encouraging them to do so on our behalf. After all, they are managing our money and should be doing so in a responsible fashion. We need to make our voice heard as investors, just as we do as citizens and consumers.

David Pitt-Watson
Chair of the UN Environment Programme Finance Initiative
Executive Fellow of Finance, London Business School, UK

How can we render private corporations accountable for the the damage they might cause to the environment?

As in any system, they need to be called to account. In part, that depends on law makers. But we also have a role as investors, just as we do as citizens, workers and consumers. Together, investors have made a big impact. For example, the pressure exerted by investors on several European oil companies has meant that those companies are now supportive of carbon tax and have come to the negotiating table. CalPERS in the USA has demanded that capital expenditure on carbon be reviewed by all the companies in which it invests.[lii] AP4 in Sweden has simply decarbonised its investments.[liii] There are many other examples.

We should never forget that, in our market system, it is the shareholders to whom the boards of companies are accountable. Investors therefore can have a huge impact. So, any pension holder needs to be sure that their fund manager has taken this into account. After all, in an unsustainable world, it is difficult to see how pensions will be paid.

David Pitt-Watson
Chair of the UN Environment Programme Finance Initiative
Executive Fellow of Finance, London Business School, UK

The veneer of immunity to public pressure and judicial action for environmental devastation of private corporations is starting to flake off. For instance, a new movement of climate litigators is taking action to hold the historically biggest carbon polluters liable for the climate chaos they have wrought and to force these companies to change their deadly business model. We can't be afraid to prosecute large, powerful companies when they break laws. Political leaders need to reach out to the public if they need support — public pressure is the only way to stand up to companies with deep pockets. Once again, it is fundamentally important that trade agreements that undermine the rule of law and the ability of national prosecutors to stand for the public interest be stopped in their tracks.

Stephanie Brancaforte
Global Campaign Leader on Climate & Energy at Greenpeace

How can we price environmental services and incorporate them into the measure of the GDP so that their degradation is no longer considered an externality?

There are many kinds of environmental services. The problems of pricing them vary according to the service in question. For climate change, the problem is relatively simple analytically. A ton of CO_2 put into the atmosphere affects the whole world with little lag in time; hence, we can estimate a social cost of CO_2 that is applicable everywhere in the world (this does not mean that the derivation of this figure is not difficult in practice. However, reasonable estimates exist, and they do not differ by more than a factor of two or three). On the other hand, the effect of uniformed land on the productivity of adjacent farms (which has been shown to be generally positive) varies enormously from place to place, so we would in principle have to have separate estimates for each point.

Prof. Kenneth Arrow
Joan Kenney Professor of Economics and Emeritus
Professor of Operations Research
Stanford University, USA
Winner of the 1972 Nobel Memorial Prize in Economics

We need to change our societal goals from the growth of GDP to improvement of well-being, more broadly defined. In addition, since 1978, the global economy has not been growing at all, according to the genuine progress indicator. We have seen several decades of 'uneconomic growth' where GDP is growing, but real economic welfare, after the costs of GDP growth are subtracted, has been stagnant. To achieve genuine progress and the real improvement of well-being, we need a new development paradigm that adequately accounts for the non-marketed costs and benefits from natural and social capital. It is well overdue to leave GDP behind as a proxy for economic well-being and consider what we really want to grow and improve. We need to take much more seriously the important distinction between growth in GDP and real sustainable development.

Prof. Robert Costanza
Professor and Chair in Public Policy at the Australian National
University, Australia

What types of incentives do governments need to reverse in order to transition to a sustainable economy? How can that be done?

It is easy to state the general principle and very difficult to implement it. In a market-driven economy, incentives are driven by prices. To the extent that there are externalities, the actual prices create the wrong incentives. These can be corrected by appropriate taxes and subsidies. No doubt, more direct controls, such as fuel efficiency standards, will also be needed in practice.

One may also be concerned about exhaustible resources, even if there are no externalities. As for fossil fuels, my view is that any appropriate climate change policy will require a shift to solar and other renewable resources, so that current fossil fuel reserves will not be used up. Metals may be a problem, but unlike fuels, they can be recycled. Finally, if food scarcity becomes an issue, we can expect the price system to lead to a shift from eating meat to eating vegetables and grain if need be. Personally, I am optimistic that the shift to birth rates below reproduction levels, as already manifest in Europe, China and the USA, will prevent a degradation in food consumption.

Prof. Kenneth Arrow
Joan Kenney Professor of Economics and Emeritus
Professor of Operations Research
Stanford University, USA
Winner of the 1972 Nobel Memorial Prize in Economics

It is essential for businesses to be aware of their impact on the natural world. Those that fail to recognise this and adapt their practices accordingly will be left behind. Through initiatives such as the Natural Capital Coalition, from the World Business Council on Sustainable Development (WBCSD), businesses are starting to understand the impact they have and the extent to which they are dependent on the natural environment. We have no Planet B to fall back on, so being aware of our finite natural resources and the functionality of our ecosystems is vital if we are to move towards a truly sustainable economy.

Pricing externalities and putting a value on natural capital helps, but ultimately, there is no future for the old way of take — make — dispose. Embracing a new, more inclusive model of growth is fundamental to our very existence. This increasingly means moving to a circular economy and a system that brings people in and doesn't shut them out. It means innovative models where we can grow without continuing to deplete the world's resources, where smart design means that raw materials are reusable time and again without quality or value suffering.

At the heart of this must be businesses driven by purpose, existing to serve the best interests of society. Without this clarity of purpose, leaders will not be able to make decisions for long-term gain in the best interests of the many not the few. Continuing to pursue short-term goals at the expense of future sustainability will have a profound and indelible cost, a cost that, ultimately, we simply cannot afford to pay.

Paul Polman
CEO of Unilever

How can governments encourage investments in sustainable sectors?

Governments can play a central role by providing the right incentives. The key is to get prices right. This balances environmental and economic concerns, ensuring that a country's resources are efficiently allocated across different sectors and that adequate account is taken of intergenerational effects. Take global warming, for example. Here, the central problem is that no single firm or household has a significant effect on future global climate, yet collectively they do. So, for example, energy prices should reflect future climate effects. In this way, environmental effects factor into individual level decisions. This pricing aligns private and social costs, thereby encouraging firms and households to economise on energy use and shift to cleaner fuels. To take another example, many of the world's fisheries are overexploited not only because of government support for the industry, but also because fishermen do not take into account their effect on depleting fish stocks for future generations. Again, getting the prices right is crucial — making sure that the price of fish fully reflects the costs of catching it and the costs of depleting the resource for future generations.

At the IMF, we have been focusing on providing practical tools to help governments put principle into practice. For example, we have developed a database for over 150 countries of the environmental costs of different fossil fuel products (global warming, public health costs from air pollution, broader costs like congestion and accidents associated with the use of road fuels in vehicles) and the set of energy taxes needed to properly reflect these environmental costs. At a global level, we estimate that getting energy prices right — moving from existing energy prices to prices that fully recover supply and environmental costs — would reduce CO_2 emissions by almost a quarter and fuel-related air pollution deaths by almost 60%. At the same time, these reforms would raise substantial new revenues estimated at 3.6% of global GDP, which can be used to lower other burdensome taxes or reduce debt.

Vitor Gaspar
Director of the Fiscal Affairs Department at the International
Monetary Fund
Former Finance Minister of Portugal (2011–2013)

Governments and world leaders have a vital role in setting the overall framework that will drive transition to a sustainable economy. The Paris agreement confirmed the long-term goal of limiting global warming to 2°C, or better still 1.5°C. Policy needs to support this transition. As the Friends of Fossil Fuel Subsidy Reform communiqué, released in Paris, sets out, the elimination of fossil fuel subsidies would make a significant contribution to this shared objective.[liv] By keeping prices artificially low, fossil fuel subsidies encourage wasteful consumption, disadvantage renewable energy and depress investment in energy efficiency.

Equally, we need consistent carbon pricing, so the true cost of pollution is paid. As the work of the New Climate Economy has indicated, carbon pricing works and does not harm the world economy. Programmes such as the WBCSD's Low-Carbon Technology Partnership Initiatives and advocacy efforts from hundreds of CEOs have changed the landscape of corporate climate action forever. We now know how to close between 65 and 96% of the emissions gap[lv] in the period to 2030.[lvi] The Paris agreement confirms that we must do this. Businesses can now press forward with their ambitious plans knowing that the governments of the world have set a clear direction and will implement the policy frameworks to support them.

Of course, Paris was just the beginning. It now falls to all of us, whether in business, government, finance or civil society, to work together to take the promises on paper and turn them into action on the ground. We have seen the impact the Global Commission on Climate and the Economy[lvii] has had in reframing the narrative on climate action and economic growth. Business will need to give governments confidence that economies can grow inclusively and sustainably and that policies that reward sustainable behaviour are better for the bottom line. The business case for sustainability is now beyond dispute.

Paul Polman
CEO of Unilever

A stable policy environment that sends the right long-term signals to the private sector, aligned with the 1.5°C climate ambition and the SDGs, will be critical in making the transition to a low-carbon and sustainable world. By putting the right policy frameworks in place, governments can help business go further and faster.

The adoption of the SDGs and the Paris agreement on climate were critical preliminary steps. Going forward, a review process will be needed to strengthen commitments over time and hold both national governments and companies accountable for achieving the goals that were defined. Robust and stable carbon pricing coupled with the elimination of fossil fuel subsidies are also clear prerequisites for a fast-paced transition to a low-carbon economy. There is no single political solution. The choice of political instruments and technologies will need to be adapted to local, national and regional contexts. We need ongoing collaboration and dialogue to remove policy barriers and reach the necessary scale and impact.

Peter Bakker
President of the World Business Council
for Sustainable Development

Governments can encourage investment in sustainable sectors through regulation, market-based instruments and nudging (e.g., eco-labelling) as well as through well-targeted state aid. The European Commission for Competition modernised its state aid rules in 2014 to facilitate aid for sustainable investment. The rules that allow EU countries to give aid without prior Commission approval (general block exemption regulations) were simplified and their scope significantly widened to cover renewable energies, district heating and energy efficiency, for example. This will facilitate and speed up implementation of such measures. Potentially more distortive aid will be assessed under the guidelines for environmental protection and energy. These guidelines support EU countries in reaching their 2020 climate targets, while addressing market distortions that might result by promoting a gradual move to market-based support for renewable energy, for example. In specific circumstances, they allow for relief for energy-intensive companies from charges levied for renewables support. They include new provisions on aid to energy infrastructure and generation capacity. Sustainable sectors can also be supported with other types of aid like research, development, innovation and risk financing aid.

Margrethe Vestager
Commissioner for Competition, European Union

A major aspect of British Columbia's Liquefied Natural Gas (LNG) strategy is to foster innovative approaches to managing natural gas sector emissions. In 2014, new legislation ensured that LNG facilities will have an emissions cap, making them the cleanest in the world. Central to this is a GHG-emission intensity benchmark for LNG facilities. The benchmark can be met through flexible options, such as purchasing offsets or paying a set price per tonne of GHG emissions that would be dedicated to a technology fund. Both these approaches serve as incentives to invest in emission reduction projects in the natural gas and other sectors in British Columbia. Money from the new technology fund will go towards the development of clean technologies with a significant potential to reduce British Columbia's emissions in the long term. This will drive investment in British Columbia-based offset projects, including forest management, natural gas vehicles, community energy systems, industrial energy efficiency and waste management.

Mary Polak
Minister of the Environment of British Columbia, Canada

In what ways can the private sector drive the transition towards a sustainable world?

Business has historically led the scaling up of technological progress. By putting its innovative potential and financial resources at the service of society and the environment, business can improve lives and help protect our climate and ecosystems. Business is a critical implementation partner for governments in addressing the societal and environmental challenges we face.

In September 2015, world leaders adopted the SDGs — an all-encompassing agenda to eradicate poverty, promote peace and equity, boost inclusive growth and protect our environment. Achieving the SDGs require leadership and collaborative action by all stakeholders: businesses, governments and civil society alike. To match the scale of our socioeconomic and environmental challenges, sustainability must become an integral part of every company's decision-making and disclosures. A performance picture that incorporates the environmental and social impacts of a company alongside its financial results will guide investors in allocating assets and incentivise more companies to become sustainable. This will ultimately help us achieve the SDGs faster by accelerating the shift to a clean thriving economy and safeguarding the future of our planet.

As for businesses, embracing the SDGs as a growth opportunity will open new markets and present new investment opportunities that will unlock the unrealised market potential that significantly outweighs initial investment costs. Forward-looking companies around the world are becoming increasingly aware of these opportunities and taking ambitious action by developing low-carbon technologies, following science-based emission reduction targets, eliminating deforestation from their supply chains or investing in nature-based solutions.

We must change our system so that investors ask companies to do more and reward them by allocating their capital to the most sustainable operators.

Peter Bakker
President of the World Business Council for Sustainable Development

Business played an important part in shaping the SDGs and the historic agreement at COP21, and business will play an important role in realising them. However, it is clear that we need more businesses to embrace the sustainable development agenda and treat it as an important driver of core business strategies and investment decisions. Sustainable business models are vital to long-term inclusive growth and value creation. Our voice, and our leadership, in supporting governments to take decisive action to implement the sustainability agenda is paramount. Our actions send market signals that the world really can change path, and our business leaders are committed to making it happen.

Technology is changing to the extent that we can now do things cost effectively that 5 or 10 years ago were impossible. Business must be at the forefront of this technological progress and must lead by doing — encouraging others to embrace this sustainable technology.

During the course of last year, we saw collective leadership from companies like retailers Marks & Spencer and Ikea, luxury goods company Kering and DSM, to name a few, and coalitions including the World Business Council for Sustainable Development, We Mean Business, and the B Team, demonstrate the pivotal role of business in driving forward the changes we have to make. This leadership must continue to ensure we achieve the goals set out at COP21. I believe we will see increasing numbers of businesses pledge to supporting a more sustainable future and taking steps in every part of their organisation to play their part in achieving these goals.

Paul Polman
CEO of Unilever

The transition to sustainability affects everyone, public and private sector alike. We need new energy sources and better energy usage. Transport, energy and buildings need to adapt. And so does farming, manufacturing and services. All this is a fantastic opportunity; in particular, an opportunity for the finance industry. It is reckoned that for climate adaptation alone, we need around $1 trillion a year. That may seem a lot, but it is not compared to the $200 trillion plus assets held in the financial system. And you can already see this beginning to happen. At the Paris conference, $600 billion of investors promised to decarbonise their investment out of brown into green.[lviii] In 2015, $40 billion worth of green bonds were issued to support new green investment.[lix] These funds are being redirected towards green opportunities not just because those who manage them are environmentally responsible, but also because they realise green business is such a potentially profitable option.

David Pitt-Watson
Chair of the UN Environment Programme Finance Initiative
Executive Fellow of Finance, London Business School, UK

The right regulatory framework can help ensure that investment in sustainability is profitable, and so encourage the private sector to focus its innovative efforts on developing sustainable practices and technology. As with other economic challenges, this may require pro-competitive coordination and competition between companies. Coordination is needed to achieve efficiencies and to open up possibilities where individual firms lack the necessary scale or range of activities. Competition is needed to ensure that maximum effort is made to benefit consumers and to avoid rent seeking. Competition policy aims to protect competition by prohibiting anti-competitive agreements and conduct while allowing the coordination that is likely to achieve efficiencies and allow consumers a fair share of the benefits. Agreements between firms to support sustainability initiatives are not necessarily anti-competitive. But even if an agreement has some anti-competitive effects, EU competition rules allow it if the benefits outweigh any negative effects for consumers on the market involved. EU competition policy is thus an essential tool to ensure that markets stay as competitive and open as possible while allowing the cooperation that benefits consumers overall. This allows firms developing attractive, sustainable technologies to grow as fast as possible and spread their solutions far and wide.

Margrethe Vestager
Commissioner for Competition, European Union

Would the development of social institutions to defend the public interest (*e.g.*, protection of natural resources) be effective in holding governments and businesses accountable?

In places where there are strong traditions of civil society and the rule of law, business and government have a much harder job getting away with collusion that harms the public interest. There is no question that institutions that defend the public interest are chronically under-resourced and politically vulnerable. In many countries, the laws and tools we need to ensure basic environmental protections exist on the books. What is most often lacking is a truly renewable resource: political will, which fortunately can be generated by citizen pressure. Civil society's main hope is the guerrilla organising power of the Internet to enable rapid organising and the timely leaking of secret damaging draft deals that invariably elicit public condemnation.

Stephanie Brancaforte
Global Campaign Leader on Climate & Energy at Greenpeace

Chapter 10

Religion

Most human beings consider themselves religious,[lx] and in many parts of the world, religions play an important role in bringing people together and in promoting moral and ethical ways of living. Though environmentalism is often seen as a secular form of political activism, it has been at the centre of the moral and ethical frameworks and ways of life promoted by various religions.

In the same way that people should care for and treat one another with respect, they should do the same to the environment. Indeed, many religions have highlighted our interdependence with and responsibility to protect the environment, and have cautioned about the consequences of its degradation.

As religions are united in their respect for the environment, they can promote environmentally friendly mentalities and galvanise sustainable actions. For example, religious leaders played a key role in supporting the Paris Climate Agreement by collecting the signatures of around 1.8 million people calling for climate justice in the run-up to the COP21 climate conference,[lxi] and they have since continued in their united efforts to promote its implementation through various coordinated actions and declarations.[lxii]

Do you believe that major world religions can find common ground and effectively cite people to take action and change their behaviour to the environment?

All the major world religions teach us to be contented, which can be a powerful antidote to the greed with which we are inclined to exploit the environment and its resources as if they had no end. If we compare changes in the climate and damage to the environment to war and violence, we see that violence has an immediate impact on us. The trouble is that damage to the environment takes place more stealthily, so we don't see it until it is often too late. Trying to restore it at that point is very difficult. We need to educate ourselves and make caring for the environment, even in small ways like remembering to turn off the lights when we leave a room, a part of our lives.

His Holiness the Dalai Lama

Yes, of course. And this is what I have been doing with many people around the world, not just Muslims. For example, we were recently in Salt Lake City talking about this in the Parliament of World Religions. We were coming together. And once again, it's not just about religious organisations or religious people, it has to be about crossing the board with atheists, agnostics, Asian spiritualities and monotheisms because we need to come together and try to find common ground. And the common ground is reached as soon as you are talking about God, about transcendence. You understand that the environment is a gift that you have to care about it, that you have to take care of.

But if we are obsessed with the legal framework of religions, we usually don't understand the ethical reference when it comes to respecting nature and the Earth. This means we also often forget the meaning of khilafah as being viceregent on Earth, meaning that we don't have the ownership of nature, we are just managing it. And we have to manage it in the best way we can, to respect the ethical frame and reference, to arrive at this intellectual and spiritual revolution. But of course, if we are serious about these teachings, they can play a major role in ethical concerns, applied ethics, and translation into this change. But it's also by not simplifying the problem in Radical Reform (my book, Radical Reform: Islamic Ethics and Liberation, 2009) that I'm also connecting our struggle for the environment with our understanding of the global economy. Because if you just disconnect the two and you come with very simplistic discourse that could be counter-productive, you can say, 'you know what, we have to respect nature, we have lots of hadiths in Islam that are telling us to protect the species and all this', but it's deeper than that. And simplistic answers to complex issues are not going to help.

Prof. Tariq Ramadan
HH Sheikh Hamad Bin Khalifa Al Thani
Professor of Contemporary Islamic Studies
University of Oxford, UK

Have the anti-religious and anti-spiritual ideologies of the twentieth century contributed to our environmental problems?

Many of the problems we face are a result of our materialistic way of life. To change that, we need a more holistic education, an education that incorporates inner values, such as a compassionate concern for others' well-being. We need a greater sense that all seven billion human beings alive today belong to one human family. We need to talk to each other just as fellow human beings. We all want to have a happy life and that is our right. Sometimes, difficult circumstances help us gain more experience in fulfilling that goal.

His Holiness the Dalai Lama

Concern for the environment is an area that unites the world's religions. Each of the world's major religions affirms the goodness of the natural world. Each religion has an ethic of earth care, calling for humanity to sustain the earth that sustains us. This is a sacred obligation.

These religions all recognise the harmony and interdependence of all natural systems and forms of life, including human life. As Pope Francis puts it, we are part of nature, so if we harm nature, we end up harming ourselves. This also means that all creatures have intrinsic values in their existence, their life, their beauty, their interdependence and so must be respected.

I believe that the world's religions played a vital role during the COP21 negotiations. Everyone I spoke to stressed the importance of

Pope Francis's encyclical, *Laudato si*, which laid out the moral case for protecting creation. Other religious leaders also issued powerful statements in the run-up to Paris–Christians, Jews, Muslims, Buddhists and Hindus, for example. This is an issue where the world's religions stood together, and world leaders listened.

Cardinal Peter Turkson
President of the Pontifical Council for Justice and Peace
Archbishop Emeritus of Cape Coast, Ghana

I don't think it's only anti-religious and anti-spiritual ideologies. I think that even within religious discourse, you sometimes see a discourse that transforms anything religious into a form of formalism. And because it's very formal and technical in the way it deals with the rules, it has nothing to do with a spiritual dimension or understanding the very goal. So, any scientific or religious understanding that transforms everything into technical answers or legal frameworks does not understand the ethical reference, or more importantly, the philosophy of the goals, and it undermines anything to do with the environment. So, I wouldn't say it's only scientism or materialism that is the ultimate reason why we are facing this. Some religious teachings or some religious scholars do not pay attention to the priority of that.

Prof. Tariq Ramadan
HH Sheikh Hamad Bin Khalifa Al Thani
Professor of Contemporary Islamic Studies
University of Oxford, UK

Why has environmentalism been seen as a secular topic thus far? How can religion be used to encourage people to care for and take care of nature?

I don't believe that environmentalism is simply a secular topic. Caring for the earth is first and foremost a moral issue, which puts it in the domain of religion. The different religions all affirm the moral imperative to combat climate change and they call upon believers to take action.

At a personal level, we know that combating climate change calls for the inculcation of Earth-sensitive virtues for the development of a true ecological sensibility. And religious communities have always been great seedbeds for nurturing virtue. This means that people of faith can be pioneers when it comes to ecological virtue. They can lead by example — such as by adopting more modest lifestyles and making a conscious effort to reduce their carbon footprints.

Cardinal Peter Turkson
President of the Pontifical Council for Justice and Peace
Archbishop Emeritus of Cape Coast, Ghana

I think there are many reasons. The first is that in the Islamic framework, for example, things are very clear when it comes to what is halal (allowed) and what is haram (forbidden). And there is only ethical concern when it comes to the environment. So, in prioritising the legal, it puts the ethical as secondary goal. This has an impact. And this is why we have to come back with the centrality of the ethical teachings in order to bring out the centrality of the environment. Because very often, when Muslims ask about environmental issues, they are aware of the verses of the Koran and of the prophetic traditions, but it doesn't seem to be as important as it is. So, this is explained by the priority given to the legal as opposed to the ethical sphere.

Secondly, scholars talk about priorities by saying 'that in dealing with poverty, a lack of education, and a deep crisis', the environment is not the primary problem. It's mainly arguing that this is an issue for industrialised societies, not understanding it as something that is essential in the way we deal with the Islamic reference, at least in Muslim-majority countries.

Thirdly, when we are obsessed with the legal situation and when we prioritise technical issues over ethical ones, this is reflected in the way we look at the world. So, we don't talk about the way we deal with the universe and with nature as we should and give a technical answer to social problems.

Prof. Tariq Ramadan
HH Sheikh Hamad Bin Khalifa Al Thani
Professor of Contemporary Islamic Studies
University of Oxford, UK

Could mosques become an effective network for raising awareness about our environmental problems?

Yes, of course. There are many examples of this around the world, such as in the way we build mosques. For example, in Malaysia, there is a green mosque in Perlis that is completely powered by renewable energy. There are also similar examples in northern France and in Germany. Changing the way mosques are built can have a positive effect on awareness. Secondly, the teachings of scholars or imams, and the organisations promoting environmentally friendly attitudes have to be central in everything. So, the way mosques are built, the religious instruction in mosques, and the collaboration between people and their surroundings, environment and their neighbourhood are critical in raising awareness about our environmental problems.

Prof. Tariq Ramadan
HH Sheikh Hamad Bin Khalifa Al Thani
Professor of Contemporary Islamic Studies
University of Oxford, UK

Could churches become an effective network for raising awareness about our environmental problems?

Definitely. Given their role as schools of virtue, religious communities can be in the vanguard of ecological education. Religions can also incorporate an environmental sensibility into religious liturgies and practices. As an example of this, Pope Francis decided to follow the example of the Orthodox Church and designate 1 September as an annual day of prayer for the care of creation. And of course, religious communities can lead by example by decarbonising their own houses of worship and other properties. Religious believers can enact change through the economic and political decisions they make. We know that every economic decision constitutes a moral decision. Religious consumers can buy goods that are produced in a way that respects nature. Religious business owners can make sure that all social costs are accounted for in business activities. Religious investors can choose to invest in renewables rather than fossil fuels. And religious believers can also make their voices heard on this issue in the political domain. Overall, 84% of people around the world identify with a religious tradition. This is the world's most powerful lobby! If we all stand together, then we can save the planet from destruction.

Cardinal Peter Turkson
President of the Pontifical Council for Justice and Peace
Archbishop Emeritus of Cape Coast, Ghana

Chapter 11

Philosophy

Sustain, sustainable, sustainability: *verb*: to continue over a period of time; *adjective*: causing little or no damage; *noun*: the idea that goods and services should be produced in ways that do not use resources that cannot be replaced.

Verb, adjective, noun?

Perhaps, it is all three. But perhaps more importantly, it is a moral and ethical paradigm against which action — individual, corporate and government — should be evaluated. Many suggest our goal should be to leave things better than we found them. But is that possible? The human footprint on the planet is already so large. Perhaps, sustainability means managing your own behaviour, your own decisions, so that others are not denied basic dignities and necessities. Should we ask: does my action in anyway deny another their basic dignity and necessities — clean air to breathe, safe and available water to drink, healthy and nutritional food to eat?

In the beginning of the anti-pollution environmental movement in the USA, the focus was moral. One of our oldest and most important environmental laws, the Clean Water Act, set a legal and enforceable goal. Water bodies of the USA — rivers, lakes, streams — should be fishable and swimmable.

Today, in setting pollution standards, we ask what will it cost polluters to reduce their pollution. Will the benefits of less pollution be greater than the cost of reducing the pollution? If the benefits are not greater, then some argue the pollution reductions must be curtailed until the benefits justify the costs. But cost: benefit analyses are not as objective as some suggest. How do you value the life of an older person living longer because of less air pollution? What is the dollar amount assigned to that benefit? Some suggest you can use a lower value because the value of an elderly life is less, since death is closer. Understanding the costs and the benefits associated with pollution reduction is not wrong, but limiting the setting of pollution standards to those situations where benefits exceed costs will not deliver on the moral commitment of fishable and swimmable.

As the political arguments against the science of climate change grew louder and louder, my colleagues and I began to say, 'It doesn't matter what you think about the science, there are clean energy jobs to be created if we commit to reducing GHG'. But, of course, it does matter what people think, and simply giving them a pass on respecting the overwhelming body of science would be like saying 'It doesn't matter what you think about the segregation of races'. It does matter and no one should be given a pass. Sustainability must be defined as a moral and ethical commitment. Anything less denies the fundamental value of life.

Carol Browner
Former Administrator of the US Environmental Protection
Agency (1993–2001)
Director of the White House Office of Energy and Climate Change
Policy (2009–2011)

Transitioning towards more sustainable societies also implies changes in our ways of thinking and acting in relation to the environment. Some have argued that our societies have become anthropocentric, that they view everything from a human perspective and act in ways that benefit us alone at the expense of other species. As our population and technological mastery increases our influence over other species and ecosystems, anthropocentrism also reminds us that human advancement should not and cannot be at the expense of other species. This is especially so when we consider the reality that many of our societal functions depend on other species and ecosystems.

Has humanity come to see itself not only as separate but also superior to nature?

Superior to nature? Less than 20% of humanity enjoys the benefits of the welfare state. The remaining 80% lives below the levels of a dignified life and an important percentage of them are in painful situations of extremely poverty. They have no access to crucial human needs, even to what is necessary to survive. At present, 3.1 million children die of hunger every year,[lxiii] while at the same time, over 1.7 trillion dollars is spent on armaments and military expenses.[lxiv] This is the balance of the neoliberal system that has substituted the democratic principles that according to UNESCO's Constitution should guide humanity with market laws and the United Nations with plutocratic groups (G6, G7, G8, G20). Article number 1 of the UNESCO's Constitutions has a farsighted definition of education: it is to be 'free and responsible'. However, there are still many countries (and several states in North America) in which creationism, dogmatism and fanaticism are accepted in teaching and prevent the fulfilment of this goal.

The moment from when the quality of the Earth was influenced by human activities (the Anthropocene) it has been inadmissible, from the point of view of intergenerational responsibilities, not to take into account the processes, particularly social and environmental, that are potentially irreversible. President Obama and Pope Francis have both warned that the present generation is the first to face the effects of climate change and the last one that can try to stop them.

Prof. Federico Mayor Zaragoza
Former Director-General of UNESCO (1987–1999)
President of the Foundation for a Culture of Peace.

Is our increasing distance from nature the source of our environmental problems? Is there any way we can reconnect with nature?

Children today can probably name 20 television shows but will have a hard time naming 10 endangered species in their country. Baba Dioum has said that we conserve only what we love, we love only what we understand and we understand only what we are taught. We need children to know more about the value of nature to their well-being and we need to help them access nature better. Our surveys show that one in three Chileans have never visited a protected area, and that this number rises to one in two for low-income communities. So last year, we established 2nd October as our National Day of the Environment, in which our parks system would be free to the public, and we would make a special effort to take low-income students to parks on that day. We believe that this is a cornerstone for future conservation, so that we will protect what we love.

Michelle Bachelet
President of Chile

How can we reconcile an increasingly urbanised world with an increasingly urgent need to understand our dependence on our environment?

As an anthropologist, I have to question the conventional distinction between humanity and nature. Humans are natural phenomena. Why would we regard a termite mound as natural but a city as unnatural? Yes, we do damage to other occupants of the planet, just as elephants wreak havoc on the plant life as they move through the bush, but that does not make either unnatural. We should resist the temptation to label things we like as 'natural' and those we don't like as 'unnatural'. As J. Meyer argues, we should resist appeals to nature as the source from which social, economic, and political principles should be derived 'for precisely the same reason they are powerful — they cede enormous authority over human affairs to something deemed "nature". At the very least, any democratic politics would be imperilled by an acceptance of these claims'.[lxv] Having said that,

I find myself depressed by the endless discourse on sustainability as 'damage control', doing what we do with the minimum of damage to the non-human elements of the environment. I am much more energised by the idea of 'regenerative sustainability' elaborated by the Canadian geographer John Robinson, which sets out to positively improve the condition of the environment and the humans who live in it.

Prof. Steve Rayner
James Martin Professor of Science and Civilization
Director of the Institute for Science, Innovation and Society
University of Oxford, UK

How can we encourage people to care for and to take care of nature?

The need to take care of nature and the environment is urgent. It's a matter of human survival because this planet is our only home. We have to take ecology seriously. Although the climate does change naturally, the rate and extent of recent change is an evident result of human activity. In today's world, we are all much more interdependent than we used to be. Therefore, leaders around the world must confront the issue of global warming and initiate action to reduce the emission of GHGs for all our benefit. But on a personal and family level, too, we need to develop a much clearer awareness of our actions and their consequences, so that taking care of and limiting damage to the natural environment becomes an ordinary part of our daily life. That is the proper way, and it can only be achieved through education.

His Holiness the Dalai Lama

How can we motivate people to think of the long-term repercussions of their actions on future generations?

By talking to them about their children and grandchildren, and by reminding them of their own childhoods and of the memories they have of their parents' world.

Brice Lalonde
Executive Coordinator of the UN Conference on Sustainable
Development (Rio+20; 2012)
Former French Ambassador on Climate Change Negotiations
(2007–2010)
Former French Minister for the Environment (1988–1992)

How will our morality and ways of thinking need to change if we are to transition to environmentally sustainable societies?

First, we must recognise our response to climate change as a shared commitment to the common good; we are all connected. Or put more simply, engagement is not an option — it is our responsibility to ourselves and to each other.

While each community will come to this work from their own unique histories, traditions and perspectives, we must come *together* in our shared work.

At Georgetown, we come to this work through the lens of our Catholic and Jesuit identity. In 2015, Pope Francis issued his encyclical focused on the environment and the poor, *Laudato Si*, the most anticipated encyclical in our lifetime. It offers us both a historical grounding and a transformative vision of the Roman Catholic Church's teachings on environmental challenges and the future of our planet. In *Laudato Si*, the Holy Father frames the challenge of climate change in these terms:

> It is hard for us to accept that the way natural ecosystems work is exemplary … our industrial system, at the end of its cycle of production and consumption, has not developed the capacity to absorb and reuse waste and by-products. We have not yet managed to adopt a circular model of production capable of preserving resources for present and future generations.[lxvi]

What Pope Francis describes here is our current lack — and present urgent need — for a circular economy, an economy that seeks to ultimately eliminate waste through sustainable design, engineering, and manufacturing processes. So while Georgetown might come to this work from a particular tradition, we share a goal and a responsibility with institutions and communities around the world: environmentally sustainable societies. This is the shared goal that we must seek out together.

Dr. John J. DeGioia
President, Georgetown University

If we exploit the environment in extreme ways, even though we may get some monetary or other benefit from it now, in the long run, we and future generations will suffer. Environmental and climate change now pose some of the most serious threats to the health of our planet and people. They will have a direct impact on all of us. Many people have simply not been aware of what we human beings have been doing and the effect our actions have had on nature. When I lived in Tibet, people were very careful not to harm animals because they were aware that they were sentient beings like us, but we did not pay much attention to the environment. We were a small population living in a huge land and by and large we thought nature looked after itself.

Our general carelessness about pollution is illustrative. Unlike the bloodshed and violence of war, the force of which immediately makes an impression on our minds, the damage we humans are doing to the atmosphere happens gradually, so we do not really notice it. Our dependence on fossil fuel is such that although we were warned long ago about the threat of CO_2 in the atmosphere, we have done little to stop it. Now, time is running out. Deserts will spread, ice caps and glaciers, such as those in my homeland Tibet, will melt, coastal areas will flood and millions will be forced from their homes. In such circumstances, concerns about freedom, democracy and human rights will no longer have much meaning.

His Holiness the Dalai Lama

Chapter 12

Education

Though governments and businesses can make it easier for our societies to become more sustainable, any lasting change requires both participation and understanding from citizens. Indeed, people cannot effectively act on a matter they do not understand. Promoting an understanding of sustainable development and all the societal benefits that this implies from a young age may be essential in ensuring that young and future generations can contribute fully to these changes.

In the same way that sustainability relates to a diverse set of subjects because of the many different causes of and potential solutions to environmental and climate change, the educational system should reflect these interrelations. The increasing importance of sustainability will mean that problems and solutions will have to be dealt with as a whole, rather than in many individual fields of study, as these come to reflect our planet's increased interdependence. And thus, ensuring that the educational system can adequately teach students to understand the challenges of the coming decades and century may be crucial in ensuring we emerge resilient and can transition towards more sustainable societies.

What are the benefits of education on individuals and on societies? How can we ensure that all children have a secondary school education and the opportunity to pursue higher education?

Education has a variety of benefits. At the individual level, people with an education earn higher wages, are less likely to commit crimes and lead healthier lives. In particular, educating girls can have profound effects on societies and their children. Better educated mothers, particularly those who complete secondary school, are more likely to survive childbirth and their children are more likely to live past the age of five. Additionally, both the number of schooling years and the levels of skills learned have a great impact on economic growth and productivity. New research has shown that students' maths and science abilities, measured by international exams, can explain the different pace of economic growth across different countries and regions.[lxvii]

Since the Education for All goals were declared in 1990 and the Millennium Development Goals in 2000, both of which set out the ambitious goal of universal access to primary school across the globe, we have made tremendous progress. Today, over 90% of all children are enrolled in primary schools, largely due to building new schools, making them free and requiring attendance.[lxviii] However, the new SDGs aim for a universal education that runs from early childhood to the end of secondary school. This ambitious new goal will need a diverse set of actors working together and channelling resources and energy into secondary school access. But it's also important to focus on quality learning opportunities. In many countries, the rapid expansion of primary education has resulted in little improvement in learning. It has been estimated that 250 million children in the world don't have even basic literacy and numeracy skills — 130 million of whom have attended 4 years of school.[lxix] So, focused efforts must address improving quality alongside increasing access to both primary and secondary schools.

Dr. Rebecca Winthrop
Director of the Center for Universal Education
Brookings Institution, USA

What is the role of the education systems in facilitating our transition towards more sustainable societies?

Enhancing awareness, knowledge and skills is vital in protecting the environment in the context of sustainable development, which is predicated on an understanding of the true value of our environment to our economies and societies. This connection, while it is often instinctively felt, has only in recent times begun to be appreciated in wider circles. It has taken on its own momentum and now forms the basis for the SDGs and the 2030 Agenda, but this understanding has its roots in education.

The importance of education is seen throughout the seventeen SDGs. Education is incorporated into many targets, but there is also an entire goal devoted to it. SDG four seeks to achieve inclusive quality education for all, and this speaks to the centrality of knowledge in achieving a more sustainable and equitable future for all. Higher education institutions play critical roles in education for sustainable development. They promote sharing of knowledge, skills and technological innovations, and help close the gap between science and policy. More than this, these institutions educate future leaders who will drive and influence the development agenda for decades to come. This is why UNEP has engaged with universities in multiple ways. One major programme, the Green University Partnership on Environment and Sustainability, has 750 higher education partners across the world and aims to promote the integration of environment and sustainability concerns into teaching, research, community engagement, student engagement and the management of universities.

Achim Steiner
Director of the Oxford Martin School, University of Oxford, UK
Former Executive Director of the UN Environment Programme
(2006–2016)

Why is pursuing higher education likely to become a necessity over the next few decades?

Higher education has always brought extraordinary value to both individuals and societies: it brings unique resources for growing and developing talent; seeking solutions to problems of public health, policy and economics; and imagining what each of us can contribute to our collective work of building a better, more peaceful, more equitable and more just world.

As we face the urgent and serious problem of climate change and its impact upon our planet, the role of higher education becomes ever more important. We will need a proficient and dedicated citizenry and workforce to adequately engage this crisis — and to help mitigate its effects, especially upon our most vulnerable sisters and brothers.

Higher education will be at the heart of the research — the inquiry and discovery — necessary for creating a more sustainable planet. Perhaps, never before has the creativity and persistence of our researchers been more essential to the well-being of our global community.

Dr. John J. DeGioia
President, Georgetown University, USA

For citizens to be able to exercise their political rights, critical thinking and complex knowledge will increasingly become a necessity. There are two reasons for this: The first is the evolution of communication technologies and pace, leading to an extreme simplification of messages. The second reason is the growing complexity of the challenges that mankind is facing in a contest of growing uncertainties. Climate change is a perfect example of such a complexity, requiring a combination of scientific, political, economic and social knowledge, extremely difficult to acquire in the current education systems. Our societies are facing challenges that have no simple solutions, problems that require a wide spectrum of academic knowledge, immense wisdom and tolerance. Issues such as large-scale migrations, non-territorial terrorism, the reconfiguration of family models, biotechnologies, the new frontiers of science and governing large metropolises require better educated citizens.

Dr. Alessia Lefébure
Director of the Alliance Programme
Columbia University, USA

McKinsey has estimated that we are facing a massive global skills gap. While most new entrants to the workforce will come from developing regions such as sub-Saharan Africa and South Asia, too many young people lack the secondary and tertiary education employers require to take on more complex careers. In these regions, there will be an over-supply of low-skilled workers and an undersupply of highly skilled workers.[lxx]

Dr. Rebecca Winthrop
Director of the Center for Universal Education
Brookings Institution, USA

What is the role of higher education in researching more sustainable practices and in advocating for policy changes?

The percentage of the population participating in higher education is growing faster than ever everywhere in the world. According to UNESCO data, the gross tertiary enrolment ratio has increased between 1995 and 2011 from 15 to 30% worldwide, reaching figures above 70% in North America and Europe, above 60% in Japan, Hong Kong and Taiwan, not to mention South Korea, whose ratio is the highest in the world. China has moved from 6 to 25% in only 20 years. Universities are where most of tomorrow's leaders receive education and training and shape their values and beliefs. The role of higher education is thus crucial in providing broad and informed analysis to all rising generations about complex matters that require more than just raw data and basic knowledge. The role of the faculty, especially in research-based universities, has changed. From knowledge provider, the faculty has become the bestower of meaning by analysis, translation, bridging and providing historical context to current issues.

Dr. Alessia Lefébure
Director of the Alliance Programme
Columbia University, USA

What values should we be teaching our children through the educational system?

UNESCO's Constitution refers very clearly to the main political values we all need. In 1992, I asked the President of the European Commission, Mr. Jacques Delors, to chair an International Commission on 'Education in the XXI Century'. In summary, the recommendations were: learning to be, learning to know, learning to do and learning to live together. I added learn to undertake because taking risks without knowledge is dangerous, but knowledge without taking risks is useless.[lxxi]

Prof. Federico Mayor Zaragoza
Former Director-General of UNESCO (1987–1999)
President of the Foundation for a Culture of Peace

Our government programme focuses on facing inequality and promoting sustainable and inclusive development. In our educational system, we should promote values on sustainability. Sustainability implies inclusiveness, that is, is not to discriminate on grounds of gender, race or social origin. This means designing a society for those who need the most help. In this approach, environmental conservation comes naturally.

Our Ministry of the Environment's Department of Environmental Education has many programmes to promote environmental protection, from preschool programmes that include recycling to a school certification system for primary and secondary schools that awards different levels of excellence. A recent innovation was our first ever intergenerational dialogue between elderly people and schoolchildren to discuss environmental issues. This year we are embarking in an ambitious environmental education programme creating the Adriana Hoffman's Academy of Environmental Education, which will provide e-learning tools for citizens to learn about protecting the environment.

Michelle Bachelet
President of Chile

Six decades ago, I was growing up in southern Bangladesh. My father, Father of the Nation, Bangabandhu Sheikh Mujibur Rahman, used to talk about the value of pristine nature. He told us how the lives and livelihoods of people are intricately linked to the land, the rivers, the wetlands and the sea in the Bangladesh riverine delta. People in our villages still believe that conservation and protection of environment is a time-honoured responsibility, not just a necessity. The concept of taking care of mother Earth is imbibed in the ethos, art, culture and way of life of Bengali people. That spirit has been inserted deep in Bengali minds and ways of living over centuries through the works of our poets such as Tagore, Nazrul, Jibanananda and Jasimuddin.

Like many other societies, ours is built on respect for elders as part of shared societal or communal responsibility. Akin to that, across generations, our people have believed that if they took care of nature, nature would take care of them. When we talk about environmental conservation or addressing climate change, this goes far beyond viewing climate as a global or community public good. For our people, land is just not a resource or capital, it is part of our inheritance. We cannot sustain and prosper by giving any less attention to nature. We must teach the same values to our children. And remind them that mother earth does not need us to exist, but we need her to exist.

H.E. Sheikh Hasina
Prime Minister of Bangladesh

What types of twenty-first century skills should the educational system be teaching our children?

In Canada, provinces and territories are primarily responsible for the organisation, delivery, and assessment of education at the elementary and secondary levels, for technical and vocational education and for postsecondary education. The federal government, however, plays a crucial role in education, providing financial support touching all levels of learning, both directly to individuals and indirectly through provincial and territorial governments for higher education.

The Government of Canada believes all Canadian children deserve a real and fair chance to succeed, and all Canadians should be able to live with dignity. While it is not known exactly what the future will bring, the Government of Canada will work collaboratively and in partnership with all stakeholders, especially provinces and territories, to create a highly adaptable workforce with the right mix of skills, including both technical and essential skills.

In particular, learning about the global transition to a low-carbon economy as the world acts on climate change will transcend all levels of education in preparing for careers.

Workers, especially youth, must have the skills to evolve with their jobs and adapt to workplace change. And that's why education and training are important priorities for the Government of Canada. The Government will focus on young people and will increase investments in youth training and employment and make post-secondary education more affordable.

In particular, the Government is committed to strengthening employment opportunities for youth doing co-ops, business programs and internships in STEM, increasing overall investments in skills development and improving essential skills.

H.E. Justin Trudeau
Prime Minister of Canada

The world around us is changing rapidly, and our children have to learn to cope. This entails comprehensive personal development alongside the basic acquisition of knowledge in the school setting. The children of today are the citizens and workers of tomorrow. They will have to find their way on the labour market and in society. To assist them on their journey, it is crucial that they develop characteristics such as responsiveness, creativity and commitment to cope with change.

Dr. Jet Bussemaker
Minister of Education, Culture and Science of the Netherlands

How can we encourage the educational system to be more flexible and better adapted to a constantly changing world?

It starts with the teacher in the classroom. A range of studies have shown that the teacher, more than any other factor, is responsible for determining the quality of education. The same applies here. Teachers have to keep up with the times and incorporate the ever-changing outside world into the classroom experience for their pupils. Fortunately, most teachers do this already. In addition to these didactic skills, however, the curriculum is also crucial. It should provide scope for personal growth, for the development of characteristics like responsiveness, creativity and commitment. A curriculum that focuses solely on knowledge acquisition is an anachronism.

Dr. Jet Bussemaker
Minister of Education, Culture and Science of the Netherlands

Do you believe that the standardisation of the curriculum, a practice common in many countries, is leading to increasing uniformity of thought? How can we reform the educational system to promote a plurality of thought?

The standardisation of the curriculum can take place only when educational context is not correct and is connected exclusively to economically, ideologically or religiously driven systems. Each human being is unique and able to think, to imagine, to anticipate, to invent, to create! These free and responsible citizens, anticipating truly democratic systems, will contribute to the common destiny by not placing the reins of power in the hands of the very few, as happens nowadays, but in the hands of the community, led by scientists, teachers, artists and intellectuals.

Prof. Federico Mayor Zaragoza
Former Director-General of UNESCO (1987–1999)
President of the Foundation for a Culture of Peace

In the Netherlands, schools have plenty of latitude to structure their own curricula. The government determines what children have to learn, teachers and schools determine how they learn it. The system works well, according to the OECD, which sees this freedom as one of the strengths of the Dutch approach to education, combined with supervision by an inspectorate. However, freedom must not be confused with license. Dutch schools have the responsibility to teach their pupils good citizenship. That means plurality of thought, listening to each other and understanding each other, for the society of tomorrow begins in the classroom of today.

Dr. Jet Bussemaker
Minister of Education, Culture and Science of the Netherlands

Do you believe that the educational system must evolve from one where subjects are taught in academic silos to a more open one that allows for a greater understanding of our planet's interconnectedness? What changes will have to be made to achieve this interdisciplinarity?

The educational system, will now, without any doubt, open up progressively because, for the first time in the history, the human beings can express themselves freely. Since the beginning of time, under an absolute male power, most humans were born, lived and died within the space of a few square kilometers. They were silent, obedient and fearful. The educational system reflected the immense social inequalities and, in many cases, was accessible only to the richest and those living in big cities. The ideologies and beliefs of the teachers were strictly reflected in the learning programmes. In the past few years, mainly because of digital technology, citizens are becoming world citizens because they know reality in depth, they are aware of what is happening in the world as a whole. And they can participate. And as the cornerstone of the new era, women, until very recently left completely out of the decision-making process, are also being educated in such a way that before long the new beginning enshrined in the Earth Charter will be feasible.[lxxii]

Prof. Federico Mayor Zaragoza
Former Director-General of UNESCO (1987–1999)
President of the Foundation for a Culture of Peace

How do you believe students can be taught that we live on an interdependent planet where the repercussions of our current environmental crisis (climate change) will eventually affect all nations?

They don't need to be taught, they are already living it. In Tuvalu, what else do you want to teach children suffering from the rising sea level, where everyday they see the sea coming closer to their doorstep? Is there any lesson in the classroom they need to learn? They are already learning from their actual lives. And they are reading books, looking at their iPhones and iPads and reading the science saying Do something! Do something because the Earth is already 1°C hotter than pre-industrial times[lxxiii] and there are many risks and consequences if it continues to get hotter'. Everybody, even young children, can see that the plantations at their homes in Tuvalu were growing very well 5 years ago, but they're not growing now. It's all yellow leaves every morning. Why? Because of sea salinity coming from the water sources, and they know that the freshwater in the ground tastes and smells bad. You don't need teachers to tell them that this is because of climate change; they are already living the dangers of global warming. But you need to educate them on options, what options to disguise help: how can they elevate the level of the land so their gardens can grow better, so that they can feed themselves and their children. And that's what I'm calling education: to adapt. It's very expensive, but it is necessary.

We need cooperation. The children living on small islands may be the first to suffer, but I tell you, before they are middle-aged, I know you will be suffering the same fate. The small islands will be the first, but all communities in the world are going to face the same difficulties if we don't effectively implement the Paris agreement. That is the reality of what science is telling us, what we have a duty to do. We are all one family and we must work as a family to ensure that our gardens continue to grow, to provide food. Okay, industries may need to adapt, but we must all work together. You cannot let the small islands like Tuvalu drown because one day you will suffer the same way. I think we need to bring this down to the human level: it is not about industries, not about saving industries, but it is about preventing wars, radicalism and extremism. Why? Because if we don't act to prevent climate change, we will all be struggling over resources and it's going to get worse.

H.E. Enele Sopoaga
Prime Minister of Tuvalu

How can we encourage children to foster their love of nature into adulthood?

The value of nature in the development of our food and farming is well known: indeed, numerous studies demonstrate the lasting impact of getting children out into the countryside before the age of eleven. Yet nature's inherent ability to support our health and well-being is undervalued and not fully recognised. The sheer awe you feel seeing a plant growing on the windowsill, hearing birdsong, watching a butterfly emerging from a chrysalis, feeds the imagination of children and awaken their inner connections with nature. However, harnessing this to create a lifelong love of nature is challenging.

In an increasingly urban society, space for nature is diminishing and growing the connections between children, education, food and farming is essential in order to ensure we have farmers, scientists and responsible consumers of the future. The great thing about nature is its capacity to arouse all our senses; the sounds of the dawn chorus or the rain on the ground, the stunning sights of a sunrise across a landscape, the smell of freshly mown grass and the dampness of the woods, the touch of prickly plant or a smooth leaf, or the taste of our food from our farms or in the wild such as blackberries on hedges. These are the experiences and opportunities to embed a true appreciation and respect for nature throughout our life. Bringing children and families out on to farm, such as we do at LEAF, on our Open Farm Sunday, helps people discover the story behind their food and lets nature feed their senses.

Caroline Drummond
CEO, LEAF UK

How can we foster a sense of equality and togetherness among children through the educational system as we seek to build a socially inclusive world?

Children need to be taught from an early age both at home and in schools about equality, human rights and responsible behaviour. Sustainability education should be part of the basic curriculum in schools. From a young age, people should be conscious of ecological and social concerns and receive information about the impact of their behaviour and their own ability to make choices. This education should also include information on all the benefits of sustainable behaviour. For instance, sustainable agriculture does not only protect the soil, it also brings climate benefits and increases jobs and incomes. Eating fish or vegetable proteins also has considerable climate benefits, is healthier and saves funds in the family budget.

Governments need to take active steps for developing education and encouraging scientific research as well as supporting voluntary measures for citizens to play their part in building sustainable societies. The choices private citizens make in their everyday life are significant. Being privately conscious and socially active is good policy for sustainable development.

Tarja Halonen
Former President of Finland (2000–2012)

How can service learning and education encourage students to be better citizens?

We are witnessing an increasing disconnection between the story institutions tell and the needs of today's students. For the most part, institutional communication highlights the short-term, on-campus experience prospective students can expect to enjoy. However, the need for the student to learn skills, knowledge and behaviours that can grow over time tends to be left behind. Universities don't just provide students with a short-term experience. They also provide them tools for the future, and it is crucial that the learning on campus has a long life cycle. Training students to handle complexity and uncertainty over the long term is a difficult task that could be addressed through a better use of diversity.

In many countries, universities have listed among their top priorities developing ethnic, racial, sexual, religious, socioeconomic or age diversity, but the main goal is to guarantee access and equal opportunities to underrepresented groups. In spite of the good intentions and beyond the official discourse, once these individuals are admitted to university, little is done to bring their diversity into the daily learning experience. In most cases, diversity could be seen as a dormant resource. However, it is through diversity that students learn the complexity of the decision-making process and the necessity to consider the variety of conflicting perspectives and opinions. Future leaders should be capable of transforming the ordinary into the extraordinary. Universities should not limit themselves to training responsible leaders. They should become the place that nurtures visionaries and leaders who can anticipate challenges, push boundaries and are ready to offer the creative restlessness needed to imagine a different world.

Dr. Alessia Lefébure
Director of the Alliance Program
Columbia University, USA

Service learning, project-based learning, or what we often call more generally 'hands-on minds-on learning' has been shown to be an effective way for children to acquire both academic and non-academic skills. Our current research looking at new models of education shows that many innovative and effective education programmes and schools utilise project-based learning to improve student learning. Many such programmes focus on solving problems in the community with projects that are developed and executed by the students.[lxxiv]

Dr. Rebecca Winthrop
Director of the Center for Universal Education
Brookings Institution, USA

How can students fill the gap between knowledge and action when it comes to transitioning to a sustainable society?

University communities have a unique responsibility to be the stewards and creators of knowledge and to help our students learn how to thoughtfully engage with complex and urgent issues. We also have the unique position of being at the vanguard of discovery — of cutting-edge knowledge and technologies. These dynamics have an extraordinary track record of exciting innovation and inspiring young talent, especially when it is most needed in our societies.

While we live in an age of unprecedented challenge in terms of climate change, we also live in an age of unprecedented opportunity to tackle this challenge at the frontiers of nearly every field of study or discipline: the arts and humanities, the sciences, business, finance and policy all have a role to play. For any young person who asks what contribution they can make, the opportunities are vast, cutting-edge and more exciting than ever.

Dr. John J. DeGioia
President, Georgetown University, USA

Chapter 13

Advice and Skills
for the Next Generation

Many of the issues covered in this book examine changes our societies are likely to make over the next few decades to become more sustainable. The policies enacted and the mechanisms set in motion today will affect present generations minimally, compared to their effect on the young and future ones. As we consider the legacy we leave behind to future generations, it is crucial that we remind them not to repeat our past mistakes and that we leave the right institutions in place to ensure that their needs are considered and that our planet is preserved.

What advice do you have for present and future generations on living sustainably and on protecting our environment?

There is now overwhelming scientific and technological evidence that unless dramatic measures are taken to halt the current state of environmental degradation, the world as we know it will cease to exist. Current records show there has been a continued rise in world temperatures over the last century. The past 50 years have been the hottest in world history and temperatures continue to rise. Estimates are that if the current rise in global temperatures is not kept under

2°C above pre-industrial levels within the next 30 years or so, the world will be so unbearably and irreversibly altered.

We therefore need urgently to curb the use of environmentally degrading products, such as fossil fuels, coal, natural gas and the other chemicals that deplete the ozone layer and upset world weather trends.

In many parts of the world, the rains no longer come when expected, and when they do come, they are torrential and cause floods. Similarly, there are long droughts that reduce the length of the planting season, resulting in low harvests; this also results in the drying up of river beds, leaving less water for drinking and pasture. Dry seasons also trigger bush fires that spiral out of control and cause havoc; the winters are cold and severe, leading to shutdowns in many cities because of unprecedented snowfalls that block pathways and make transportation impossible.

There is the urgent need for mankind to adopt more climate-resilient products that will help safeguard the environment from continued depletion and at the same time adopt mitigation and adaption measures in terms of food crops, manufacturing and other industrial products to help ensure a more sustainable world.

John Kufuor
Former President of Ghana (2001–2009)

If it is true that we are living unsustainably — using more living resources than the planet can regenerate and dangerously trespassing planetary boundaries — then we are jeopardising the very natural systems that all life on Earth depends on. It is therefore also true that awareness of the problems and the solutions has never been greater. In addition, science has never been clearer and commitments to remedy the situation have never been stronger. The goal is crystal clear: we need to decouple human development from environmental destruction. We have taken nature for granted for too long.

Climate change is triggering more extreme weather events that cost lives and billions of dollars, pollution in major cities and polluted water and food are harming our health, and fishermen are pulling up empty nets. Finally, we are beginning to react. For the first time, in 2015, the world's governments agreed to integrate economic, social and environmental agendas in the SDGs. The SDGs will drive hundreds of billions in investment. In Paris, almost 200 countries, including for the first time all major polluters, have agreed to reduce emissions by 2030 and eventually phase out the use of fossil fuel by the end of the century. Many major global corporations have voluntarily committed to green their supply chains under the pressure from millions of consumers.

We are in the middle of a major transition out of our current unsustainable and suicidal development model. Translating these unprecedented commitments into action is now the challenge. The scale and pace of transition will define success or failure. It is this generation, not the past one and not the next one, that is the responsible and has the opportunity to trigger the most unprecedented revolution of our civilisation. The goal is to redefine our relationship with the planet and allow us to build a prosperous and just future for all in harmony with nature. We must, we can.

Dr. Marco Lambertini
Director-General of WWF International

For the present generation, my main advice would be to educate yourselves to the degree necessary to understand risks linked to climate change, assess your vulnerability, manage that risk and communicate this to your policy-makers and pressure them as best you can to resolve the underlying problems.

Prof. Andy Pitman
ARC Centre of Excellence for Climate System Science
University of New South Wales, Australia

Many actions are required for future sustainability, but they can be broadly listed in four categories:

- Measure what is going on for understanding and policy.
- Understand the causes, consequences and interactions of bio-physical human systems.

- Act by investing and creating incentives that will change what and how we produce and consume.
- Adapt strategies based on successes and failures, environmental needs and socioeconomic priorities.

Within these four broad approaches, I highlight two critical pathways:

- Promote appropriate incentives so that users of natural resources face the appropriate signals about the costs they impose on others from their actions. This could take many different forms and might range from stewardship payments to farmers who provide ecosystem services that would otherwise not be supplied or the elimination of fossil fuel energy subsidies.
- Radically improve the quality of decision-making, especially in terms of risks, by the public, private and civil sectors. This requires greater transparency about decisions; deeper and broader community engagement in sustainability decisions, and the requisite understanding that goes with this engagement; focusing on evidence and the separation of facts and values; and the much greater use of appropriate methods of decision-making that considers systemic risks (such as across food, energy, environment and water), and the consequences of such decisions on the resilience of anthropogenic and natural systems.

Prof. Quentin Grafton
Professor of Economics at the Australian National University,
Australia
UNESCO Chair in Water Economics and Transboundary
Water Governance

We need a new economic paradigm for sustainable well-being. Individual behaviour must change, but it must be in the context of a new regime of rules, norms and institutions that allow and encourage sustainable behaviour. The culture must evolve in the appropriate direction and our challenge is to design and implement the models that this evolution can make use of. We need a broad civil society movement to enable and direct this cultural change, and new social institutions (such as common asset trusts) to implement it.

Prof. Robert Costanza
Professor and Chair in Public Policy at the Australian National
University, Australia

I would suggest that they should examine their fundamental value system (as should the present generation). We'll never solve the sustainability challenge by continuing to focus on material growth, and increasingly disconnecting ourselves from the rest of the natural world around us. We need a new definition of well-being (there is a lot of research on this question) and need to reattach ourselves to the biosphere (the rest of life) and organise our societies and economies as if life matters (not just 'resources' and 'ecosystem services'). Humans are capable of doing this — indigenous cultures around the world had these sorts of value systems — and we need to integrate this type of value system with more contemporary technologies.

Prof. Will Steffen
Climate Change Institute
Australian National University, Australia

Recognise that (un)sustainability is a collective problem that demands collective solutions. While living a seemingly sustainable lifestyle may feel good and serve as an example to others, one's personal impact on ecological trends is negligible. No person or city or country can be sustainable for long in isolation from global trends. Individuals cannot implement the policies needed for sustainability (e.g., individuals cannot provide better public transportation or implement a carbon tax). Recognise that government intervention in markets is necessary for market efficiency and true cost pricing. Governments must implement sustainability-oriented policies for the common good, often in the face of strong corporate lobbies for inaction.

Sustainability and a stable environment are political goals that require a functioning democracy. Citizens have an obligation to themselves and future generations to be well informed about sustainability-related issues and to be politically engaged to ensure that governments act in the long-term public interest.

Prof. William Rees
Professor Emeritus and former Director of the School
of Community and Regional Planning
University of British Columbia, Canada

The goal of sustainability is inclusive intergenerational well-being: the well-being of people around the world today and in future generations. The challenge is that the goal of intergenerational well-being cannot be met if we draw down our natural capital. But I see around me all kinds of efforts and strong progress toward that goal. I think we can accomplish it, but there is much, much more to be done and done quickly.

Prof. Pamela Matson
Dean of the School of Earth, Energy & Environmental Studies
Stanford University, USA

The severity of different environmental problems is going to be different for future generations. However, the same principles will apply.

Future generations will need to price it right. The best way to unclog congested roads, for example — or congested airports for that matter — is to implement charges that progressively rise and fall during peak periods for using the infrastructure. Policy-makers will also need to put in place the right incentives for urban development — avoid subsidising development through tax incentives for housing and making sure that property developers are charged for the new infrastructure requirements (such as roads and schools). And efficiently pricing water will become increasingly important with greater stress on water resources from population pressure and climate-induced changes in regional supplies.

Vitor Gaspar
Director of the Fiscal Affairs Department
International Monetary Fund
Former Finance Minister of Portugal (2011–2013)

It is likely that the first message we will need to communicate to future generations will be this: we offer a sincere apology for the reckless way in which the most affluent of us — in the most affluent countries — consumed the finite resources of the planet with profoundly inadequate consideration for the consequences for future generations. This suggests that one valuable piece of advice might be: don't do what we did. On a more positive note, it might also be useful to emphasise the crucial importance of strengthening awareness and respect of the fragility and interdependence of human ecologies and all other living beings.

Prof. John Wiseman
Deputy Director of the Melbourne Sustainable Society Institute
University of Melbourne, Australia

I think we should be advising our own generations that we have to leave a world behind that is in as good a shape as when we got it, in terms of our generation, so that the future generations can continue to have a healthy ecosystem, and clean air and clean water. And then, future generations will also have to figure out how they should live and work so that they also leave behind the same kind of environment for the generations that succeed them.

Janos Pasztor
UN Assistant Secretary-General for Climate Change Issues
(2015–2016)

Avoiding further deterioration of the environment and the implementation of sustainable development cannot be postponed because points of no return may otherwise soon be reached. I recommend reading the 'Declaration on the Responsibilities of the Present Generations towards Future Generations'[lxxv] adopted by the General Conference of UNESCO in 1997 at the initiative of Commandant Jacques Cousteau. More than advice, I think that today what is needed is examples of suitable attitudes and everyday behaviour. It is necessary to realise that the future can be invented. President John Fitzgerald Kennedy said in a speech in June 1963: 'No problem of human destiny is beyond human beings. Man's reason and spirit have often solved the seemingly unsolvable — and we believe they can do it again'.

Prof. Federico Mayor Zaragoza
Former Director-General of UNESCO (1987–1999)
President of the Foundation for a Culture of Peace

I would advise all those young people in school and at university that they have the opportunity to think of new ways of developing, that they can innovate and imagine a new and better world. They can think of new means of industrialisation that do not depend on CO_2 emissions, of new means of governance, of new ways to power our cities and protect the environment, and thus, it is our responsibility today to educate them and to help them become conscious of the inadequacy of our current model.

Hakima El Haite
Minister for the Environment of Morocco

I'm not sure current generations have a lot to offer to future generations in terms of advice on living sustainability! The past 50 or 60 years have perhaps been the most destructive and myopic in human history. I hope that this will change soon, we have a wonderful opportunity in the coming years to set the world on course to a safer, sustainable and more prosperous future — but this requires strong leadership. My advice for all generations would be to hold your leaders to account — demand the action necessary to protect our planet and our shared home. In addition, we each need to hold ourselves to account and think of ways to live more sustainably. I recall the passion with which the late Nobel Laurate Wangari Maathai would urge us all to 'reduce, reuse, recycle'.

Mary Robinson
President of the Mary Robinson Foundation for Climate Justice
Former President of Ireland (1990–1997)
Former UN High Commissioner for Human Rights (1997–2002)

Don't just wait for the politicians to act. Every one has a responsibility here. And the experience of many others is that it gets relatively easier. The more you have done, the more you realise that you can still do. Conscious consumers have real power and can change the market.

Connie Hedegaard
Former European Commissioner for Climate Action (2010–2014)
Former Danish Minister of Climate and Energy (2007–2009) *and of*
the Environment (2004–2007)

If our aim is to make the world a better place for the present and future generations and to make our way of life more sustainable, the general public must become more actively involved. Science and technology have brought us many marvellous gifts, no doubt, but these are matched, if not outweighed, by many urgent and ongoing tragedies, such as human starvation and the extinction of other species. We must learn to work together to take care of this planet, which is our only home. And we must learn to make more prudent and judicious use of the limited resources available to us.

In the past, human beings took part in destroying the environment because we didn't know any better. But today, we have access to much more information to help us understand the damage we do through our reckless and irresponsible behaviour. That's why it's essential that we take the opportunity to reassess what we have inherited, what we are responsible for now, and what we hope to pass on to coming generations.

His Holiness the Dalai Lama

'If you don't end up living the way you think, you end up thinking the way you live' my father often said. New generations get it! They understand the impact of the climate on the planet and their lives. They know we need to do things better and more efficiently, using less resources and producing way less CO_2 emissions. The fantastic opportunity at hand is to improve living conditions around the world, while at the same time decoupling this growth from CO_2 emissions.

Future generations are fortunate to live their lives in this period and lead the transformation.

José María Figueres
President and Chairman of the Carbon War Room and
Former President of Costa Rica (1994–1998)

I would offer future generations the same advice as current ones: that they learn the wisdom, learn to love the environment, live a convivial existence, monitor their ecological footprint, feel like citizens of the world, participate in public affairs and think of future generations.

Brice Lalonde
Executive Coordinator of the UN Conference on Sustainable
Development (Rio+20; 2012)
Former French Ambassador on Climate Change Negotiations
(2007–2010)
Former French Minister for the Environment (1988–1992)

Across communities and societies, it is our responsibility to make the world liveable for posterity. We cannot go by the proximity factor: that our actions will not affect us! We remain optimistic that the global efforts like the 2030 Agenda or the recent global climate agreement will secure us a world liveable for all across divides. And there is just no choice for any: all people in all lands must do it together. Our climate is indivisible. If I have to leave words to our children, they are these: protect our environment and the mother earth for our existence and for the existence of humanity on this planet.

H.E. Sheikh Hasina
Prime Minister of Bangladesh

In transitioning towards a more sustainable planet, world leaders see the need for new ways of thinking about the goals that are being pursued, and this requires everyone in the world to understand the interconnections between diet, lifestyle, health and prosperity. This means that we should all be ready to think through these connections: to become enlightened thinkers whoever we are and wherever we are working. To do this, we should be valuing, sharing and explaining the results of experience, observation, analysis and know-how. We should be helping everyone to appreciate that they do not have to be trapped in the thought paradigms of others. We should be helping each person to appreciate the usefulness of their own experiences and reflections on them that have real meaning in the context of their own lives. We can all see the need to be enlightened thinkers on food and nutrition once we appreciate that the food people eat determines the kind of person they are now and will become in future. To obtain maximum nutritional benefits from food systems, we need to be sure that all people can access diets with the right combinations of nutrients (avoiding too much fat, too much sugar, and too much salt and any other substances which can damage people's health).

The food and nutrition challenge of today is — quite simply — to secure the transformation of food systems so that they enable nutritious diets to be accessible to all, backed by quality health services and accompanied at all times by real progress with women's empowerment. Enlightened thinking is critical for transformation around nutrition, health and climate change. Enlightened thinkers working in the field of nutrition recognise that what they think, eat and do matters not just to them but to others with whom they live, who they influence, to their children, to their relatives and then to their wider communities.

As world leaders look ahead, they increasingly recognise the importance of acting in ways that empower people, so they can be agents of transformation. They call upon people everywhere to contribute to the 2030 Agenda for Sustainable Development. People can do this in many ways — enlightened thinking, education, organising and managing, communication and monitoring. Once people are committed to being active, they are in a position to contribute to the growing worldwide movement for nutritional health. They can request decision-makers to find ways that enable food production, distribution, processing and marketing to reflect the need for all people to enjoy the benefits of good nutrition — and not just a select few.

They can take these requests to businesses and civil society organisations. They can be agents of change.

In conclusion, an initiative to empower all people everywhere to become thought leaders will unleash new potential in the long-term quest for sustainable development of all people and planet. These thought leaders will shape the contribution of current generations and pave the way for a sustainable future for all.

Dr. David Nabarro
UN Secretary-General's Special Representative
on Food Security and Nutrition
Special Adviser to the UN Secretary-General on the 2030
Agenda for Sustainable Development and Climate Change

You are leaders! I no longer want to hear people say 'Youth today are the leaders of tomorrow'. That is, I believe, out of date, old-fashioned. You must say, 'Youth today, young generations are leaders in their own right'. The world is yours, you must also be welcomed and work in collaboration with national leaders, community leaders, church leaders, business leaders, whether you are young or you are at university you have a role to play. The young generation must take up ownership of the world and its role in the survival and security of humankind. Not only in your nation, but also to your colleagues, your brothers, your sisters everywhere in the world. You must move forward as one family of the world and help each other.

H.E. Enele Sopoaga
Prime Minister of Tuvalu

References

i. UNFCCC (2015). Paris agreement, 12 December (https://unfccc. int/resource/docs/2015/cop21/eng/109r01 pdf)
ii. Paris Deal: Epic Fail on a Planetary Scale, *New Internationalist*, 2015, 12 December (https://newint.org/features/web-exclusive/2015/ 12/12/cop21-paris-deal-epi-fail-on-planetary-scale/). Final COP21 text a disaster for the world's most vulnerable and future generations, *Global Justice Now*, 2015, 12 December (http://www.globaljustice. org.uk/news/2015/dec/12/final-cop-21-text-disaster-worlds-most-vulnerable-and-future-generations).
iii. Policies which subsidise the use of renewable energy.
iv. Technological tools which allow the efficient use and management of electric grids.
v. Sachs, J. (2015). *The Age of Sustainable Development*. Columbia University Press, 203.
vi. (https://www.whitehouse.gov/blog/2014/06/20/overwhelming-consensus-climate-scientists-worldwide);
(www.epa.gov/cleanpowerplan/clean-power-plan-existing-power-plants);
(www.georgetownclimate.org/clean-energy/clean-power-plan-tool-kit);
(www.theglobeandmail.com/report-on-business/industry-news/ energy-and-resources/china-now-the-largest-installer-of-clean-energy/ article28237771/);
(www.bloomberg.com/news/articles/2015-12-30/china-to-suspend-new-coal-mine-approvals-amid-pollution-fight);

(www.georgetownclimate.org/georgetown-at-the-un-climate-change-conference-in-paris-cop21).

vii. (https://www.iea.org/newsroomandevents/pressreleases/2015/october/renewables-to-lead-world-power-market-growth-to-2020.html).

viii. (energy.georgetownclimate.org/view-state-climate-and-energy-profiles);
(www.georgetownclimate.org/clean-energy/clean-power-plan-tool-kit)
(www1.nyc.gov/sandytracker/);
(www.georgetownclimate.org/adaptation/clearinghouse).

ix. IUCN (2015). 'Conservation successes overshadowed by more species declines'. IUCN red list update, 23 June.

x. WWF Global (n.d.). How many species are we losing? (http://wwf.panda.org/about_our_earth/biodiversity/biodiversity/);
De Vos, J. M., Joppa, L. N., Gittleman, J. L. *et al.* (2015). Estimating the normal background rate of species extinction, *Conservation Biology*, 29: 452–462.

xi. Barnosky, A., Matzke, N., Tomiya, S. *et al.* (2011). Has the Earth's sixth mass extinction already arrived? *Nature*, 471: 51–57.

xii. Convention on Biological Diversity (2010). The strategic plan for biodiversity 2011–2020 and the Aichi biodiversity targets, 29 October.

xiii. To ensure that market 'demand' for the species is reduced.

xiv. OECD (n.d.). Water use in agriculture (http://www.oecd.org/agriculture/wateruseinagriculture.htm).

xv. UN FAO (n.d.). Food loss and food waste (http://www.fao.org/food-loss-and-food-waste/en/).

xvi. French law forbids food waste by supermarkets, *The Guardian*, 2016, 4 February (https://www.theguardian.com/world/2016/feb/04/french-law-forbids-food-waste-by-supermarkets).

xvii. Could these apps solve America's huge food waste problem? Fortune, 2015, 16 April (http://fortune.com/2015/04/16/could-these-apps-solve-americas-huge-food-waste-problem/).

xviii. A form of cropping used to preserve biodiversity, prevent soil erosion, improve soil fertility and suppress weeds, among other things, using specific types of crops.

xix. For information, including over 80 case studies, please refer to Agriculture for Impact's Sustainable Intensification Database (ag4impact.org/database)

xx. See the Biotechnology section of the Agriculture for Impact Sustainable Intensification Database for examples and case studies (ag4impact.org/database).

xxi. New Genetics, Food and Agriculture: Scientific Discoveries — SocietalDilemas(2003). (http://www.icsu.org/publications/reports-and-reviews/new-genetics-food-and-agriculture-scientific-discoveries-societal-dilemas-2003/new-genetics-food-and-agriculture-scientific-discoveries-societal-dilemas-2003).

xxii. A form of irrigation that maximises the productivity of water on a given piece of land.

xxiii. The State of World Fisheries and Aquaculture (2014). UN Food and Agricultural Organisation, Rome (http://www.fao.org/3/a-i3720e.pdf).

xxiv. 'Crude density is the population size per unit area. Social density is more complex, consisting of the interactions between people, and between people and other parts of the biosphere.' Ian Pool.

xxv. Rajanatram, J., Marcus, J., Flaxman, A. *et al.* (2010). Neonatal, post-neonatal and childhood under-5 mortality for 187 countries, 1970–2010: a systematic analysis of progress towards MDG-4, *Lancet*, 375: 1998–2008.

xxvi. Sibada, A., Woubalem, Z., Hogan, D. *et al.* (2003). The proximate determinants of the decline to below replacement fertility in Addis Ababa, Ethiopia, *Studies in Family Planning*, 34: 1–7.

xxvii. Bloom, D., Canning, D. and Sevilla, J. (2003). *The Demographic Dividend: A New Perspective on the Economic Consequences of Population Change*, RAND; Higgins, M. and Williamson, J. (1997). Age structure and dependence on foreign capital, *Population and Development Review*, 23: 261–293; Mason, A. and Lee, R. (2006). Reform and support systems for the elderly in developing countries, capturing the second demographic dividend, Genus, 62: 11–35. I have a short policy-oriented review of these: Pool I. (2007). Demographic dividends: determinants of development or merely windows of opportunity, *Ageing Horizons*, 7: 28–35.

xxviii. Cleland, J. (2006). The continuing challenge of population growth. In Hobcraft, J. (ed.) *The ICPD Vision: How Far Has the 11-Year Journey Taken Us?* UNFPA.

xxix. Economist Intelligence Unit (2007). The silent epidemic: an economic study of diabetes in developed and developing countries, *The Economist*.

xxx. Ian Pool reviewed the Ghana programme for UNFPA in 1992.

xxxi. Eckert-Jaffe, O., Joshi, H., Lynch, K. *et al.* (2002). Timing of births and socioeconomic status in France and Britain: social policies and occupational polarisation, *Population*, 57: 475–508.

xxxii. Hardin, G. (1968). The tragedy of the commons. *Science*, 162: 1243–1248.

xxxiii. Official governmental aid, usually to assist with international development programmes.

xxxiv. Economic growth from environmental degradation.

xxxv. The United States, Russia, China, Australia, India, Germany, Ukraine, Kazakhstan, Colombia, Canada (http://www.mining-technology.com/features/feature-the-worlds-biggest-coal-reserves-by-country/).

xxxvi. China and France Joint Presidential Statement on Climate Change (2015). 2 November (http://www.diplomatie.gouv.fr/en/french-foreign-policy/climate/2015-paris-climate-conference-cop21/article/china-and-france-joint-presidential-statement-on-climate-change-beijing-02-11).

xxxvii. Displacement Solutions (2013). The peninsula principles: on climate displacement within states, 18 August (http://displacementsolutions.org/wp-content/uploads/2014/12/Peninsula-Principles.pdf).

xxxviii. UNFCCC (2015). Adoption of the Paris agreement COP21, 12 December: 8, 17; (https://unfccc.int/resource/docs/2015/cop21/eng/109r01.pdf).

xxxix. The International Consortium of Investigative Journalists, 'Luxembourg Leaks: Global Companies' Secrets Exposed' (https://www.icij.org/project/luxembourg-leaks).

xl. Oxfam (2014). Hidden hunger in South Africa (https://www.oxfam.org/sites/www.oxfam.org/files/file_attachments/hidden_hunger_in_south_africa_0.pdf).

xli. UN and Climate Change Press Release (2014). Green Climate Fund exceeds initial capitalization target of $10 billion, 10 December (http://www.un.org/climatechange/blog/2014/12/green-climate-fund-surpasses-10-billion-goal/).

xlii. UN Habitat Press Release (2016). UN-Habitat launches the World Cities Report 2016, urbanization and development: emerging futures, 18 May (http://unhabitat.org/un-habitat-launches-the-world-cities-report-2016/); UN Habitat World Cities report 2016 (http://wcr.unhabitat.org/main-report/).

xliii. The urban heat effect is the effect which leads urban areas to be warmer than their surroundings because of increased human activity.

xliv. Department of Economic and Social Affairs (2014). World urbanization prospects: the 2014 revision, highlights: 1: UN (http://esa.un.org/unpd/wup/Publications/Files/WUP2014-Highlights.pdf).

xlv. Satterthwaite, D. (2008). Cities' contribution to global warming: notes on the allocation of greenhouse gas emissions. *Environment and Urbanization*, 20: 539–549.

xlvi. The New Climate Economy Report (2014). Cities (http://2014.newclimateeconomy.report/wp-content/uploads/2014/08/NCE-cities-web.pdf).

xlvii. See (https://www.washingtonpost.com/news/wonk/wp/2014/09/22/how-compact-cities-help-curb-climate-change/).

xlviii. UNEP (2015). Renewables re-energized: green energy investments worldwide surge 17% to $270 billion in 2014, 31 March (http://www.unep.org/newscentre/default.aspx?DocumentID=26788&ArticleID=34875).

xlix. LSE (2014). Cities: Copenhagen: green economy leader report (https://files.lsecities.net/files/2014/05/Copenhagen-GEL_20May Final_ExecSum_1page-layout.pdf).

l. Copenhagen Commune (n.d.). Morten Kabell and political priorities (https://kabell.kk.dk/artikel/morten-kabell-and-political-priorities).

li. Sustainable Development Knowledge Platform (n.d.). Open working group proposal for sustainable development goals, UN (https://sustainabledevelopment.un.org/focussdgs.html).

lii. Brown, A. (2015). Investors demand more thorough disclosure on carbon risks, *IR Magazine*, April 20 (http://www.irmagazine.com/articles/sustainability/20719/investors-call-sec-demand-more-thorough-disclosure-carbon-risks/).

liii. Liinanki, C. (2014). Pensions In Nordic region: time for action on carbon, *Investment & Pensions Europe*, November (http://www.ipe.com/pensions/pensions-in/nordic-region/pensions-in-nordic-region-time-for-action-on-carbon/10004145.fullarticle).

liv. Friends of Fossil Fuel Subsidy (2015). Reform Communiqué (http://fffsr.org/communique/).

lv. The gap between the pledges to reduce GHG emissions by 2030 and the goal of keeping temperature rises below 2°C.

lvi. World Business Council for Sustainable Development (2015). Global low-carbon initiative reveals action plans developed by 223 organisations: ambitions could achieve 65% of the emissions reduction needed to stay under 2°C, 7 December. (http://www.wbcsd.org/Pages/

EDocument/EDocumentDetails.aspx?ID=16643&NoSearchContext Key=true).

lvii. See The Global Commission on Climate and the Economy annual reports (http://newclimateeconomy.net).

lviii. UNFCCC (2015). Lima-Paris Action Agenda matures into major force driving climate action, December (http://newsroom.unfccc. int/lpaa/lpaa/massive-mobilization-by-non-state-stakeholders-summarized-at-cop21/).

lix. CleanTechnica (2015). Labeled green bonds issuance crosses $40 billion,24December(http://cleantechnica.com/2015/12/24/labeled-green-bonds-issuance-crosses-40-billion-2015/).

lx. Pew Research (2012). The global religious landscape, 18 December (http://www.pewforum.org/2012/12/18/global-religious-landscape-exec/).

lxi. Religions for Peace International (n.d.) Faith-based leaders deliver petitions to President Francois Hollande in Paris (http://www.religionsforpeaceinternational.org/what-we-do/protect-earth).

lxii. Interfaith Climate Change Statement (2016). To world leaders (http://www.interfaithstatement2016.0rg/statement).

lxiii. UN World Food Programme (n.d.). Hunger statistics (https://www. wfp.org/hunger/stats).

lxiv. Stockholm International Peace Research Institute (2013). Military Expenditure, SIPRI Yearbook 2013 (https://www.sipri.org/ yearbook/2013/03).

lxv. Meyer, J. (2001). *Political Nature: Environmentalism and the Interpretation of Western Thought*. MIT Press. p. 1.

lxvi. Francis, (2013). 'Laudato Si', sec. 22. Libreria Editrice Vaticana.

lxvii. Hanushek, E. (2013). Economic growth in developing countries: the role of human capital, Economics of Education Review (http:// hanushek.stanford.edu/sites/default/files/publications/Education%20 and%20Economic%20Growth.pdf).

lxviii. UN (2012). Millennium development goal progress report: 16–19 (http://www.un.org/millenniumgoals/pdf/MDG%20Report%20 2012.pdf).

lxix. UNESCO EFA Global Monitoring Report 2013/4 (2014). Teaching and Learning: Achieving Quality for All, p. 5 (http://unesdoc.unesco.org/images/0022/002256/225660e.pdf).

lxx. McKinsey Global Institute (2012). The world at work: jobs, pay, and skills for 3.5 billion people, June (http://www.mckinsey.com/ global-themes/employment-and-growth/the-world-at-work).

lxxi. 'I recommend as references for a good education the World Plan of Action on Education in Human Rights and Democracy (Montreal, 1993), the Convention on the Human Rights of the Children (UN, 1989), Education for all throughout Life (UNESCO, 1990), the Declaration and Programme of Action on a Culture of Peace (General Assembly, 1991) and the Earth Charter (Federico Mayor, 2000).' Federico Mayor.

lxxii. Earth Charter, UNESCO, 6 (http://www.unesco.org/education/tlsf/mods/theme_a/img/02_earthcharter.pdf).

lxxiii. UK Met Office (2015). Global climate in context as the world approaches 1°C above pre-industrial for the first time November (http://www.metoffice.gov.uk/research/news/2015/global-average-temperature-2015).

lxxiv. The Ashoka changemaker schools in particular use these methods to help develop empathy (https://www.ashoka.org/meet-changemaker-schools).

lxxv. (http://portal.unesco.org/en/ev.php URL_ID=13178&URL_DO=DO_TOPIC&URL_SECTION=201.html).

Abbreviations

COPs	Conference of the Parties
ETS	Emissions Trading Scheme
EUA	Environmental Upgrade Agreement
GCF	Green Climate Fund
GHG	Greenhouse Gas
GMO	Genetically Modified Organism
GNH	Gross National Happiness
GPSs	Global Positioning Systems
ICLEIs	International Council for Local Environmental Initiatives
IUCN	International Union for the Conservation of Nature
LDCs	Less Developed Countries
LEAF	Linking Environment and Farming
LNG	Liquefied Natural Gas
MDCs	More Developed Countries
MDGs	Millennium Development Goals

MI	Motivational Interviewing
NGO	Non-governmental Organization
ODA	Official Development Assistance
PoWPAs	Programme of Work on Protected Areas
SDGs	Sustainable Development Goals
SP	Scenario Planning
STEM	Science, Technology, Engineering and Mathematics
TFR	Total Fertility Rate
UNEA	UN Environment Assembly
UNEP	UN Environment Programme
UNESCO	UN Educational, Scientific and Cultural Organization
UNFCCC	UN Framework Convention on Climate Change
WBCSD	World Business Council on Sustainable Development
WHO	World Health Organization
WWF	World Wildlife Fund

Acknowledgements

I would first like to thank the contributors, without whom this book could not have been published. All of them lead very busy lives and I am deeply grateful to them for having taken the time to contribute to this book. Creating a book composed exclusively of interviews on a given topic is a novel concept, and I would like to thank them for having believed in its realisation.

I would also like to thank Hakima El Haite, the Moroccan Environment Minister, who allowed me to go to the COP21 international climate conference in Paris and to conduct several of the interviews featured in this book.

At King's College London, I would like to thank Dr. Adrian Blau, Prof. Nick Clifford, Dr. Humeira Iqtidar and Prof. Mark Pennington for providing useful feedback on various parts of the book.

I would be remiss if I did not also thank Philly Lim May Li and Suraj Kumar, my editors at World Scientific, for their amazing efforts in ensuring this book was ready for publication as quickly as it was.

I would also like to thank Prof. Rick van der Ploeg at the University of Oxford and Prof. Richard Green at the Imperial College London Business School for taking the time to read the book and for providing a kind recommendation.

Finally, I would like to thank my family for their support. The work related to the development of this book took around 18 months of sustained work and their encouragement has been valuable throughout this time. My uncle Ali provided invaluable advice in ensuring that this book could be as good as it could be, and of course, I would like to thank my parents, Karima and Reda, for having believed in this book from the start and for their support in encouraging me to see it through.